ABRAHAM LINCOLN

Born February 12, 1809, in Kentucky, to illiterate parents, Abraham Lincoln was raised in rural Kentucky and Indiana. Often unable to attend school, he obtained an informal education through wide-ranging reading, including Daniel Defoe's *Robinson Crusoe*, Mason Locke Weems's *The Life and Memorable Actions of George Washington*, the plays of Shakespeare, and other classics of literature. After a failed business venture, he worked as a hired hand, but also surveyed land and wrote deeds for his neighbors. He was first elected to the Illinois House of Representatives as a Whig in 1834, after an unsuccessful campaign in 1832. He began studying law on his own and earned his license in 1836, opening a general practice in civil and criminal law. Lincoln first debated Stephen A. Douglas in 1838, in support of his law partner John T. Stuart's campaign for Congress against Douglas. Their most famous series of debates took place twenty years later, before audiences numbering 10,000 and more. These debates were collected and published in the spring of 1860; in November he was elected president of a country divided over the issue of slavery. As Commander in Chief of the Union, he prosecuted the Civil War, issued the Emancipation Proclamation on New Year's Day, 1863, and began addressing the momentous task of Reconstruction after the devastating war ended. But less than a week after Lee's surrender to Grant at Appomattox on April 9, 1865, Lincoln was assassinated by the popular actor John Wilkes Booth at Ford's Theater in Washington, D.C.

Herbert Mitgang is author of the three-volume *The Journalist's Lincoln* and of the play *Mister Lincoln*.

BANTAM CLASSICS
Ask your bookseller for these other American Classics

Selected Writings of Abraham Lincoln

Selected and with an Introduction
by Herbert Mitgang

BANTAM BOOKS

NEW YORK · TORONTO · LONDON · SYDNEY · AUCKLAND

SELECTED WRITINGS OF ABRAHAM LINCOLN
A Bantam Classic Book / July 1992

Grateful acknowledgement is made for permission
to reprint this text which has been excerpted
from *The Collected Works of Abraham Lincoln*
by Roy P. Basler. Copyright © 1953 by Rutgers,
The State University.

Lincoln, Abraham. Sixteenth president
of the United States. Photo by
Mathew Brady. The National Portrait
Gallery, Smithsonian Institution.

ISBN 0-553-21407-1

Published simultaneously in the United States and Canada

Bantam Books are published by Bantam Books, a division of Bantam Double-
day Dell Publishing Group, Inc. Its trademark, consisting of the words "Bantam
Books" and the portrayal of a rooster, is Registered in U.S. Patent and Trademark Office and in other countries. Marca Registrada. Bantam Books, 666
Fifth Avenue, New York, New York 10103.

PRINTED IN THE UNITED STATES OF AMERICA

OPM   0 9 8 7 6 5 4 3 2 1

Contents

Introduction by Herbert Mitgang

I. THE PRAIRIE LAWYER   1

II. THE COMMANDING PRESIDENT   143

IV. THE SYMBOL OF AMERICA   277

Introduction

"In times like the present, men should utter nothing for which they would not willingly be responsible through time and in eternity."

Written by President Abraham Lincoln in the middle of the Civil War, these words illustrate the compassion, literary style, and far-seeing vision of a man whose language both illuminated his own time and looked to the future.

"*We* cannot escape history," he said in his second annual message to Congress. "No personal significance, or insignificance, can spare one or another of us. The fiery trial through which we pass, will light us down, in honor or dishonor, to the latest generation."

Present generations read Lincoln for many reasons—even some that are surprising. These selections clearly show that he was the greatest writer among all the Presidents (without, of course, a ghost writer) and a master of the English language. He was an outstanding Constitutionalist; no other President referred so often to the documents of the original Framers. He was a Commander-in-Chief in the White House; the orders to his Generals display an instinctive knowledge of military leadership and tactics. He was a humanist who saw blacks and whites as individuals, not simply as members of different races, and who respected the dignity of the laboring class in the workplace. He had forward-thinking ideas about the role of women in society. And so we read and study Lincoln today not only for his eloquence but also for his sense of history, for his hopes for peace, and for his appeal to people everywhere to be touched by what he called "the better angels of our nature."

Lincoln came out of the American soil and experience. He was born on a patch of Kentucky scarred by deep ravines and eroded earth. His impoverished family traveled to Indiana, hoping to do better on a homestead where title came from the government.

The Lincolns were strugglers in a pioneering nation. Thomas and Nancy Lincoln would recognize the contrast between poverty and privilege today. When he was a candidate for President, Lincoln was asked about his boyhood years. "Why it is a great piece of folly to attempt to make anything out of my early life. It can all be condensed into a single sentence, and that sentence you will find in Gray's 'Elegy': 'The short and simple annals of the poor.' "

It was on this rough road that the sixteenth President of the United States traveled to greatness. Leaving his boyhood behind him in Kentucky and Indiana, Lincoln arrived in New Salem, Illinois, in the summer of 1831. He was twenty-two. Prophetically, an election was going on, and because he could make "a few rabbit tracks" with the pen, he become voting clerk. Less than a year later, he was in politics.

A self-announced candidate for election to the state legislature in 1832, he first joined the contest and then volunteered in the militia for the Black Hawk Indian uprising. His unit was officially designated "Captain Abraham Lincoln's Company of the First Regiment of the Brigade of Mounted Volunteers," and he won military election as a company leader. After his discharge as a private—his own company had disbanded and he had reenlisted to obtain the benefit of service—he returned to New Salem to face the voters. Running as a Whig in a Democratic-dominated state, he was defeated. However, he received an almost unanimous vote in his own precinct of New Salem, 227 votes against 3.

Lincoln revealed himself—and was seen by the public—for the first time in the *Sangamo Journal*, Springfield. From its first issue, the editors spoke for the Whigs and became close personal and political friends of Lincoln. The *Sangamo Journal*—so called after the river and county of Sangamon—remained Lincoln's hometown paper and forum all through his political youth and maturity.

Springfield and the county were thinking in terms of commerce and expanded business opportunities. In the written announcement for office that ran in the *Sangamo Journal* in 1832, Lincoln spoke for his constituents, making a point of improving the navigation on the Sangamon. The newcomer signed himself, "Your friend and fellow-citizen, A. LINCOLN." It was a phrase he would use on the stump and in letters many times in future years.

After his initial defeat for the state legislature, he was appointed postmaster of New Salen in 1833. Here he continued his meager education by reading the newspapers before distributing them. He became an inveterate newspaper reader and frequently wrote letters to the editor. On his second bid for political office, he was elected to the state legislature in 1834, and reelected for a second, third, and fourth term. After helping to move the Illinois capital to Springfield, he moved to the burgeoning town. Here, he studied hard and was admitted to the Illinois bar in 1837. He continued to practice law right up to the time he was elected President in 1860.

The importance of Lincoln's legal career cannot be exaggerated. It helped to form his thinking and develop his writing. The law enhanced his respect for the rights of citizens under the Constitution. He represented every kind of litigant in every legal forum in the state, including the supreme court and the federal courts. Two views of Lincoln as attorney have been presented in modern biographies. One holds that he was only a slick country lawyer, who once falsified evidence in a murder trial to save his client from the gallows; the other holds that he was really only a big-time lawyer representing railroad interests. Both are oversimplifications.

Lincoln's widespread law practice indicates that he handled minor as well as major cases; that he was meticulous in preparing complex written documents and was an outstanding courtroom advocate—especially in front of juries; and that other members of the Illinois bar regularly sought his counsel for their appellate work. Like other lawyers in the young United States, he followed the rights, rules, and regulations that were rooted in the British common law.

In his Springfield practice, his legal fees were considered fair and on the modest side. According to his fee book, the fees ranged from $2.50 to fifty dollars for handling cases in the 1840s. In the 1850s, his fees rose as his practice grew in complexity. When he appeared before the state supreme court, his fees sometimes went to a hundred dollars. Lincoln did insist on being compensated for his work, and sued at least a half-dozen clients for failing to pay promptly. The highest fee he ever billed the Illinois Central Railroad, which he represented a number of times in cases involving rights-of-way, was $5,000. The railroad refused to pay; he was forced to sue and obtain a judgment against his wealthiest client. But some of his fellow lawyers on the Eighth Judicial Circuit—which he rode with horse and buggy from courthouse to courthouse for months at a time— said his fees were generally too low.

In the course of his legal career, Lincoln engaged in every kind of litigation, civil and criminal, dull and dramatic, and earned respect from his peers as one of the leading trial lawyers in Illinois. His highly personal "Notes for a Law Lecture," written in 1850, disclose facts about his professionalism and what he believed it meant to practice law faithfully. These notes include important revelations about his character—views that stood him in good stead both as a lawyer and as a public servant in the state legislature, Congress, and the White House. His ideology of ethical behavior in one's life and profession is as relevant today as when he penned it.

I am not an accomplished lawyer. I find quite as much material for a lecture, in those points wherein I have failed, as in those wherein I have been moderately successful.

The leading rule for the lawyer, as for the man, of every calling, is *diligence*. Leave nothing for to-morrow, which can be done to-day. Never let your correspondence fall behind. Whatever piece of business you have in hand, before stopping, do all the labor pertaining to it which can *then* be done. . . .

Discourage litigation. Persuade your neighbors to compromise whenever you can. Point out to them how the *nominal* winner is often a *real* loser—in fees, and expenses, and waste of time. As a peace-maker the lawyer has a superior opertunity [sic] of being a good man. There will still be business enough.

Never stir up litigation. A worse man can scarcely be found than one who does this. Who can be more nearly a fiend than he who habitually overhauls the Register of deeds, in search of defects in titles, whereon to stir up strife, and put money in his pocket? A moral tone ought to be infused into the profession, which should drive such men out of it.

The matter of fees is important far beyond the mere question of bread and butter involved. Properly attended to fuller justice is done to both lawyer and client. An exorbitant fee should never be claimed. As a general rule, never take your whole fee in advance, nor any more than a small retainer. When fully paid before hand, you are more than a common mortal if you can feel the same interest in the case, as if something was still in prospect for you, as well as for your client.

Then, in words that show the combination of velvet and steel that characterized many of his major arguments in the courts and as Chief Executive and Commander-in-Chief, he concludes:

There is a vague popular belief that lawyers are necessarily dishonest. I say *vague*, because when we consider to what extent *confidence*, and *honors* are resposed in, and conferred upon law-yers by the people, it appears improbable that their *impression* of dishonesty is very distinct and vivid. Yet the impression, is common—almost universal. Let no young man, choosing the law for a calling, for a moment yield to this popular belief. Resolve to be honest at all events; and if, in your own judgment, you can not be an honest lawyer, resolve to be honest without being a lawyer. Choose some other occupation, rather than one in the choosing of which you do, in advance, consent to be a knave.

In the midst of his legal career, Lincoln never relaxed his habits of study and reading. One by one he took up the natural sciences and thoroughly acquainted himself with abstruse metaphysics. He had been a surveyor while studying the law, and this required a knowledge of higher forms of mathematics. All his life he remained an indefatigable student, never suffering any subject to which he directed his attention to pass without profound investigation.

The influence of nearly a quarter of a century of legal practice upon Lincoln's life, mind, and writing has been overlooked by many historians. Yet respect for the law—especially his lawful oath to preserve, protect, and defend the Constitution and the country—was at the core of his language and conduct as the only President who was required to save the nation from a rebellion. The common law that he advised young lawyers to study so diligently was rooted in due process, representation, and equal justice. Above all, Lincoln was a constitutionalist.

In 1846, after a rough campaign, Lincoln became a United States congressman. It had been touchy getting the congressional nomination in the first place, but Lincoln was determined in his pursuit of federal office. Before the election, he wrote one of his many letters marked confidential to a friend in a nearby county: "Now if you should hear anyone say that Lincoln don't want to go to Congress, I wish you as a personal friend of mine would tell him you have reason to believe he is mistaken. The truth is, I would like to go very much."

Lincoln's opponent was Peter Cartwright, Democrat and Methodist circuit rider. Brother Cartwright's campaign was aimed at both Lincoln and the Devil; sometimes on the stump he tried to prove they were the same fellow. He accused Lincoln of being irreverent, citing the fact that Lincoln didn't belong to any church. This issue of religion came up when he ran for President, too. Lincoln indicated that religion was personal, not political. Once he put it bluntly: "When any church will inscribe over its altar, as its sole qualification for membership, the Savior's condensed statement of the substance of both law and Gospel, 'Thou shalt love the Lord thy God with all thy heart, and with all thy soul and thy neighbor as thyself,' that church will I join with all my heart and all my soul."

On election day Lincoln received 6,340 votes, Cartwright 4,829, Walcott (Abolitionist) 249. He was ready to make his first major appearance in Washington.

There was a war on when the new congressman took his place in the Thirtieth Congress in 1847. The Mexican War, declared on May 12, 1846, was political, sectional, and imperial. The southern annexationist wing of President Polk's Democrats had led the fight to admit Texas as a slave state. Lincoln had opposed the extension of slavery since his days in the Illinois legislature. Moreover, northern Whigs and Abolitionists deplored the doctrine of Manifest Destiny, that somehow the United States had the God-given right to extend its boundaries to the Pacific Ocean.

Only two weeks after Congress assembled, Lincoln rose to make a series of accusations against the President. Mr. Polk had said that the Mexicans were the first aggressors— by an invasion of American soil and an effusion of American blood—after rejecting friendly overtures by the United States. Lincoln built his case in a series of inquiries which immediately were branded the "spot" resolutions. He demanded to know the exact spot where Americans were killed and if that spot was indeed American territory. He implied that the Mexicans across the Rio Grande had been driven from their homes by the approach of American arms and that intervention was unnecessary for the defense of Texas.

Lincoln's big blast against the war came on January 12, 1848, a few weeks after his speech. It was carefully prepared: "I condensed all I could for fear of being cut off by the hour rule, and when I got through I had spoke but forty-five minutes." He began by saying that "mere party wantonness" was not the reason for his stand against the war. His basic position was that the war was "unnecessarily and unconstitutionally commenced." The President, he said, tried to twist every silent vote for supplies to support the army into an endorsement of the war itself. He highlighted the credibility gap in the President's first war message which declared that the soil was ours when hostilities began—this, he said, was "the sheerest deception."

Constructed almost in the form of a legal brief, the speech attempted to drive a wedge between President Polk and Congress. Lincoln delved into old treaties, going back to the Louisiana Purchase, in order to explore the question of how far the boundaries of Texas extended. "That Congress did *not* understand it to extend clear to the Rio Grande," he said, "is quite certain." But nobody was really certain about the ownership of the vague borders between Texas and Mexico.

Lincoln attacked the war hawks who sought victory and glory. He said of the President that "the blood of this war, like the blood of Abel, is crying to Heaven against him . . . by fixing the public gaze upon the exceeding brightness of military glory . . . he plunged into it, and has swept, *on* and *on*, till, disappointed in his calculation of the ease with which Mexico might be subdued, he now finds himself, he knows not where . . . [T]he President is . . . wandering and indefinite. First, it is to be done by a more vigorous prossecution [sic] of the war in the vital parts of the enemies [sic] country," but then, *"the continued success of our arms*

may fail to secure a satisfactory peace." The major omission
of the President's message, he said, was when the war could
be expected to end.

The most startling section of Lincoln's most important
speech up to the time seemed to give aid and comfort to
the enemy. He preached a doctrine of people's revolution
that is especially intriguing when considered from a post-
Civil War perspective.

Any people anywhere, being inclined and having the power,
have the *right* to rise up, and shake off the existing government,
and form a new one that suits them better. This is a most valuable,—a most sacred right—a right, which we hope and believe,
is to liberate the world. Nor is this right confined to cases in which
the whole people of an existing government, may choose to exercise
it. Any portion of such people that *can, may* revolutionize, and
make their own, of so much of the teritory [sic] as they inhabit.
More than this, a *majority* of any portion of such people may
revolutionize, putting down a *minority*, intermingled with, or near
about them, who may oppose their movement. Such minority, was
precisely the case, of the tories of our own revolution. It is a
quality of revolutions not to go by *old* lines, or *old* laws; but to
break up both, and make new ones.

On one of the most controversial issues before the House
of Representatives—abolition of slavery in the District of
Columbia—it was Congressman Lincoln who introduced the
resolution in 1849. He advanced two novel ideas: the obligation to support and educate Negro youths and compensated emancipation by the federal government as a fair,
practical, and quick means of buying freedom for enslaved
Negroes (as blacks were called in Lincoln's time). It was a
futile effort. Long afterward, Lincoln explained that upon
"finding that I was abandoned by my former backers and
having little personal influence, I dropped the matter knowing that it was useless to prosecute the business at that
time."

Congressman Lincoln's antiwar and antislavery speeches lived to haunt him and his party. He hinted that he would be glad to run for a second term; not only did he not get the nomination, but his party's candidate was badly defeated. Still, he refused to compromise his position. He returned home to Springfield from Washington and continued to build up his law practice with William Herndon, the junior partner in Lincoln & Herndon. By now he was a family man, with four sons, in a fairly happy marriage to Mary Todd Lincoln.

The birth of the Republican party coincided with the renaissance of Lincoln in the tumult of American politics torn by the race question. In particular, he was against the extension of the "peculiar institution" into the free territories of the growing Republic. On this point he never gave an inch and was as strong as the most vehement Abolitionist. It was the unifying theme of his political life and, eventually, made him the most acceptable candidate when the new Republican party sought the best man and a winning nominee for President.

Lincoln's arguments against the introduction of slaves in the Nebraska Territory inevitably led him to discuss nearly every aspect of social, political, and moral attitudes toward the Negro—at the time totally dehumanized by the conditions of slavery in the South, our greatest national sin. In the 1850s, Lincoln was a moralist without being an Abolitionist. The issue for him was not true political and social equality and economic opportunity, but physical freedom from bondage. That is at the root of any historical paralleling between Lincoln and other moralists, then and now.

Lincoln declared in public and private:

I now do no more than oppose the extension of slavery. I am not a Know-Nothing [the Know-Nothing party was anti-Catholic and anti-immigrant]. That is certain. How could I be? How can anyone who abhors the oppression of Negroes be in favor of

degrading classes of white people? Our progress in degeneracy
appears to be pretty rapid. As a nation, we began by declaring
that "all men are created equal, except Negroes." When the
Know-Nothings get control, it will read, "All men are created
equal except Negroes, and Foreigners and Catholics." When it
comes to this I should prefer emigrating to some country where
they make no pretense of loving liberty—to Russia, for instance,
where despotism can be taken pure and without the base alloy of
hypocrisy.

Yet while Lincoln supported his national argument for
the merits of freedom on libertarian grounds by repeatedly
citing the Declaration of Independence and the Constitution,
the question of the day took emotional turns. The hypocriti-
cal and hard-hearted played on white people's racism by
using the threat of mixed marriage to deny Negro equality
on any level. Lincoln responded:

Now I protest against that counterfeit logic which concludes
that, because I do not want a black woman for a slave I must
necessarily want her for a wife. I need not have her for either. I
can just leave her alone. In some respects she is certainly not my
equal, but in her natural right to eat the bread she earns with her
own hands without asking leave of anyone else, she is my equal
and the equal of all others.

When Lincoln and Stephen Douglas debated all over
Illinois during the senatorial contest in 1858, the basic issue
was not the abolition of slavery but its expansion into free
territories. Lincoln tried to keep the campaign on the track
of slavery's evils. His main line of reasoning was that the
Negro was not to be considered a slave, but a human being
entitled to the benefits and rights in the Declaration and
Constitution. He underscored that the words "slaves" and
"Negroes" never appeared in these documents. "This is part
of the evidence that the fathers of the Government expected

and intended the institution of slavery to come to an end," he argued.

To remove the impression that he was against Negro rights of citizenship once slavery had died, he declared:

There is no reason in the world why the Negro is not entitled to all the natural rights enumerated in the Declaration of Independence, the right of life, liberty and the pursuit of happiness. I hold that he is as much entitled to these as the white man. I agree with Judge Douglas that he is not my equal in many respects—certainly not in color, perhaps not in moral or intellectual endowment. But in the right to eat the bread, without leave of anybody else, which his own hand earns, he is my equal and the equal of Judge Douglas, and the equal of every living man.

The newspapers reported "great applause."

On election day in 1858 he received more of the people's votes than Douglas, but because of districting and holdover senators, Douglas was elected by the Illinois legislature. Despite his defeat, Lincoln emerged as a man of national stature. He had struck a blow against the "house divided" along racial lines. Thereafter, he was watched by the "newspaper generals" in New York and Chicago as a fit candidate for the presidency.

At the convention in Chicago in 1860, Lincoln was nominated for President by the four-year-old Republican party on the fourth ballot. He defeated his main opponent, former Governor William Seward of New York, a strong Abolitionist, whom he later named his Secretary of State. When he heard the news of the winning ballot in the Springfield office of his longtime newspaper supporter, the *Illinois State Journal*, Lincoln said happily, "Gentlemen, you had better come up and shake my hand while you can. Honors elevate some men, you know." He accepted the Republican party platform, which included protective tariffs, a homestead law, the construction with federal help of a railroad to the Pacific, and the admission of Kansas as a state. It denied the right of any authority to give legal existence to slavery in the territories under the false guise of popular sovereignty.

On Inauguration Day, March 4, 1861, Lincoln had four years, one month, and eleven days to live before his appointment with death at Ford's Theatre on April 15, 1865. Thirty-four states were in the Union; seven had withdrawn. In his Inaugural Address, Lincoln was conciliatory to the seceding states, but below lay a bedrock of principle. Between the election and inauguration Lincoln said, "Let there be no compromise on the question of extending slavery. If there be, all our labor is lost and, ere long, must be done again." The country was aflame when he took the oath to uphold the Constitution and the laws. The language of this self-educated man now was all-important; Lincoln selected and arranged his words with the utmost care.

In the Inaugural's key sentences, he said that "the Union of these States is perpetual," even older than the Constitution; that it was his duty "to hold, occupy, and possess" the property of the United States; that "no bloodshed or violence" was called for. And he concluded, "In *your* hands, my dissatisfied fellow countrymen, and not in *mine*, is the momentous issue of civil war." But southern rabble-rousers had decided to secede from the Union by the time of the Inaugural Address, and at that point there was little Lincoln could do to change the course of history.

President Lincoln fully executed his constitutional role of Commander-in-Chief. He had to. He envisioned the task of the Army of the Potomac as pursuing and defeating the Army of Virginia, swiftly and decisively capturing Richmond, the Confederate capital. But his first Union Army commander, General George McClellan, had, in Lincoln's words, "the slows." McClellan preferred to preen and drill instead of to fight. Nor was Lincoln's flank at army headquarters in Washington properly protected. The General-in-Chief was Winfield Scott, "Old Fuss and Feathers," an elderly man who was better at napping than planning. The search for a general who would fight with audacity and without excuses continued until 1864, when Lincoln finally found his man in Ulysses S. Grant, who applied siege and *schrecklichkeit* tactics to the battlefields.

As Commander-in-Chief, Lincoln checked constantly with the military telegraph bureau in the War Department for the latest from the war fronts. He visited the army in the field, riding around the encampments on horseback and by carriage. Through field glasses he could observe enemy pickets and flags flying. During the first half of the war, the Union Army was outmaneuvered and outgeneraled by Robert E. Lee and his commanders. The Confederates were fighting on their home ground and could defend their positions more readily when attacked. Lee pushed as far north as Pennsylvania, but after the devastating Battle of Gettysburg in the first week of July 1863—the high-water mark of the Confederacy—his offensive efforts were thwarted.

Lincoln's Emancipation Proclamation was intertwined with the military and political situation. The proclamation freed all slaves in the states waging war against the Union; it exempted the border slave states and all or part of the three Confederate states controlled by the Union Army on grounds that they were not in rebellion against the United States. The proclamation of freedom had a psychological and practical effect at home; it gained Union supporters in Europe, as well. In spite of the prejudice that existed, Lincoln called early for the use of Negro troops. Between the Emancipation Proclamation in January 1863 and the end of the war, 180,000 Negroes enlisted and fought under the Union flag—"brave in action, patient under dangerous and heavy labors, and cheerful amid hardships and privations."

The Emancipation Proclamation coincided with a turn in the Union's military fortunes. After Lincoln chose General Ulysses S. Grant to lead the Union Armies, forces under General William T. Sherman made their famous march to the sea, cutting a swath through the Deep South, tearing up railroads, burning cotton bales, destroying military stores. The South was starving and losing; all roads led to surrender at Appomattox Court House on April 9, 1865.

The mighty scourge of war passed away. Lincoln had liberated Richmond five days before the end of the war, shaking hands with bowing Negroes who had been freed by "Father Abraham." He had put black men into Union blue, sometimes against the wishes of northerners, and given the ex-slaves rifles to carry and use in the field. Forevermore, Lincoln would be known as the Great Emancipator.

Lincoln's Second Inaugural Address on March 4, 1865, ranks with the Gettysburg Address as the President's most eloquent statement. Speaking in a voice that was "not heavy or coarse, but singularly clear and penetrating, with almost a metallic ring," according to a soldier standing nearby, Lincoln addressed his "fellow countrymen." The eloquence is there in the persuasive balancing of opposites and alternatives; the Emancipator is there and, even more, the man of principle and peace:

Yet, if God wills that [the war] continue, until all the wealth piled by the bond-man's two hundred and fifty years of unrequited toil shall be sunk, and until every drop of blood drawn with the lash, shall be paid by another drawn with the sword, as was said three thousand years ago, so still it must be said "the judgments of the Lord, are true and righteous altogether."

In his final words, promising to "bind up the nation's wounds; to care for him who shall have borne the battle, and for his widow, and his orphan," those present noticed that the President made no distinction between Union and Confederate. This magnanimous approach is interpreted as a guide to the Reconstruction years under Lincoln; after all, his second term of office was expected to run to March 1869.

Unknown to his audience, the President made a change

in the last two words of his Second Inaugural. He originally wrote, "to do all which may achieve and cherish a just, and a lasting peace, among ourselves, and with the world." On his handwritten manuscript he struck out the words "the world" and wrote above, "all nations." We can surmise that he did so because of the sound of the language and because Lincoln envisioned a biblical time of international amity, when brother would not rise against brother, and when swords would be beaten into plowshares.

In his lifetime and in ours, wherever people of color, ethnic minorities or people in bondage suffer, the Lincoln testament inflames dreams. On every continent his forceful words and breadth of vision cross cultural and geographic borders.

"Let free men religiously keep sacred the day of the fall of slavery," Garibaldi said to the Italian people. "Prosperity to you, Abraham Lincoln, pilot of liberty."

A contemporary of Lincoln, Karl Marx, exiled from Germany for his radical views, wrote: "In my opinion, the biggest things that are happening in the world today are, on the one hand, the movement of slaves in America started by the death of John Brown and, on the other, the movement of serfs in Russia. Lincoln is a figure *sui generis* in the annals of history. Indecisively, against his will, he reluctantly performs the *bravura aria* of his role as though asking pardon for the fact that circumstances are forcing him to play the hero. Is there no meaning in the fact that everything of significance taking shape in the New World makes its appearance in such everyday forms?"

In a poem about the assassination of Lincoln, the playwright Henrik Ibsen said that a shot was fired in the New World that reverberated all over Europe. With a sorrow resembling Walt Whitman's on the death of Lincoln—"When lilacs last in the dooryard bloom'd"—Ibsen wrote of "the bloodred honor band that crossed the breast" of the martyr Lincoln.

Prime Minister Jawaharlal Nehru of free India revealed that for years he kept on his study table a brass mold of Lincoln's right hand. "It is a beautiful hand, strong and firm and yet gentle," said the man of Asia, "and I look at it every day, and it gives me strength."

The eminent sculptor Leonard Volk had journeyed to Springfield during the presidential campaign of 1860 to make plaster casts of the candidate's hands for posterity. He worked in his subject's dining room. Molding the left hand, Volk paused a few moments to hear Lincoln tell of a scar on the thumb. "You have heard that they call me the Rail Splitter candidate," Lincoln said, "and you saw them carrying rails in the procession Saturday evening. Well, it is true that I did split rails, and one day, while I was sharpening a wedge on a log, the axe glanced and nearly took my thumb off, and there is the scar, you see."

When the sculptor requested that the right hand hold something, Lincoln went to the woodshed beyond his house. Volk heard him sawing; he returned whittling the end of a broomstick. Volk remarked that it was not necessary to whittle the edges clean. "Oh, well," said Lincoln, "I thought I would like to have it nice."

The fact that this hand, of all hands, should symbolize for Nehru of India "our thinking and our urges" indicates the continuing and powerful influence of Lincoln's humanity the world over; his language and libertarian ideas still transcend racial divides and political barriers. He personifies to other nations—as he does to Americans—the ideals of the presidency and the United States.

Lincoln was not always the great image of America in the world. The *Times* of London, which was widely reprinted on the Continent and in the British Empire, thundered sarcastically against him. "It is rarely that a man can be found to balance accurately mischief to another against advantage to himself," the British newspaper said of him in 1862. Sir John Tenniel, who late became famous for his drawings of *Alice in Wonderland*, drew ghoulish anti-Lincoln fantasies for *Punch*, including Lincoln as a "Federal Phoenix" rising from the flames of the Constitution and States' Rights. In France the Emperor Napoleon III's organ, *Le Pays*, chided the American President for dividing the Republic.

But a turning point in the world's estimate of Lincoln came on the first day of 1863 when he issued the Emancipation Proclamation. Then his stature began to grow among people and nations. "Linkum" became a name heard on continents where white men were in the minority. Even the workers of Manchester, England—in spite of the shutdown of some of their cotton mills formerly supplied by the American South with slave labor—sent resolutions of approval. Replying, Lincoln showed an awareness of the world forum for his words: "A fair examination of history has seemed to authorize a belief that the past action and influences of the United States were generally regarded as having been beneficient toward mankind."

In the last year of the President's life, the hostile European press began to take notice of the simplicity and majesty of the thoughts behind his language. The words of the Second Inaugural were widely disseminated abroad; the idea of "a lasting peace, among ourselves, and with all nations," struck a responsive chord. His assassination did not in itself make the President a world figure, although it did serve to dramatize his memory.

A day after Lincoln's death a young French lawyer, Marquis Adolphe de Chambrun, whose opinions carried weight in political and Church circles in Paris and Rome, wrote to his wife an estimate of Lincoln: "He was well aware that in a free democracy close union must always exist between the authority which represents the nation and

the nation itself. Slavery seemed to him unquestionably unjust and, for that reason, hateful. He had found in the
Declaration of Independence the principle of liberty and
equality."

In 1909, on the centenary of Lincoln's birth, the Russian
novelist Leo Tolstoy told of traveling in the Caucasus,
where he was the guest of a wild chieftain and his tribe.
The chieftain asked about the great leaders of the world
beyond his range, and Tolstoy spoke of czars and generals
from Alexander to Napoleon. Yet the mountain man said,

But you have not told us about the greatest general and ruler
of the world. We want to know something about him. He spoke
with a voice of thunder, he laughed like the sunrise and his deeds
were strong as the rock and as sweet as the fragrance of roses.
He was so great that he even forgave the crimes of his greatest
enemies and shook brotherly hands with those who had plotted
against his life. His name was Lincoln and the country in which
he lived is called America. Tell us of that man.

And the civilized man of Russia told the wild herdsman
his own view of Lincoln: "He was the only real giant in
depth of feeling and in certain moral power. He was one
who wanted to be great through his smallness. He wanted
to see himself in the world, not the world in himself."

From this vision of Lincoln in the world it is possible to
understand why the sixteenth President still stands alone in
the pantheon of American Presidents.

It is possible to realize why the first President of modern
China, Sun Yat-sen, turned to the Gettysburg Address in
formulating his basic philosophy of government: "The Three
Principles of the People correspond with the principles
stated by President Lincoln—'government of the people, by
the people, for the people.' I translated them into *min yu*
(the people to have), *min chih* (the people to govern), and
min hsiang (the people to enjoy)."

It is possible to know why, during the 1956 Hungarian uprising against Soviet domination in postwar Europe, a voice came out of the night on Hungarian radio with the words, "Four score and seven years ago." In clear English, through the static and background noises, the broadcast faded out: "The brave men, living and dead, who struggled here, have consecrated it, far above our poor power to add or detract . . ."

During the final year of the Civil War, Commander-in-Chief Lincoln's generals conducted war plunder in the South. But on Lincoln's orders, their terror tactics were inflicted almost entirely upon property and the tools and arms of war. In the most terrible war known to the civilized world up to that time, there was no Inquisition, no Dachau, no Hiroshima, no Mylai ever associated with the name of Abraham Lincoln.

—HERBERT MITGANG

1.

THE PRAIRIE LAWYER

To the People of Sangamo County

To the People of Sangamo County

FELLOW-CITIZENS: Having become a candidate for the honorable office of one of your representatives in the next General Assembly of this state, in accordance with an established custom, and the principles of true republicanism, it becomes my duty to make known to you—the people whom I propose to represent—my sentiments with regard to local affairs.

Time and experience have verified to a demonstration, the public utility of internal improvements. That the poorest and most thinly populated countries would be greatly benefitted by the opening of good roads, and in the clearing of navigable streams within their limits, is what no person will deny. But yet it is folly to undertake works of this or any other kind, without first knowing that we are able to finish them—as half finished work generally proves to be labor lost. There cannot justly be any objection to having rail roads and canals, any more than to other good things, provided they cost nothing. The only objection is to paying for them; and the objection to paying arises from the want of ability to pay.

With respect to the county of Sangamo, some more easy means of communication than we now possess, for the purpose of facilitating the task of exporting the surplus products of its fertile soil, and importing necessary articles from abroad, are indispensably necessary. A meeting has been held of the citizens of Jacksonville, and the adjacent country, for the purpose of deliberating and enquiring into the expediency of constructing a rail road from some eligible point on the Illinois river, through the town of Jacksonville, in Mor-

gan county, to the town of Springfield, in Sangamo county.
This is, indeed, a very desirable object. No other improvement that reason will justify us in hoping for, can equal in
utility the rail road. It is a never failing source of communication, between places of business remotely situated from
each other. Upon the rail road the regular progress of commercial intercourse is not interrupted by either high or low
water, or freezing weather, which are the principal difficulties that render our future hopes of water communication
precarious and uncertain. Yet, however desirable an object
the construction of a rail road through our country may be;
however high our imaginations may be heated at thoughts
of it—there is always a heart appalling shock accompanying
the account of its cost, which forces us to shrink from our
pleasing anticipations. The probable cost of this contemplated rail road is estimated at $290,000;—the bare state-
ment of which, in my opinion, is sufficient to justify the
belief, that the improvement of Sangamo river is an object
much better suited to our infant resources.

Respecting this view, I think I may say, without the fear
of being contradicted, that its navigation may be rendered
completely practicable, as high as the mouth of the South
Fork, or probably higher, to vessels of from 25 to 30 tons
burthen, for at least one half of all common years, and to
vessels of much greater burthen a part of that time. From
my peculiar circumstances, it is probable that for the last
twelve months I have given as particular attention to the
stage of the water in this river, as any other person in the
country. In the month of March, 1831, in company with
others, I commenced the building of a flat boat on the Sangamo, and finished and took her out in the course of the
spring. Since that time, I have been concerned in the mill
at New Salem. These circumstances are sufficient evidence,
that I have not been very inattentive to the stages of the
water. The time at which we crossed the mill dam, being
in the last days of April, the water was lower than it had

been since the breaking of winter in February, or than it was for several weeks after. The principal difficulties we encountered in descending the river, were from the drifted timber, which obstructions all know is not difficult to be removed. Knowing almost precisely the height of water at that time, I believe I am safe in saying that it has as often been higher as lower since.

From this view of the subject, it appears that my calculations with regard to the navigation of the Sangamo, cannot be unfounded in reason; but whatever may be its natural advantages, certain it is, that it never can be practically useful to any great extent, without being greatly improved by art. The drifted timber, as I have before mentioned, is the most formidable barrier to this object. Of all parts of this river, none will require so much labor in proportion, to make it navigable, as the last thirty or thirty-five miles; and going with the meanderings of the channel, when we are this distance above its mouth, we are only between twelve and eighteen miles above Beardstown, in something near a straight direction; and this route is upon such low ground as to retain water in many places during the season, and in all parts such as to draw two-thirds or three-fourths of the river water at all high stages.

This route is upon prairie land the whole distance;—so that it appears to me, by removing the turf, a sufficient width and damming up the old channel, the whole river in a short time would wash its way through, thereby curtailing the distance, and increasing the velocity of the current very considerably, while there would be no timber upon the banks to obstruct its navigation in future; and being nearly straight, the timber which might float in at the head, would be apt to go clear through. There are also many places above this where the river, in its zig zag course, forms such complete peninsulas, as to be easier cut through at the necks than to remove the obstructions from the bends—which if done, would also lessen the distance.

What the cost of this work would be, I am unable to say. It is probable, however, it would not be greater than is common to streams of the same length. Finally, I believe the improvement of the Sangamo river, to be vastly important and highly desirable to the people of this county; and if elected, any measure in the legislature having this for its object, which may appear judicious, will meet my approbation, and shall receive my support.

It appears that the practice of loaning money at exorbitant rates of interest, has already been opened as a field for discussion; so I suppose I may enter upon it without claiming the honor, or risking the danger, which may await its first explorer. It seems as though we are never to have an end to this baneful and corroding system, acting almost as prejudicial to the general interests of the community as a direct tax of several thousand dollars annually laid on each county, for the benefit of a few individuals only, unless there be a law made setting a limit to rates of usury. A law for this purpose, I am of opinion, may be made, without materially injuring any class of people. In cases of extreme necessity there could always be means found to cheat the law, while in all other cases it would have its intended effect. I would not favor the passage of a law upon this subject, which might be very easily evaded. Let it be such that the labor and difficulty of evading it, could only be justified in cases of the greatest necessity.

Upon the subject of education, not presuming to dictate any plan or system respecting it, I can only say that I view it as the most important subject which we as a people can be engaged in. That every man may receive at least, a moderate education, and thereby be enabled to read the histories of his own and other countries, by which he may duly appreciate the value of our free institutions, appears to be an object of vital importance, even on this account alone, to say nothing of the advantages and satisfaction to be derived from all being able to read the scriptures and other works, both of a religious and moral nature, for themselves. For my part, I desire to see the time when education, and by its means, morality, sobriety, enterprise and industry, shall become much more general than at present, and should be gratified to have it in my power to contribute something to the advancement of any measure which might have a tendency to accelerate the happy period.

With regard to existing laws, some alterations are thought to be necessary. Many respectable men have suggested that our estray laws—the law respecting the issuing of executions, the road law, and some others, are deficient in their present form, and require alterations. But considering the great probability that the framers of those laws were wiser than myself, I should prefer not meddling with them, unless they were first attacked by others, in which case I should feel it both a privilege and a duty to take that stand, which in my view, might tend most to the advancement of justice.

But, Fellow-Citizens, I shall conclude. Considering the great degree of modesty which should always attend youth, it is probable I have already been more presuming than becomes me. However, upon the subjects of which I have treated, I have spoken as I thought. I may be wrong in regard to any or all of them; but holding it a sound maxim, that it is better to be only sometimes right, than at all times wrong, so soon as I discover my opinions to be erroneous, I shall be ready to renounce them.

Every man is said to have his peculiar ambition. Whether it be true or not, I can say for one that I have no other so great as that of being truly esteemed of my fellow men, by rendering myself worthy of their esteem. How far I shall succeed in gratifying this ambition, is yet to be developed. I am young and unknown to many of you. I was born and have ever remained in the most humble walks of life. I have no wealthy or popular relations to recommend me. My case is thrown exclusively upon the independent voters of this county, and if elected they will have conferred a favor upon me, for which I shall be unremitting in my labors to compensate. But if the good people in their wisdom shall see fit to keep me in the background, I have been too familiar with disappointments to be very much chagrined. Your friend and fellow-citizen,

New Salem, March 9, 1832.

To the Editor of the Sangamo Journal

To the Editor of the Journal: New Salem, June 13, 1836.

In your paper of last Saturday, I see a communication over the signature of "Many Voters," in which the candidates who are announced in the Journal, are called upon to "show their hands." Agreed. Here's mine!

I go for all sharing the privileges of the government, who assist in bearing its burthens. Consequently I go for admitting all whites to the right of suffrage, who pay taxes or bear arms, (by no means excluding females.)

If elected, I shall consider the whole people of Sangamon my constituents, as well those that oppose, as those that support me.

While acting as their representative, I shall be governed by their will, on all subjects upon which I have the means of knowing what their will is; and upon all others, I shall do what my own judgment teaches me will best advance their interests. Whether elected or not, I go for distributing the proceeds of the sales of the public lands to the several states, to enable our state, in common with others, to dig canals and construct rail roads, without borrowing money and paying interest on it.

If alive on the first Monday in November, I shall vote for Hugh L. White for President. Very respectfully,

Protest in the Illinois Legislature on Slavery

The following protest was presented to the House, which was read and ordered to be spread on the journals, to wit:

"Resolutions upon the subject of domestic slavery having passed both branches of the General Assembly at its present session, the undersigned hereby protest against the passage of the same.

They believe that the institution of slavery is founded on both injustice and bad policy; but that the promulgation of abolition doctrines tends rather to increase than to abate its evils.

They believe that the Congress of the United States has no power, under the constitution, to interfere with the institution of slavery in the different States.

They believe that the Congress of the United States has the power, under the constitution, to abolish slavery in the District of Columbia; but that that power ought not to be exercised unless at the request of the people of said District.

The difference between these opinions and those contained in the said resolutions, is their reason for entering this protest."

DAN STONE,
A. LINCOLN,
Representatives from the county of Sangamon.
March 3, 1837

Address to the Young Men's Lyceum of Springfield, Illinois

THE PERPETUATION OF OUR POLITICAL INSTITUTIONS

As a subject for the remarks of the evening, *the perpetuation of our political institutions*, is selected.

In the great journal of things happening under the sun, we, the American People, find our account running, under date of the nineteenth century of the Christian era. We find ourselves in the peaceful possession, of the fairest portion of the earth, as regards extent of territory, fertility of soil, and salubrity of climate. We find ourselves under the government of a system of political institutions, conducing more essentially to the ends of civil and religious liberty, than any of which the history of former times tells us. We, when mounting the stage of existence, found ourselves the legal inheritors of these fundamental blessings. We toiled not in the acquirement or establishment of them—they are a legacy bequeathed us, by a *once* hardy, brave, and patriotic, but *now* lamented and departed race of ancestors. Their's was the task (and nobly they performed it) to possess themselves, and through themselves, us, of this goodly land; and to uprear upon its hills and its valleys, a political edifice of liberty and equal rights; 'tis ours only, to transmit these, the former, unprofaned by the foot of an invader; the latter, undecayed by the lapse of time, and untorn by usurpation—to the latest generation that fate shall permit the world to know. This task of gratitude to our fathers, justice to ourselves, duty to posterity, and love for our species in general, all imperatively require us faithfully to perform.

How, then, shall we perform it? At what point shall we expect the approach of danger? By what means shall we fortify against it? Shall we expect some transatlantic military giant, to step the Ocean, and crush us at a blow? Never!

All the armies of Europe, Asia and Africa combined, with all the treasure of the earth (our own excepted) in their military chest; with a Buonaparte for a commander, could not by force, take a drink from the Ohio, or make a track on the Blue Ridge, in a trial of a thousand years.

At what point then is the approach of danger to be expected? I answer, if it ever reach us, it must spring up amongst us. It cannot come from abroad. If destruction be our lot, we must ourselves be its author and finisher. As a nation of freemen, we must live through all time, or die be suicide.

I hope I am over wary; but if I am not, there is, even now, something of ill-omen amongst us. I mean the increasing disregard for law which pervades the country; the growing disposition to substitute the wild and furious passions, in lieu of the sober judgement of Courts; and the worse than savage mobs, for the executive ministers of justice. This disposition is awfully fearful in any community; and that it now exists in ours, though grating to our feelings to admit, it would be a violation of truth, and an insult to our intelligence, to deny. Accounts of outrages committed by mobs, form the every-day news of the times. They have pervaded the country, from New England to Louisiana;—they are neither peculiar to the eternal snows of the former, nor the burning suns of the latter;—they are not the creature of climate—neither are they confined to the slaveholding, or the non-slaveholding States. Alike, they spring up among the pleasure hunting masters of Southern slaves, and the order loving citizens of the land of steady habits. Whatever, then, their cause may be, it is common to the whole country.

It would be tedious, as well as useless, to recount the horrors of all of them. Those happening in the State of Mississippi, and at St. Louis, are, perhaps, the most dangerous in example, and revolting to humanity. In the Mississippi case, they first commenced by hanging the regular gamblers: a set of men, certainly not following for a livelihood, a very useful, or very honest occupation; but one which, so far from being forbidden by the laws, was actually licensed by an act of the Legislature, passed but a single year before. Next, negroes, suspected of conspiring to raise an insurrection, were caught up and hanged in all parts of the State: then, white men, supposed to be leagued with the negroes; and finally, strangers, from neighboring States, going thither on business, were, in many instances, subjected to the same fate. Thus went on this process of hanging, from gamblers to negroes, from negroes to white citizens, and from these to strangers; till, dead men were seen literally dangling from the boughs of trees upon every road side; and in numbers almost sufficient, to rival the native Spanish moss of the country, as a drapery of the forest.

Turn, then, to that horror-striking scene at St. Louis. A single victim was only sacrificed there. His story is very short; and is, perhaps, the most highly tragic, of any thing of its length, that has ever been witnessed in real life. A mulatto man, by the name of McIntosh, was seized in the street, dragged to the suburbs of the city, chained to a tree, and actually burned to death; and all within a single hour from the time he had been a freeman, attending to his own business, and at peace with the world.

Such are the effects of mob law; and such are the scenes, becoming more and more frequent in this land so lately famed for love of law and order; and the stories of which, have even now grown too familiar, to attract any thing more, than an idle remark.

But you are, perhaps, ready to ask, "What has this to do with the perpetuation of our political institutions?" I answer, it has much to do with it. Its direct consequences are, comparatively speaking, but a small evil; and much of its danger consists, in the proneness of our minds, to regard its direct, as its only consequences. Abstractly considered, the hanging of the gamblers at Vicksburg, was of but little consequence. They constitute a portion of population, that is worse than useless in any community; and their death, if no pernicious example be set by it, is never matter of reasonable regret with any one. If they were annually swept, from the stage of existence, by the plague or small pox, honest men would, perhaps, be much profited, by the operation. Similar too, is the correct reasoning, in regard to the burning of the negro at St. Louis. He had forfeited his life, by the perpetration of an outrageous murder, upon one of the most worthy and respectable citizens of the city; and had he not died as he did, he must have died by the sentence of the law, in a very short time afterwards. As to him alone, it was as well the way it was, as it could otherwise have been. But the example in either case, was fearful. When men take it in their heads to day, to hang gamblers, or burn murderers, they should recollect, that, in the confusion usually attending such transactions, they will be as likely to hang or burn some one, who is neither a gambler nor a murderer as one who is; and that, acting upon the example they set, the mob of to-morrow, may, and probably will, hang or burn some of them, by the very same mistake. And not only so; the innocent, those who have ever set their faces against violations of law in every shape, alike with the guilty, fall victims to the ravages of mob law; and thus it goes on, step by step, till all the walls erected for the defence of the persons and property of individuals, are trodden down, and disregarded. But all this even, is not the full extent of the evil. By such examples, by instances of the perpetrators of such acts going unpunished, the lawless in spirit, are encouraged to become lawless in practice; and having been used to no restraint, but dread of punishment, they thus become, absolutely unrestrained. Having ever regarded Government as their deadliest bane, they make a jubilee of the suspension of its operations; and pray for nothing so much, as its total annihilation. While, on the other hand, good men, men who love tranquility, who desire to abide by the laws, and enjoy their benefits, who would gladly spill their blood in the defence of their country; seeing their property destroyed; their families insulted, and their lives endangered; their persons injured; and seeing nothing in prospect that forebodes a change for the better; become tired of, and disgusted with, a Government that offers them no protection; and are not much averse to a change in which they imagine they have nothing to lose. Thus, then, by the operation of this mobocratic spirit, which all must admit, is now abroad in the land, the strongest bulwark of any Government, and particularly of those constituted like ours, may effectually be broken down and destroyed—I mean the *attachment* of the People. Whenever this effect shall be produced among us; whenever the vicious portion of population shall be permitted to gather in bands of hundreds and thousands, and burn churches, ravage and rob provision stores, throw printing presses into rivers, shoot editors, and hang and burn obnoxious persons at pleasure, and with impunity; depend on it, this Government cannot last. By such things, the feelings of the best citizens will become more or less alienated from it; and thus it will be left without friends, or with too few, and those few too weak, to make their friendship effectual. At such a time and under such circumstances, men of sufficient talent and ambition will not be wanting to seize the opportunity, strike the blow, and overturn that fair fabric, which for the last half century, has been the fondest hope, of the lovers of freedom, throughout the world.

I know the American People are *much* attached to their Government;—I know they would suffer *much* for its sake;—I know they would endure evils long and patiently, before they would ever think of exchanging it for another. Yet, notwithstanding all this, if the laws be continually despised and disregarded, if their rights to be secure in their persons and property, are held by no better tenure than the caprice of a mob, the alienation of their affections from the Government is the natural consequence; and to that, sooner or later, it must come.

Here then, is one point at which danger may be expected.

The question recurs "how shall we fortify against it?" The answer is simple. Let every American, every lover of liberty, every well wisher to his posterity, swear by the blood of the Revolution, never to violate in the least particular, the laws of the country; and never to tolerate their violation by others. As the patriots of seventy-six did to the support of the Declaration of Independence, so to the support of the Constitution and Laws, let every American pledge his life, his property, and his sacred honor;—let every man remember that to violate the law, is to trample on the blood of his father, and to tear the character of his own, and his children's liberty. Let reverence for the laws, be breathed by every American mother, to the lisping babe, that prattles on her lap—let it be taught in schools, in seminaries, and in colleges;—let it be written in Primmers, spelling books, and in Almanacs;—let it be preached from the pulpit, proclaimed in legislative halls, and enforced in courts of justice. And, in short, let it become the *political religion* of the nation; and let the old and the young, the rich and the poor, the grave and the gay, of all sexes and tongues, and colors and conditions, sacrifice unceasingly upon its altars.

While ever a state of feeling, such as this, shall universally, or even, very generally prevail throughout the nation, vain will be every effort, and fruitless every attempt, to subvert our national freedom.

When I so pressingly urge a strict observance of all the laws, let me not be understood as saying there are no bad laws, nor that grievances may not arise, for the redress of which, no legal provisions have been made. I mean to say no such thing. But I do mean to say, that, although bad laws, if they exist, should be repealed as soon as possible, still while they continue in force, for the sake of example, they should be religiously observed. So also in unprovided cases. If such arise, let proper legal provisions be made for them with the least possible delay; but, till then, let them if not too intolerable, be borne with.

There is no grievance that is a fit object of redress by mob law. In any case that arises, as for instance, the promulgation of abolitionism, one of two positions is necessarily true; that is, the thing is right within itself, and therefore deserves the protection of all law and all good citizens; or, it is wrong, and therefore proper to be prohibited by legal enactments; and in neither case, is the interposition of mob law, either necessary, justifiable, or excusable.

But, it may be asked, why suppose danger to our political institutions? Have we not preserved them for more than fifty years? And why may we not for fifty times as long?

We hope there is no *sufficient* reason. We hope all dangers may be overcome; but to conclude that no danger may ever arise, would itself be extremely dangerous. There are now, and will hereafter be, many causes, dangerous in their tendency, which have not existed heretofore; and which are not too insignificant to merit attention. That our government should have been maintained in its original form from its establishment until now, is not much to be wondered at. It had many props to support it through that period, which now are decayed, and crumbled away. Through that period, it was felt by all, to be an undecided experiment; now, it is understood to be a successful one. Then, all that sought celebrity and fame, and distinction, expected to find them in the success of that experiment. Their *all* was staked upon it:—their destiny was *inseparably* linked with it. Their ambition aspired to display before an admiring world, a practical demonstration of the truth of a proposition, which had hitherto been considered, at best no better, than problematical; namely, *the capability of a people to govern themselves*. If they succeeded, they were to be immortalized; their names were to be transferred to counties and cities, and rivers and mountains; and to be revered and sung, and toasted through all time. If they failed, they were to be called knaves and fools, and fanatics for a fleeting hour; then to sink and be forgotten. They succeeded. The experiment is successful; and thousands have won their deathless names in making it so. But the game is caught; and I believe it is true, that with the catching, end the pleasures of the chase. This field of glory is harvested, and the crop is already appropriated. But new reapers will arise, and *they*, too, will seek a field. It is to deny, what the history of the world tells us is true, to suppose that men of ambition and talents will not continue to spring up amongst us. And, when they do, they will as naturally seek the gratification of their ruling passion, as others have *so* done before them. The question then, is, can that gratification be found in supporting and maintaining an edifice that has been erected by others? Most certainly it cannot. Many great and good men sufficiently qualified for any task they should undertake, may ever be found, whose ambition would aspire to nothing beyond a seat in Congress, a gubernatorial or a presidential chair; *but such belong not to the family of the lion, or the tribe of the eagle*. What! think you these places would satisfy an Alexander, a Caesar, or a Napoleon? Never! Towering genius disdains a beaten path. It seeks regions hitherto unexplored. It sees *no distinction* in adding story to story, upon the monuments of fame, erected to the memory of others. It *denies* that it is glory enough to serve under any chief. It *scorns* to tread in the footsteps of *any* predecessor, however illustrious. It thirsts and burns for distinction; and, if possible, it will have it, whether at the expense of emancipating slaves, or enslaving freemen. Is it unreasonable then to expect, that some man possessed of the loftiest genius, coupled with ambition sufficient to push it to its utmost stretch, will at some time, spring up among us? And when such a one does, it will require the people to be united with each other, attached to the government and laws, and generally intelligent, to successfully frustrate his designs.

Distinction will be his paramount object; and although he

would as willingly, perhaps more so, acquire it by doing good as harm; yet, that opportunity being past, and nothing left to be done in the way of building up, he would set boldly to the task of pulling down.

Here then, is a probable case, highly dangerous, and such a one as could not have well existed heretofore.

Another reason which *once was;* but which, to the same extent, is *now no more,* has done much in maintaining our institutions thus far. I mean the powerful influence which the interesting scenes of the revolution had upon the *passions* of the people as distinguished from their judgment. By this influence, the jealousy, envy, and avarice, incident to our nature, and so common to a state of peace, prosperity, and conscious strength, were, for the time, in a great measure smothered and rendered inactive; while the deep rooted principles of *hate,* and the powerful motive of *revenge,* instead of being turned against each other, were directed exclusively against the British nation. And thus, from the force of circumstances, the basest principles of our nature, were either made to lie dormant, or to become the active agents in the advancement of the noblest of cause—that of establishing and maintaining civil and religious liberty.

But this state of feeling *must fade, is fading, has faded,* with the circumstances that produced it.

I do not mean to say, that the scenes of the revolution *are now* or *ever will be* entirely forgotten; but that like every thing else, they must fade upon the memory of the world, and grow more and more dim by the lapse of time. In history, we hope, they will be read of, and recounted, so long as the bible shall be read;—but even granting that they will, their influence *cannot be* what it heretofore has been. Even then, they *cannot be* so universally known, nor so vividly felt, as they were by the generation just gone to rest. At the close of that struggle, nearly every adult male had been a participator in some of its scenes. The consequence was, that of those scenes, in the form of a husband, a father, a son or a brother, a *living history was* to be found in every family—a history bearing the indubitable testimonies of its own authenticity, in the limbs mangled, in the scars of wounds received, in the midst of the very scenes related—a history, too, that could be read and understood alike by all, the wise and the ignorant, the learned and the unlearned. But *those* histories are gone. They *can* be read no more forever. They *were* a fortress of strength; but, what invading foemen could *never do,* the silent artillery of time *has done;* the levelling of its walls. They are gone. They *were* a forest of giant oaks; but the all resistless hurricane has swept over them, and left only, here and there, a lonely trunk, despoiled of its verdure, shorn of its foliage; unshading and unshaded, to murmur in a few more gentle breezes, and to combat with its mutilated limbs, a few more ruder storms, then to sink, and be no more.

They *were* the pillars of the temple of liberty; and now, that they have crumbled away, that temple must fall, unless we, their descendants, supply their places with other pillars, hewn from the solid quarry of sober reason. Passion has helped us; but can do so no more. It will in future be our enemy. Reason, cold, calculating, unimpassioned reason, must furnish all the materials for our future support and defence. Let those materials be moulded into *general intelligence, sound morality* and, in particular, *a reverence for the constitution and laws;* and, that we improved to the last; that we remained free to the last; that we revered his name to the last; that, during his long sleep, we permitted no hostile foot to pass over or desecrate his resting place; shall be that which to learn the last trump shall awaken our WASHINGTON.

Upon these let the proud fabric of freedom rest, as the rock of its basis; and as truly as has been said of the only greater institution, *"the gates of hell shall not prevail against it."*

January 27, 1838

My Childhood-Home I See Again

My childhood-home I see again,
   And gladden with the view;
And still as mem'ries crowd my brain,
   There's sadness in it too.

O memory! thou mid-way world
   'Twixt Earth and Paradise,
Where things decayed, and loved ones lost
   In dreamy shadows rise.

And freed from all that's gross or vile,
   Seem hallowed, pure, and bright,
Like scenes in some enchanted isle,
   All bathed in liquid light.

As distant mountains please the eye,
   When twilight chases day—
As bugle-tones, that, passing by,
   In distance die away—

As leaving some grand water-fall
   We ling'ring, list it's roar,
So memory will hallow all
   We've known, but know no more.

Now twenty years have passed away,
   Since here I bid farewell
To woods, and fields, and scenes of play
   And school-mates loved so well.

Where many were, how few remain
   Of old familiar things!
But seeing these to mind again
   The lost and absent brings.

The friends I left that parting day—
  How changed, as time has sped!
Young childhood grown, strong manhood grey,
  And half of all are dead.

I hear the lone survivors tell
  How nought from death could save,
Till every sound appears a knell,
  And every spot a grave.

I range the fields with pensive tread,
  And pace the hollow rooms;
And feel (companions of the dead)
  I'm living in the tombs.

And here's an object more of dread,
  Than ought the grave contains—
A human-form, with reason fled,
  While wretched life remains.

Poor Matthew! Once of genius bright,—
  A fortune-favored child—
Now locked for aye, in mental night,
  A haggard mad-man wild.

Poor Matthew! I have ne'er forgot
  When first with maddened will,
Yourself you maimed, your father fought,
  And mother strove to kill;

And terror spread, and neighbours ran,
  Your dang'rous strength to bind;
And soon a howling crazy man,
  Your limbs were fast confined.

How then you writhed and shrieked aloud,
  Your bones and sinnews bared;
And fiendish on the gaping crowd,
  With burning eye-balls glared.

And begged, and swore, and wept, and prayed,
  With maniac laughter joined—
How fearful are the signs displayed,
  By pangs that kill the mind!

And when at length, tho' drear and long,
  Time soothed your fiercer woes—
How plaintively your mournful song,
  Upon the still night rose.

I've heard it oft, as if I dreamed,
  Far-distant, sweet, and lone;
The funeral dirge it ever seemed
  Of reason dead and gone.

To drink it's strains, I've stole away,
  All silently and still,
Ere yet the rising god of day
  Had streaked the Eastern hill.

Air held his breath; the trees all still
  Seemed sorr'wing angels round.
Their swelling tears in dew-drops fell
  Upon the list'ning ground.

But this is past, and nought remains
  That raised you o'er the brute.
Your mad'ning shrieks and soothing strains
  Are like forever mute.

Now fare thee well: more thou the cause
  Than subject now of woe.
All mental pangs, but time's kind laws,
  Hast lost the power to know.

And now away to seek some scene
  Less painful than the last—
With less of horror mingled in
  The present and the past.

The very spot where grew the bread
  That formed my bones, I see.
How strange, old field, on thee to tread,
  And feel I'm part of thee!

c. February 1846

Handbill Replying to Charges of Infidelity

To the Voters of the Seventh Congressional District.

FELLOW CITIZENS:

A charge having got into circulation in some of the neighborhoods of this District, in substance that I am an open scoffer at Christianity, I have by the advice of some friends concluded to notice the subject in this form. That I am not a member of any Christian Church, is true; but I have never denied the truth of the Scriptures; and I have never spoken with intentional disrespect of religion in general, or of any denomination of Christians in particular. It is true that in early life I was inclined to believe in what I understand is called the "Doctrine of Necessity"—that is, that the human mind is impelled to action, or held in rest by some power, over which the mind itself has no control; and I have sometimes (with one, two or three, but never publicly) tried to maintain this opinion in argument. The habit of arguing thus however, I have, entirely left off for more than five years. And I add here, I have always understood this same opinion to be held by several of the Christian denominations. The foregoing, is the whole truth, briefly stated, in relation to myself, upon this subject.

I do not think I could myself, be brought to support a man for office, whom I knew to be an open enemy of, and scoffer at, religion. Leaving the higher matter of eternal consequences, between him and his Maker, I still do not think any man has the right thus to insult the feelings, and injure the morals, of the community in which he may live. If, then, I was guilty of such conduct, I should blame no man who should condemn me for it; but I do blame those, whoever they may be, who falsely put such a charge in circulation against me.

July 31, 1846.

"Spot" Resolutions in the U.S. House of Representatives

Whereas the President of the United States, in his message of May 11th. 1846, has declared that "The Mexican Government not only refused to receive him" (the envoy of the U.S.) "or listen to his propositions, but, after a long continued series of menaces, have at last invaded *our teritory*, and shed the blood of our fellow *citizens* on *our own soil*"

And again, in his message of December 8, 1846 that "We had ample cause of war against Mexico, long before the breaking out of hostilities. But even then we forbore to take redress into our own hands, until Mexico herself became the aggressor by invading *our soil* in hostile array, and shedding the blood of our *citizens*"

And yet again, in his message of December 7–1847 that "The Mexican Government refused even to hear the terms of adjustment which he" (our minister of peace) "was authorized to propose; and finally, under wholly unjustifiable pretexts, involved the two countries in war, by invading the teritory of the State of Texas, striking the first blow, and shedding the blood of our *citizens* on *our own soil*"

And whereas this House desires to obtain a full knowledge of all the facts which go to establish whether the particular spot of soil on which the blood of our *citizens* was so shed, was, or was not, *our own soil*, at that time; therefore

Resolved by the House of Representatives, that the President of the United States be respectfully requested to inform this House—

First: Whether the spot of soil on which the blood of our *citizens* was shed, as in his messages declared, was, or was not, within the teritories of Spain, at least from the treaty of 1819 until the Mexican revolution

Second: Whether that spot is, or is not, within the teritory which was wrested from Spain, by the Mexican revolution.

Third: Whether that spot is, or is not, within a settlement of people, which settlement had existed ever since long before the Texas revolution, until it's inhabitants fled from the approach of the U.S. Army.

Fourth: Whether that settlement is, or is not, isolated from any and all other settlements, by the Gulf of Mexico, and the Rio Grande, on the South and West, and by wide uninhabited regions on the North and East.

Fifth: Whether the *People* of that settlement, or a *majority* of them, or *any* of them, had ever, previous to the bloodshed, mentioned in his messages, submitted themselves to the government or laws of Texas, or of the United

States, by *consent*, or by *compulsion*, either by accepting office, or voting at elections, or paying taxes, or serving on juries, or having process served upon them, or in *any other way*.

Sixth: Whether the People of that settlement, did, or did not, flee from the approach of the United States Army, leaving unprotected their homes and their growing crops, *before* the blood was shed, as in his messages stated; and whether the first blood so shed, was, or was not shed, within the *inclosure* of the People, or some of them, who had thus fled from it.

Seventh: Whether our *citizens*, whose blood was shed, as in his messages declared, were, or were not, at that time, *armed* officers, and *soldiers*, sent into that settlement, by the military order of the President through the Secretary of War—and

Eighth: Whether the military force of the United States, including those *citizens*, was, or was not, so sent into that settlement, after Genl. Taylor had, more than once, intimated to the War Department that, in his opinion, no such movement was necessary to the defence or protection of Texas.

December 22, 1847

Speech in the U.S. House of Representatives on the War with Mexico

Mr. Chairman:

Some, if not all the gentlemen on, the other side of the House, who have addressed the committee within the last two days, have spoken rather complainingly, if I have rightly understood them, of the vote given a week or ten days ago, declaring that the war with Mexico was unnecessarily and unconstitutionally commenced by the President. I admit that such a vote should not be given, in mere party wantonness, and that the one given, is justly censurable, if it have no other, or better foundation. I am one of those who joined in that vote; and I did so under my best impression of the *truth* of the case. How I got this impression, and how it may possibly be removed, I will now try to show. When the war began, it was my opinion that all those who, because of knowing too *little*, or because of knowing too *much*, could not conscientiously approve the conduct of the President, in the beginning of it, should, nevertheless, as good citizens and patriots, remain silent on that point, at least till the war should be ended. Some leading democrats, including Ex President Van Buren, have taken this same view, as I understand them; and I adhered to it, and acted upon it, until since I took my seat here; and I think I should still adhere to it, were it not that the President and his friends will not allow it to be so. Besides the continual effort of the President to argue every silent vote given for supplies, into an endorsement of the justice and wisdom of his conduct—besides that singularly candid paragraph, in his late message in which he tells us that Congress, with great unanimity, only two in the Senate and fourteen in the House dissenting, had declared that, "by the act of the Republic of Mexico, a state of war exists between that Government and the United States," when the same journals that informed him of this, also informed him, that when that declaration stood disconnected from the question of supplies, sixtyseven in the House, and not fourteen merely, voted against it—besides this open attempt to prove, by telling the *truth*, what he could not prove by telling the *whole truth*—demanding of all who will not submit to be misrepresented, in justice to themselves, to speak out—besides all this, one of my colleagues (Mr. Richardson) at a very early day in the session brought in a set of resolutions, expressly endorsing the original justice of the war on the part of the President. Upon these resolutions, when they shall be put on their passage I shall be *compelled* to vote; so that I can not be silent, if I would. Seeing this, I went about preparing myself to give the vote understandingly when it should come. I carefully examined the President's messages, to ascertain what he himself had said and proved upon the point. The result of this examination was to make the impression, that taking for true, all the President states as facts, he falls far short of proving his justification; and that the President would have gone farther with his proof, if it had not been for the small matter, that the *truth* would not permit him. Under the impression thus made, I gave the vote before mentioned. I propose now to give, concisely, the process of the examination I made, and how I reached the conclusion I did. The President, in his first war message of May 1846, declares that the soil was *ours* on which hostilities were commenced by Mexico; and he repeats that declaration, almost in the same language, in each successive annual message, thus showing that he esteems that point, a highly essential one. In the importance of that point, I entirely agree with the President. To my judgment, it is the *very point*, upon which he should be justified, or condemned. In his message of Decr. 1846, it seems to have occurred to him, as is certainly true, that title—ownership—to soil, or any thing else, is not a simple fact; but is a conclusion following one or more simple facts; and that it was incumbent upon him, to present the facts, from which he concluded, the soil was ours, on which the first blood of the war was shed.

Accordingly a little below the middle of page twelve in the message last referred to, he enters upon that task; forming an issue, and introducing testimony, extending the whole, to a little below the middle of page fourteen. Now I propose to try to show, that the whole of this,—issue and evidence— is, from beginning to end, the sheerest deception. The issue, as he presents it, is in these words "But there are those

who, conceding all this to be true, assume the ground that
the true western boundary of Texas is the Nueces, instead
of the Rio Grande; and that, therefore, in marching our
army to the east bank of the latter river, we passed the
Texan line, and invaded the teritory of Mexico." Now this
issue, is made up of two affirmatives and no negative. The
main deception of it is, that it assumes as true, that *one*
river or the *other* is necessarily the boundary; and cheats the
superficial thinker entirely out of the idea, that *possibly* the
boundary is somewhere *between* the two, and not actually
at either. A further deception is, that it will let in *evidence*,
which a true issue would exclude. A true issue, made by
the President, would be about as follows "I say, the soil
was ours, on which the first blood was shed; there are those
who say it was not."

I now proceed to examine the Presidents evidence, as
applicable to such an issue. When that evidence is analized,
it is all included in the following propositions:

1. That the Rio Grande was the Western boundary of
Louisiana as we purchased it of France in 1803.

2. That the Republic of Texas always *claimed* the Rio
Grande, as her Western boundary.

3. That by various acts, she had claimed it *on paper*.

4. That Santa Anna, in his treaty with Texas, recognised the Rio Grande, as her boundary.

5. That Texas *before*, and the U. S. *after*, annexation
had *exercised* jurisdiction *beyond* the Nueces—*between* the
two rivers.

6. That our Congress, *understood* the boundary of Texas
to extend beyond the Nueces.

Now for each of these in it's turn.

His first item is, that the Rio Grande was the Western
boundary of Louisiana, as we purchased it of France in
1803; and seeming to expect this to be disputed, he argues
over the amount of nearly a page, to prove it true; at the
end of which he lets us know, that by the treaty of 1819,

we sold to Spain the whole country from the Rio Grande eastward, to the Sabine. Now, admitting for the present, that the Rio Grande, was the boundary of Louisiana, what, under heaven, had that to do with the *present* boundary between us and Mexico? How, Mr. Chairman, the line, that once divided your land from mine, can *still* be the boundary between us, *after* I have sold my land to you, is, to me, beyond all comprehension. And how any man, with an honest purpose only, of proving the truth, could ever have *thought* of introducing such a fact to prove such an issue, is equally incomprehensible. His next piece of evidence is that "The Republic of Texas always *claimed* this river (Rio Grande) as her western boundary." That is not true, in fact. Texas *has* claimed it, but she has not *always* claimed it. There is, at least, one distinguished exception. Her state constitution,—the republic's most solemn, and well considered act—that which may, without impropriety, be called her last will and testament revoking all others— makes no such claim. But suppose she had always claimed it. Has not Mexico always claimed the contrary? so that there is but *claim* against *claim*, leaving nothing proved, until we get back of the claims, and find which has the better *foundation*. Though not in the order in which the President presents his evidence, I now consider that class of his statements, which are, in substance, nothing more than that Texas has, by various acts of her convention and congress, claimed the Rio Grande, as her boundary, *on paper*. I mean here what he says about the fixing of the Rio Grande as her boundary in her old constitution (not her state constitution) about forming congressional districts, counties &c &c. Now all of this is but naked *claim;* and what I have already said about claims is strictly applicable to this. If I should claim your land, by word of mouth, that certainly would not make it mine; and if I were to claim it by a deed which I had made myself, and with which, you had had nothing to do, the claim would be quite the same, in substance—or rather, in utter nothingness. I next consider the President's statement that Santa Anna in his *treaty* with Texas, recognised the Rio Grande, as the western boundary of Texas. Besides the position, so often taken that Santa Anna, while a prisoner of war—a captive—*could* not bind Mexico by a treaty, which I deem conclusive—besides this, I wish to say something in relation to this treaty, so called by the President, with Santa Anna. If any man would like to be amused by a sight of that *little* thing, which the President calls by that *big* name, he can have it, by turning to Niles' Register volume 50, page 336. And if any one should suppose that Niles' Register is a curious repository of so mighty a document, as a solemn treaty between nations, I can only say that I learned, to a tolerable degree of certainty, by enquiry at the State Department, that the President himself, never saw it any where else. By the way, I believe I should not err, if I were to declare, that during the first ten years of the existence of that document, it was never, by any body, *called* a treaty—that it was never so called, till the President, in his extremity, attempted, by so calling it, to wring something from it in justification of himself in connection with the Mexican war. It has none of the distinguishing features of a treaty. It does not call itself a treaty. Santa Anna does not therein, assume to bind Mexico; he assumes only to act as the President-Commander-in-chief of the Mexican Army and Navy; stipulates that the then present hostilities should cease, and that he would not *himself* take up arms, nor *influence* the Mexican people to take up arms, against Texas during the existence of the war of independence. He did not recognise the independence of Texas; he did not assume to put an end to the war; but clearly indicated his expectation of it's continuance; he did not say one word about boundary, and, most probably, never thought of it. It *is* stipulated therein that the Mexican forces should evacuate the teritory of Texas, *passing to the other side of the Rio Grande;* and in another article, it is stipulated that, to prevent collisions between the armies, the Texan army should not approach nearer than within five leagues—of *what* is not said—but clearly, from the object stated it is—of the Rio Grande. Now, if this is a treaty, recognising the Rio Grande, as the boundary of Texas, it contains the singular feature, of stipulating, that Texas shall not go within five leagues of *her own* boundary.

Next comes the evidence of Texas before annexation, and the United States, afterwards, *exercising* jurisdiction *beyond* the Nueces, and *between* the two rivers. This actual *exercise* of jurisdiction, is the very class or quality of evidence we want. It is excellent so far as it goes; but does it go far enough? He tells us it went *beyond* the Nueces; but he does not tell us it went *to* the Rio Grande. He tells us, jurisdiction was exercised *between* the two rivers, but he does not tell us it was exercised over *all* the teritory between them. Some simple minded people, think it is *possible*, to cross one river and go *beyond* it without going *all the way* to the next—that jurisdiction may be exercised *between* two rivers without covering *all* the country between them. I know a man, not very unlike myself, who exercises jurisdiction over a piece of land between the Wabash and the Mississippi; and yet so far is this from being *all* there is between those rivers, that it is just one hundred and fifty-two feet long by fifty wide, and no part of it much within a hundred miles of either. He has a neighbor between him and the Mississippi,—that is, just across the street, in that direction—whom, I am sure, he could neither *persuade* nor *force* to give up his habitation; but which nevertheless, he could certainly annex, if it were to be done, by merely standing on his own side of the street and *claiming* it, or even, sitting down, and writing a *deed* for it.

But next the President tells us, the Congress of the United States *understood* the state of Texas they admitted into the union, to extend *beyond* the Nueces. Well, I suppose they did. *I* certainly so understood it. But how *far* beyond? That Congress did *not* understand it to extend clear to the Rio Grande, is quite certain by the fact of their joint resolutions, for admission, expressly leaving all questions of boundary to future adjustment. And it may be added, that Texas herself, is proved to have had the same understanding of it, that our Congress had, by the fact of the exact conformity of her new constitution, to those resolutions.

I am now through the whole of the President's evidence; and it is a singular fact, that if any one should declare the President sent the army into the midst of a settlement of Mexican people, who had never submited, by consent or by force, to the authority of Texas or of the United States, and that *there*, and *thereby*, the first blood of the war was shed, there is not one word in all the President has said, which would either admit or deny the declaration. This strange omission, it does seem to me, could not have occurred but by design. My way of living leads me to be about the courts of justice; and there, I have sometimes seen a good lawyer, struggling for his client's neck, in a desparate case, employing every artifice to work round, befog, and cover up, with many words, some point arising in the case, which he *dared* not admit, and yet *could* not deny. Party bias may help to make it appear so; but with all the allowance I can make for such bias, it still does appear, to me, that just such, and from just such necessity, is the President's struggle in this case.

Some time after my colleague (Mr. Richardson) introduced the resolutions I have mentioned, I introduced a preamble, resolution, and interrogatories, intended to draw the President out, if possible, on this hitherto untrodden ground. To show their relevancy, I propose to state my understanding of the true rule for ascertaining the boundary between Texas and Mexico. It is, that *wherever* Texas was *exercising* jurisdiction, was hers; and *wherever* Mexico was exercising jurisdiction, was hers; and that *whatever* separated the actual exercise of jurisdiction of the one, from that of the other, was the true boundary between them. If, as is probably true, Texas was exercising jurisdiction along the western bank of the Nueces, and Mexico was exercising it along the eastern bank of the Rio Grande, then *neither* river was the boundary; but the uninhabited country between the two, was. The extent of our teritory in that region depended, not on any *treaty-fixed* boundary (for no treaty had attempted it) but on revolution. Any people anywhere, being inclined and having the power, have the *right* to rise up, and shake off the existing government, and form a new one that suits them better. This is a most valuable,—a most sacred right—a right, which we hope and believe, is to liberate the world. Nor is this right confined to cases in which the whole people of an existing government, may choose to exercise it. Any portion of such people that *can*, *may* revolutionize, and make their *own*, of so much of the teritory as they inhabit. More than this, a *majority* of any portion of such people may revolutionize, putting down a *minority*, intermingled with, or near about them, who may oppose their movement. Such minority, was precisely the case, of the tories of our own revolution. It is a quality of revolutions not to go by *old* lines, or *old* laws; but to break up both, and make new ones. As to the country now in question, we bought it of France in 1803, and sold it to Spain in 1819, according to the President's statements. After this, all Mexico, including Texas, revolutionized against Spain; and still later, Texas revolutionized against Mexico. In my view, just so far as she carried her revolution, by obtaining the *actual*, willing or unwilling, submission of the people, *so far*, the country was hers, and no farther. Now sir, for the purpose of obtaining the very best evidence, as to whether Texas had actually carried her revolution, to the place where the hostilities of the present war commenced, let the President answer the interrogatories, I proposed, as before mentioned, or some other similar ones. Let him answer, fully, fairly, and candidly. Let him answer with *facts*, and not with arguments. Let him remember he sits where Washington sat, and so remembering, let him answer, as Washington would answer. As a nation *should* not, and the Almighty *will* not, be evaded, so let him attempt no evasion—no equivocation. And if, so answering, he can show that the soil was ours, where the first blood of the war was shed—that it was not within an inhabited country, or, if within such, that the inhabitants had submitted themselves to the civil authority of Texas, or of the United States, and that the same is true of the site of Fort Brown, then I am with him for his justification. In that case I, shall be most happy to reverse the vote I gave the other day. I have a selfish motive for desiring that the President may do this. I expect to give some votes, in connection with the war, which, without his so doing, will be of doubtful propriety in my own judgment, but which will be free from the doubt if he does so. But if he *can* not, or *will* not do this—if on any pretence, or no pretence, he shall refuse or omit it, then I shall be fully convinced, of what I more than suspect already, that he is deeply conscious of being in the wrong—that he feels the blood of this war, like the blood of Abel, is crying to Heaven against him. That originally having some strong motive—what, I will not stop now to give my opinion concerning—to involve the two countries in a war, and trusting to escape scrutiny, by fixing the public gaze upon the exceeding brightness of military glory—that attractive rainbow, that rises in showers of blood—that serpent's eye, that charms to destroy—he plunged into it, and has swept, *on* and *on*, till, disappointed in his calculation of the ease with which Mexico might be subdued, he now finds himself, he knows not where. How like the half insane mumbling of a fever-dream, is the whole war part of his late message! At one time telling us that Mexico has nothing whatever, that we can get, but teritory; at another, showing us how we can support the war, by levying contributions on Mexico.

At one time, urging the national honor, the security of the future, the prevention of foreign interference, and even, the good of Mexico herself, as among the objects of the war; at another, telling us, that "to reject indemnity, by refusing to accept a cession of teritory, would be to abandon all our just demands, and to wage the war, bearing all it's expenses, *without a purpose or definite object.*" So then, the national honor, security of the future, and every thing but teritorial indemnity, may be considered the *no-purposes,* and *indefinite,* objects of the war! But, having it now settled that teritorial indemnity is the only object, we are urged to seize, by legislation here, all that he was content to take, a few months ago, and the whole province of lower California to boot, and to still carry on the war—to take *all* we are fighting for, and *still* fight on. Again, the President is resolved, under all circumstances, to have full teritorial indemnity for the expenses of the war; but he forgets to tell us how we are to get the *excess,* after those expenses shall have surpassed the value of the *whole* of the Mexican teritory. So again, he insists that the separate national existence of Mexico, shall be maintained; but he does not tell us *how* this can be done, after we shall have taken *all* her teritory. Lest the questions, I here suggest, be considered speculative merely, let me be indulged a moment in trying to show they are not. The war has gone on some twenty months; for the expenses of which, together with an inconsiderable old score, the President now claims about one half of the Mexican teritory; and that, by far the better half, so far as concerns our ability to make any thing out of it. *It* is comparatively uninhabited; so that we could establish land offices in it, and raise some money in that way. But the other half is already inhabited, as I understand it, tolerably densely for the nature of the country; and all it's lands, or all that are valuable, already appropriated as private property. How then are we to make any thing out of these lands with this incumbrance on them? or how, remove the incumbrance? I suppose no one will say we should kill the people, or drive them out, or make slaves of them, or even confiscate their property. How then can we make much out of this part of the teritory? If the prossecution of the war has, in expenses, already equalled the *better* half of the country, how long it's future prossecution, will be in equalling, the less valuable half, is not a *speculative*, but a *practical* question, pressing closely upon us. And yet it is a question which the President seems to never have thought of. As to the mode of terminating the war, and securing peace, the President is equally wandering and indefinite. First, it is to be done by a more vigorous prossecution of the war in the vital parts of the enemies country; and, after apparently, talking himself tired, on this point, the President drops down into a half despairing tone, and tells us that "with a people distracted and divided by contending factions, and a government subject to constant changes, by successive revolutions, *the continued success of our arms may fail to secure a satisfactory peace.*" Then he suggests the propriety of wheedling the Mexican people to desert the counsels of their own leaders, and trusting in our protection, to set up a government from which we can secure a satisfactory peace; telling us, that *"this may become the only mode of obtaining such a peace."* But soon he falls into doubt of this too; and then drops back on to the already half abandoned ground of "more vigorous prossecution." All this shows that the President is, in no wise, satisfied with his own positions. First he takes up one, and in attempting to argue us *into* it, he argues himself *out* of it; then seizes another, and goes through the same process; and then, confused at being able to think of nothing new, he snatches up the old one again, which he has some time before cast off. His mind, tasked beyond it's power, is running hither and thither, like some tortured creature, on a burning surface, finding no position, on which it can settle down, and be at ease.

Again, it is a singular omission in this message, that it,

no where intimates *when* the President expects the war to terminate. At it's beginning, Genl. Scott was, by this same President, driven into disfavor, if not disgrace, for intimating that peace could not be conquered in less than three or four months. But now, at the end of about twenty months, during which time our arms have given us the most splendid successes—every department, and every part, land and water, officers and privates, regulars and volunteers, doing all that men *could* do, and hundreds of things which it had ever before been thought men could *not* do,—after all this, this same President gives us a long message, without showing us, that, *as to the end*, he himself, has, even an immaginary conception. As I have before said, he knows not where he is. He is a bewildered, confounded, and miserably perplexed man. God grant he may be able to show, there is not something about his conscience, more painful than all his mental perplexity!

January 12, 1848

To Mary Todd Lincoln

Dear Mary: Washington, April 16–1848–

In this troublesome world, we are never quite satisfied. When you were here, I thought you hindered me some in attending to business; but now, having nothing but business—no variety—it has grown exceedingly tasteless to me. I hate to sit down and direct documents, and I hate to stay in this old room by myself. You know I told you in last sunday's letter, I was going to make a little speech during the week; but the week has passed away without my getting a chance to do so; and now my interest in the subject has passed away too. Your second and third letters have been received since I wrote before. Dear Eddy thinks father is *"gone tapila."* Has any further discovery been made as to the breaking into your grand-mother's house? If I were she, I would not remain there alone. You mention that your uncle John Parker is likely to be at Lexington. Dont forget to present him my very kindest regards.

I went yesterday to hunt the little plaid stockings, as you wished; but found that McKnight has quit business, and Allen had not a single pair of the description you give, and only one plaid pair of any sort that I thought would fit "Eddy's dear little feet." I have a notion to make another trial to-morrow morning. If I could get them, I have an excellent chance of sending them. Mr. Warrick Tunstall, of St. Louis is here. He is to leave early this week, and to go by Lexington. He says he knows you, and will call to see you; and he voluntarily asked, if I had not some package to send to you.

I wish you to enjoy yourself in every possible way; but is there no danger of wounding the feelings of your good father, by being so openly intimate with the Wickliffe family?

Mrs. Broome has not removed yet; but she thinks of doing so to-morrow. All the house—or rather, all with whom you were on decided good terms—send their love to you. The others say nothing.

Very soon after you went away, I got what I think a very pretty set of shirt-bosom studs—modest little ones, jet, set in gold, only costing 50 cents a piece, or 1.50 for the whole.

Suppose you do not prefix the "Hon" to the address on your letters to me any more. I like the letters very much, but I would rather they should not have that upon them. It is not necessary, as I suppose you have thought, to have them to come free.

And you are entirely free from head-ache? That is good—good—considering it is the first spring you have been free from it since we were acquainted. I am afraid you will get so well, and fat, and young, as to be wanting to marry again. Tell Louisa I want her to watch you a little for me. Get weighed, and write me how much you weigh.

I did not get rid of the impression of that foolish dream about dear Bobby till I got your letter written the same day. What did he and Eddy think of the little letters father sent them? Dont let the blessed fellows forget father.

A day or two ago Mr. Strong, here in Congress, said to me that Matilda would visit here within two or three weeks. Suppose you write her a letter, and enclose it in one of mine; and if she comes I will deliver it to her, and if she does not, I will send it to her. Most affectionately

To Mary Todd Lincoln

My dear wife: Washington, June 12. 1848–

On my return from Philadelphia, yesterday, where, in my anxiety I had been led to attend the whig convention I found your last letter. I was so tired and sleepy, having ridden all night, that I could not answer it till to-day; and now I have to do so in the H.R. The leading matter in your letter, is your wish to return to this side of the Mountains. Will you be a *good girl* in all things, if I consent? Then come along, and that as *soon* as possible. Having got the idea in my head, I shall be impatient till I see you. You will not have money enough to bring you; but I presume your uncle will supply you, and I will refund him here. By the way you do not mention whether you have received the fifty dollars I sent you. I do not much fear but that you got it; because the want of it would have induced you say something in relation to it. If your uncle is already at Lexington, you might induce him to start on earlier than the first of July; he could stay in Kentucky longer on his return, and so make up for lost time. Since I began this letter, the

H.R. has passed a resolution for adjourning on the 17th. July, which probably will pass the Senate. I hope this letter will not be disagreeable to you; which, together with the circumstances under which I write, I hope will excuse me for not writing a longer one. Come on just as soon as you can. I want to see you, and our dear—*dear* boys very much. Every body here wants to see our dear Bobby.

Affectionately

To Mary Todd Lincoln

My dear wife: Washington, July 2. 1848.

Your letter of last sunday came last night. On that day (sunday) I wrote the principal part of a letter to you, but did not finish it, or send it till tuesday, when I had provided a draft for $100 which I sent in it. It is now probable that on that day (tuesday) you started to Shelbyville; so that when the money reaches Lexington, you will not be there. Before leaving, did you make any provision about letters that might come to Lexington for you? Write me whether you got the draft, if you shall not have already done so, when this reaches you. Give my kindest regards to your uncle John, and all the family. Thinking of them reminds me that I saw your acquaintance, Newton, of Arkansas, at the Philadelphia Convention. We had but a single interview, and that was so brief, and in so great a multitude of strange faces, that I am quite sure I should not recognize him, if I were to meet him again. He was a sort of Trinity, three in one, having the right, in his own person, to cast the three votes of Arkansas. Two or three days ago I sent your uncle John, and a few of our other friends each a copy of the speech I mentioned in my last letter; but I did not send any to you, thinking you would be on the road here, before it would reach you. I send you one now. Last wednesday, P.H. Hood & Co, dunned me for a little bill of $5.38 cents, and Walter Harper & Co, another for $8.50 cents, for goods which they say you bought. I hesitated to pay them, because my recollection is that you told me when you went away, there was nothing left unpaid. Mention in your next letter whether they are right.

Mrs. Richardson is still here; and what is more, has a baby—so Richardson says, and he ought to know. I believe Mary Hewett has left here and gone to Boston. I met her on the street about fifteen or twenty days ago, and she told me she was going soon. I have seen nothing of her since.

The music in the Capitol grounds on saturdays, or, rather, the interest in it, is dwindling down to nothing. Yesterday evening the attendance was rather thin. Our two girls, whom you remember seeing first at Carusis, at the exhibition of the Ethiopian Serenaders, and whose peculiarities were the wearing of black fur bonnets, and never being seen in close company with other ladies, were at the music yesterday. One of them was attended by their brother, and the other had a member of Congress in tow. He went home with her; and if I were to guess, I would say, he went away a somewhat altered man—most likely in his pockets, and in some other particular. The fellow looked conscious of guilt, although I believe he was unconscious that every body around knew who it was that had caught him.

I have had no letter from home, since I wrote you before, except short business letters, which have no interest for you.

By the way, you do not intend to do without a girl, because the one you had has left you? Get another as soon as you can to take charge of the dear codgers. Father expected to see you all sooner; but let it pass; stay as long as you please, and come when you please. Kiss and love the dear rascals.
Affectionately

To Thomas Lincoln and John D. Johnston

My dear father: Washington, Decr. 24th. 1848–

Your letter of the 7th. was received night before last. I very cheerfully send you the twenty dollars, which sum you say is necessary to save your land from sale. It is singular that you should have forgotten a judgment against you; and it is more singular that the plaintiff should have let you forget it so long, particularly as I suppose you have always had property enough to satisfy a judgment of that amount. Before you pay it, it would be well to be sure you have not paid it; or, at least, that you can not prove you have paid it. Give my love to Mother, and all the connections. Affectionately your Son

Dear Johnston:

Your request for eighty dollars, I do not think it best, to comply with now. At the various times when I have helped you a little, you have said to me "We can get along very well now" but in a very short time I find you in the same difficulty again. Now this can only happen by some defect in your *conduct*. What that defect is, I think I know. You are not *lazy*, and still you *are* an *idler*. I doubt whether since I saw you, you have done a good whole day's work, in any one day. You do not very much dislike to work; and still you do not work much, merely because it does not seem to you that you could get much for it. This habit of uselessly wasting time, is the whole difficulty; and it is vastly important to you, and still more so to your children that you should break this habit. It is more important to them, because they have longer to live, and can keep out of an idle habit before they are in it; easier than they can get out after they are in.

You are now in need of some ready money; and what I

propose is, that you shall go to work, "tooth and nails" for some body who will give you money for it. Let father and your boys take charge of things at home—prepare for a crop, and make the crop; and you go to work for the best money wages, or in discharge of any debt you owe, that you can get. And to secure you a fair reward for your labor, I now promise you, that for every dollar you will, between this and the first of next May, get for your own labor, either in money, or in your own indebtedness, I will then give you one other dollar. By this, if you hire yourself at ten dollars a month, from me you will get ten more, making twenty dollars a month for your work. In this, I do not mean you shall go off to St. Louis, or the lead mines, or the gold mines, in California, but I mean for you to go at it for the best wages you can get close to home in Coles county. Now if you will do this, you will soon be out of debt, and what is better, you will have a habit that will keep you from getting in debt again. But if I should now clear you out, next year you will be just as deep in as ever. You say you would almost give your place in Heaven for $70 or $80. Then you value your place in Heaven very cheaply for I am sure you can with the offer I make you get the seventy or eighty dollars for four or five months work. You say if I furnish you the money you will deed me the land, and, if you dont pay the money back, you will deliver possession. Nonsense! If you cant now live *with* the land, how will you then live without it? You have always been kind to me, and I do not now mean to be unkind to you. On the contrary, if you will but follow my advice, you will find it worth more than eight times eighty dollars to you. Affectionately Your brother

Proposal in the U.S. House of Representatives for Abolition of Slavery in the District of Columbia

Mr. LINCOLN appealed to his colleague [Mr. WENTWORTH] to withdraw his motion, to enable him to read a proposition which he intended to submit, if the vote should be reconsidered.

Mr. WENTWORTH again withdrew his motion for that purpose.

Mr. LINCOLN said, that by the courtesy of his colleague, he would say, that if the vote on the resolution was reconsidered, he should make an effort to introduce an amendment, which he should now read.

And Mr. L. read as follows:

Strike out all before and after the word "Resolved" and insert the following, towit: That the Committee on the District of Columbia be instructed to report a bill in substance as follows, towit:

Section 1. Be it enacted by the Senate and House of Representatives of the United States of America, in Congress assembled: That no person not now within the District of Columbia, nor now owned by any person or persons now resident within it, nor hereafter born within it, shall ever be held in slavery within said District.

Section 2. That no person now within said District, or now owned by any person, or persons now resident within the same, or hereafter born within it, shall ever be held in slavery without the limits of said District: *Provided,* that officers of the government of the United States, being citizens of the slave-holding states, coming into said District on public business, and remaining only so long as may be reasonably necessary for that object, may be attended into, and out of, said District, and while there, by the necessary servants of themselves and their families, without their right to hold such servants in service, being thereby impaired.

Section 3. That all children born of slave mothers within said District on, or after the first day of January in the year of our Lord one thousand, eight hundred and fifty shall be free; but shall be reasonably supported and educated, by the respective owners of their mothers or by their heirs or representatives, and shall owe reasonable service, as apprentices, to such owners, heirs and representatives until they respectively arrive at the age of——years when they shall be entirely free; and the municipal authorities of Washington and Georgetown, within their respective jurisdictional limits, are hereby empowered and required to make all suitable and necessary provisions for enforcing obedience to this section, on the part of both masters and apprentices.

Section 4. That all persons now within said District lawfully held as slaves, or now owned by any person or persons now resident within said District, shall remain such, at the will of their respective owners, their heirs and legal representatives: *Provided* that any such owner, or his legal representative, may at any time receive from the treasury of the United States the full value of his or her slave, of the class in this section mentioned, upon which such slave shall be forthwith and forever free: and *provided further* that the President of the United States, the Secretary of State, and the Secretary of the Treasury shall be a board for determining the value of such slaves as their owners may desire to emancipate under this section; and whose duty it shall be to hold a session for the purpose, on the first monday of each calendar month; to receive all applications; and, on satisfactory evidence in each case, that the person presented for valuation, is a slave, and of the class in this section mentioned, and is owned by the applicant, shall value such slave at his or her full cash value, and give to the applicant an order on the treasury for the amount; and also to such slave a certificate of freedom.

Section 5. That the municipal authorities of Washington and Georgetown, within their respective jurisdictional limits, are hereby empowered and required to provide active and efficient means to arrest, and deliver up to their owners, all fugitive slaves escaping into said District.

Section 6. That the election officers within said District of Columbia, are hereby empowered and required to open polls at all the usual places of holding elections, on the first monday of April next, and receive the vote of every free white male citizen above the age of twentyone years, having resided within said District for the period of one year or more next preceding the time of such voting, for, or against this act; to proceed, in taking said votes, in all respects not herein specified, as at elections under the municipal laws; and, with as little delay as possible, to transmit correct statements of the votes so cast to the President of the United States. And it shall be the duty of the President to canvass said votes immediately, and, if a majority of them be found to be for this act, to forthwith issue his proclamation giving notice of the fact; and this act shall only be in full force and effect on, and after the day of such proclamation.

Section 7. That involuntary servitude for the punishment of crime, whereof the party shall have been duly convicted shall in no wise be prohibited by this act.

Section 8. That for all the purposes of this act the jurisdictional limits of Washington are extended to all parts of the District of Columbia not now included within the present limits of Georgetown.

Mr. LINCOLN then said, that he was authorized to say, that of about fifteen of the leading citizens of the District of Columbia to whom this proposition had been submitted, there was not one but who approved of the adoption of such a proposition. He did not wish to be misunderstood. He did not know whether or not they would vote for this bill on the first Monday of April; but he repeated, that out

of fifteen persons to whom it had been submitted, he had
authority to say that every one of them desired that some
proposition like this should pass.

January 10, 1849

Notes on the Practice of Law

I am not an accomplished lawyer. I find quite as much
material for a lecture, in those points wherein I have failed,
as in those wherein I have been moderately successful.

The leading rule for the lawyer, as for the man, of every
calling, is *diligence*. Leave nothing for to-morrow, which
can be done to-day. Never let your correspondence fall
behind. Whatever piece of business you have in hand, before stopping, do all the labor pertaining to it which can
then be done. When you bring a common-law suit, if you
have the facts for doing so, write the declaration at once.
If a law point be involved, examine the books, and note
the authority you rely on, upon the declaration itself, where
you are sure to find it when wanted. The same of defences
and pleas. In business not likely to be litigated—ordinary
collection cases, foreclosures, partitions, and the like,—
make all examinations of titles, and note them, and even
draft orders and decrees in advance. This course has a
triple advantage; it avoids omissions and neglect, *saves*
your labor, when once done; performs the labor out of court
when you *have* leisure, rather than in court, when you have
not. Extemporaneous speaking should be practiced and cul-
tivated. It is the lawyer's avenue to the public. However
able and faithful he may be in other respects, people are
slow to bring him business, if he cannot make a speech.
And yet there is not a more fatal error to young lawyers,
then relying too much on speech-making. If any one, upon

his rare powers of speaking, shall claim exemption from the drudgery of the law, his case is a failure in advance.

Discourage litigation. Persuade your neighbors to compromise whenever you can. Point out to them how the *nominal* winner is often a *real* loser—in fees, and expenses, and waste of time. As a peace-maker the lawyer has a superior opertunity of being a good man. There will still be business enough.

Never stir up litigation. A worse man can scarcely be found than one who does this. Who can be more nearly a fiend than he who habitually overhauls the Register of deeds, in search of defects in titles, whereon to stir up strife, and put money in his pocket? A moral tone ought to be infused into the profession, which should drive such men out of it.

The matter of fees is important far beyond the mere question of bread and butter involved. Properly attended to fuller justice is done to both lawyer and client. An exorbitant fee should never be claimed. As a general rule, never take your whole fee in advance, nor any more than a small retainer. When fully paid before hand, you are more than a common mortal if you can feel the same interest in the case, as if something was still in prospect for you, as well as for your client. And when you lack interest in the case, the job will very likely lack skill and diligence in the performance. Settle the *amount* of fee, and take a note in advance. Then you will feel that you are working for something, and you are sure to do your work faithfully and well. Never sell a fee-note—at least, not before the consideration service is performed. It leads to negligence and dishonesty—negligence, by losing interest in the case, and dishonesty in refusing to refund, when you have allowed the consideration to fail.

There is a vague popular belief that lawyers are necessarily dishonest. I say *vague*, because when we consider to what extent *confidence*, and *honors* are reposed in, and conferred upon lawyers by the people, it appears improbable that their *impression* of dishonesty is very distinct and vivid. Yet the impression, is common—almost universal. Let no young man, choosing the law for a calling, for a moment yield to this popular belief. Resolve to be honest at all events; and if, in your own judgment, you can not be an honest lawyer, resolve to be honest without being a lawyer. Choose some other occupation, rather than one in the choosing of which you do, in advance, consent to be a knave.

1850?

Fragments on Government

The legitimate object of government, is to do for a community of people, whatever they need to have done, but can not do, *at all*, or can not, *so well do*, for themselves—in their separate, and individual capacities.

In all that the people can individually do as well for themselves, government ought not to interfere.

The desirable things which the individuals of a people can not do, or can not well do, for themselves, fall into two classes: those which have relation to *wrongs*, and those which have not. Each of these branch off into an infinite variety of subdivisions.

The first—that in relation to wrongs—embraces all crimes, misdemeanors, and non-performance of contracts. The other embraces all which, in its nature, and without wrong, requires combined action, as public roads and highways, public schools, charities, pauperism, orphanage, estates of the deceased, and the machinery of government itself.

From this it appears that if all men were just, there still would be *some*, though not *so much*, need of government.

Government is a combination of the people of a country to effect certain objects by joint effort. The best framed and best administered governments are necessarily expensive; while by errors in frame and maladministration most of them are more onerous than they need be, and some of them very oppressive. Why, then, should we have government? Why not each individual take to himself the whole fruit of his labor, without having any of it taxed away, in services, corn, or money? Why not take just so much land as he can cultivate with his own hands, without buying it of any one?

The legitimate object of government is "to do for the people what needs to be done, but which they can not, by individual effort, do at all, or do so well, for themselves." There are many such things—some of them exist independently of the injustice in the world. Making and maintaining roads, bridges, and the like; providing for the helpless young and afflicted; common schools; and disposing of deceased men's property, are instances.

But a far larger class of objects springs from the injustice of men. If one people will make war upon another, it is a necessity with that other to unite and coöperate for defense. Hence the military department. If some men will kill, or beat, or constrain others, or despoil them of property, by force, fraud, or noncompliance with contracts, it is a common object with peaceful and just men to prevent it. Hence the criminal and civil departments.

———

dent truth. Made so plain by our good Father in Heaven, that all *feel* and *understand* it, even down to brutes and creeping insects. The ant, who has toiled and dragged a crumb to his nest, will furiously defend the fruit of his labor, against whatever robber assails him. So plain, that the most dumb and stupid slave that ever toiled for a master, does constantly *know* that he is wronged. So plain that no one, high or low, ever does mistake it, except in a plainly *selfish* way; for although volume upon volume is written to prove slavery a very good thing, we never hear of the man who wishes to take the good of it, *by being a slave himself*.

Most governments have been based, practically, on the denial of equal rights of men, as I have, in part, stated them; *ours* began, by *affirming* those rights. *They* said, some men are too *ignorant*, and *vicious*, to share in government. Possibly so, said we; and, by your system, you would always keep them ignorant, and vicious. We proposed to give *all* a chance; and we expected the weak to grow stronger, the ignorant, wiser; and all better, and happier together.

We made the experiment; and the fruit is before us. Look at it—think of it. Look at it, in it's aggregate grandeur, of extent of country, and numbers of population—of ship, and steamboat, and rail-

1854?

Fragment on Slavery

If A. can prove, however conclusively, that he may, of right, enslave B.—why may not B. snatch the same argument, and prove equally, that he may enslave A?—

You say A. is white, and B. is black. It is *color*, then; the lighter, having the right to enslave the darker? Take care. By this rule, you are to be slave to the first man you meet, with a fairer skin than your own.

You do not mean *color* exactly?—You mean the whites are *intellectually* the superiors of the blacks, and, therefore have the right to enslave them? Take care again. By this rule, you are to be slave to the first man you meet, with an intellect superior to your own.

But, say you, it is a question of *interest;* and, if you can make it your *interest,* you have the right to enslave another. Very well. And if he can make it his interest, he has the right to enslave you.

1854?

Speech to the Jury
in the Rock Island Bridge Case, Chicago, Illinois

THIRTEENTH DAY

Tuesday, September 22nd, 1857. Mr. A. Lincoln addressed the jury: He said he did not purpose to assail anybody, that he expected to grow earnest as he proceeded, but not ill-natured. There is some conflict of testimony in the case, but one quarter of such a number of witnesses, seldom agree, and even if all had been on one side some discrepancy might have been expected. We are to try and reconcile them, and to believe that they are not intentionally erroneous, as long as we can. He had no prejudice against steamboats or steamboatmen, nor any against St. Louis, for he supposed they went about as other people would do in their situation. St. Louis as a commercial place, may desire that this bridge should not stand, as it is adverse to her commerce, diverting a portion of it from the river; and it might be that she supposed that the additional cost of railroad transportation upon the productions of Iowa, would force them to go to St. Louis if this bridge were removed. The meetings in St. Louis were connected with this case, only as some witnesses were in it and thus had some prejudice add color to their testimony.

The last thing that would be pleasing to him would be,

to have one of these great channels, extending almost from where it never freezes to where it never thaws, blocked up. But there is a travel from East to West, whose demands are not less important than that of the river. It is growing larger and larger, building up new countries with a rapidity never before seen in the history of the world. He alluded to the astonishing growth of Illinois, having grown within his memory to a population of a million and a half, to Iowa and the other young and rising communities of the Northwest.

This current of travel has its rights, as well as that north and south. If the river had not the advantage in priority and legislation, we could enter into free competition with it and we would surpass it. This particular line has a great importance, and the statement of its business during little less than a year shows this importance. It is in evidence that from September 8, 1856, to August 8, 1857, 12,586 freight cars and 74,179 passengers passed over this bridge. Navigation was closed four days short of four months last year, and during this time, while the river was or no use, this road and bridge were equally valuable. There is, too, a considerable portion of time, when floating or thin ice makes the river useless, while the bridge is as useful as ever. This shows that this bridge must be treated with respect in this court and is not to be kicked about with contempt.

The other day Judge Wead alluded to the strife of the contending interests, and even a dissolution of the Union. Mr. Lincoln thought the proper mood for all parties in this affair, is to "live and let live," and then we will find a cessation of this trouble about the bridge. What mood were the steamboat men in when this bridge was burned? Why there was a shouting, a ringing of bells and whistling on all the boats as it fell. It was a jubilee, a greater celebration than follows an excited election.

The first thing I will proceed to is the record of Mr. Gurney and the complaint of Judge Wead, that it did not extend back over all the time from the completion of the bridge. The principal part of the navigation after the bridge was burned passed through the span. When the bridge was repaired and the boats were a second time confined to the draw, it was provided that this record should be kept. That is the simple history of that book.

From April 19, 1856, to May 6—17 days—there were 20 accidents, and all the time since then, there has been but 20 hits, including 7 accidents; so that the dangers of this place are tapering off, and as the boatmen get cool, the accidents get less. We may soon expect, if this ratio is kept up, that there will be no accidents at all.

Judge Wead said, while admitting that the floats went straight through, there was a difference between a float and a boat, but I do not remember that he indulged us with an argument in support of this statement. Is it because there is a difference in size? Will not a small body and a large one, float the same way, under the same influence? True, a flat boat would float faster than an egg-shell, and the egg-shell might be blown away by the wind, but if under the *same influence* they would go the same way. Logs, floats, boards, various things, the witnesses say all show the same current. Then is not this test reliable? At all depths too, the direction of the current is the same. A series of these floats would make a line as long as a boat, and would show any influence upon any part, and all parts of the boat.

I will now speak of the angular position of the piers. What is the amount of the angle? The course of the river is a curve and the pier is straight. If a line is produced from the upper end of the long pier straight with the pier to a distance of 350 feet, and a line is drawn from a point in the channel opposite this point to the head of the pier, Col. Mason says they will form an angle of 20 degrees; but the angle if measured at the pier, is 7 degrees—that is, we would have to move the pier 7 degrees, and then it would be exactly straight with the current. Would that make the

navigation better or worse? The witnesses of the plaintiffs
seemed to think it was only necessary to say that the pier
was angling to the current, and that settled the matter. Our
more careful and accurate witnesses say, that though they
had been accustomed to seeing the piers placed straight with
the current, yet, they could see that here the current has
been made straight by us, in having made this slight angle—
that the water now runs just right now—that it is straight
and cannot be improved. They think that if the pier was
changed the eddy would be divided, and the navigation
improved; and that as it is, the bridge is placed in the best
manner possible.

I am not now going to discuss the question what is a
material obstruction? We do not very greatly differ about
the law. The cases produced here, are, I suppose, proper
to be taken into consideration by the Court in instructing
the jury. Some of them I think are not exactly in point, but
still I am willing to trust his honor, Judge McLean, and
take his instructions as law.

What is *reasonable* skill and care? This is a thing of
which the jury are to judge. I differ from them in saying
that they are bound to exercise no more care than they took
before the building of the bridge. If we are allowed by the
Legislature to build a bridge, which will require them to do
more than before, when a pilot comes along, it is unreasonable for him to dash on, heedless of this structure, which
has been *legally put there*. The Afton came there on the
5th, and lay at Rock Island until next morning. When the
boat lies up, the pilot has a holiday, and would not any of
these jurors have then gone around there, and got acquainted
with the place? Parker has shown here that he does not
understand the draw. I heard him say that the fall from the
head to the foot of that pier was four feet! He needs information. He could have gone there that day and have seen
there was no such fall. He should have discarded passion,

and the chances are that he would have had no disaster at all. He was bound to make himself acquainted with it.

McCammon says that "the current and the swell coming from the long pier, drove her against the long pier." Drove her towards the very pier from which the current came! It is an absurdity, an impossibility. The only reconciliation I can find for this contradiction, is in a current which White says strikes out from the long pier, and then, like a ram's horn, turns back, and this might have acted somehow in this manner.

It is agreed by all that the plaintiffs' boat was destroyed; that it was destroyed upon the head of the short pier; that she moved from the channel, where she was, with her bow above the head of the long pier, till she struck the short one, swung around under the bridge, and there was crowded under the bridge and destroyed.

I shall try to prove that the average velocity of the current through the draw with the boat in it, should be five and a half miles an hour; that it is slowest at the head of the pier,—swiftest at the foot of the pier. Their lowest estimate, in evidence, is six miles an hour, their highest twelve miles. This was the testimony of men who had made no experiment—only conjecture. We have adopted the most exact means. The water runs swiftest in high water, and we have taken the point of nine feet above low water. The water, when the Afton was lost, was seven feet above low water, or at least a foot lower than our time. Brayton and his assistants timed the instruments—the best known instruments for measuring currents. They timed them under various circumstances, and they found the current five miles an hour, and no more. They found that the water, at the upper end, ran slower than five miles; that below it was swifter than five miles, but that the average was five miles. Shall men, who have taken no care, who conjecture, some of whom speak of twenty miles an hour be believed, against those who have had such a favorable and well-improved opportunity? They should not even *qualify* the result. Several men have given their opinions as to the distance of the Carson, and I suppose if *one* should go and *measure* that distance, you would believe him in preference to all of them.

These measurements were made when the boat was not in the draw. It has been ascertained what is the area of the cross-section of the stream, and the area of the face of the piers, and the engineers say, that the piers being put there will increase the current proportionably as the space is decreased. So with the boat in the draw. The depth of the channel was 22 feet, the width 116 feet—multiply these and you have the square feet across the water of the draw, viz.: 2,552 feet. The Afton was 35 feet wide and drew five feet, making a fourteenth of the sum. Now one-fourteenth of five miles is five-fourteenths of one mile—about one-third of a mile—the increase of the current. We will call the current 5½ miles per hour.

The next thing I will try to prove that is that the plaintiffs' boat had power to run six miles an hour in that current. It has been testified that she was a strong, swift boat, able to run eight miles an hour up stream in a current of four miles an hour, and fifteen miles down stream. Strike the average and you will find what is her average—about 11½ miles. Take the 5½, miles which is the speed of the current in the draw, and it leaves the power of the boat in that draw at six miles an hour, 528 feet per minute, and 8⅘ feet to the second.

Next I propose to show that there are no cross currents. I know their witnesses say that there are cross currents— that, as one witness says, there are three cross currents and two eddies. So far as mere statement without experiment, and mingled with mistakes can go, they have proved. But can these men's testimony be compared with the nice, exact, thorough experiments of our witnesses. Can you believe that these floats go across the currents? It is inconceiveable that they could not have discovered every possible current. How do boats find currents that floats cannot discover? We assume the position then that those cross currents are not there. My next proposition is that the Afton passed between the S. B. Carson and Iowa shore. That is undisputed.

Next I shall show that she struck first the short pier, then the long pier, then the short one again and there she stopped. Mr. Lincoln cited the testimony of eighteen witnesses on this point. How did the boat strike Baker when she went in! Here is an endless variety of opinion. But ten of them say what pier she struck; three of them testify that she struck first the short, then the long, then the short pier for the last time. None of the rest substantially contradict this. I assume that these men have got the truth, because I believe it an established fact.

My next proposition is that after she struck the short and long pier and before she got back to the short pier the boat got right with her bow out. So says the Pilot Parker—that he "got her through until her starboard wheel passed the short pier." This would make her head about even with the head of the long pier. He says her head was as high or higher than the head of the long pier. Other witnesses confirm this one. The final stroke was in the splash door, aft the wheel. Witnesses differ but the majority say that she struck thus.

Court adjourned.

FOURTEENTH DAY

Wednesday, September 23, 1857.
Mr. A. Lincoln resumed. He said he should conclude as soon as possible. He said the colored map of the plaintiffs, which was brought in during the advanced stages of the trial, showed itself that the cross currents alleged did not exist; that the current as represented would drive an ascending boat to the long pier, but not to the short pier as

they urged. He explained from a model of a boat where
the splash door is, just behind the wheel. The boat struck
on the lower shoulder of the short pier, as she swung round,
in the splash door, then as she went on round she struck
the point or end of the pier, where she rested. Her engineers
say the starboard wheel then was rushing round rapidly.
Then the boat must have struck the upper point of the pier
so far back as not to disturb the wheel. It is forty feet from
the stern of the Afton to the splash door, and thus it appears
that she had but forty feet to go to clear the pier.

How was it that the Afton, with all her power, flanked
over from the channel to the short pier without moving one
inch ahead? Suppose she was in the middle of the draw,
her wheel would have been 31 feet from the short pier. The
reason she went over thus is, her starboard wheel was not
working. I shall try to establish the fact that that wheel
was not running, and, that after she struck, she went ahead
strong on this same wheel. Upon the last point the witnesses agree—that the starboard wheel was running after
she struck—and no witnesses say that it was running while
she was out in the draw flanking over. Mr. Lincoln read
from the testimony of various witnesses to prove that the
starboard wheel was not working while she was out in the
stream. Other witnesses show that the captain said something of the machinery of the wheel, and the inference is
that he knew the wheel was not working. The fact is undisputed, that she did not move one inch ahead, while she
was moving this 31 feet sideways. There is evidence proving
that the current there is only five miles an hour, and the
only explanation is that her power was not all used—that
only one wheel was working. The pilot says he ordered
the engineers to back her out. The engineers differ from him
and say that they kept one going ahead. The bow was so
swung that the current pressed it over; the pilot pressed
the stern over with the rudder, though not so fast but that the
bow gained on it, and, only one wheel being in motion, the

boat merely stood still so far as motion up and down is concerned, and thus she was thrown upon this pier.

The Afton came into the draw after she had just passed the Carson, and, as the Carson no doubt kept the true course, the Afton going around her, got out of the proper way, got across the current, into the eddy which is west of a straight line drawn down from the long pier, was compelled to resort to these changes of wheels, which she did not do with sufficient adroitness to save her. Was it not her own fault that she entered wrong? so far, wrong that she never got right. Is the defence to blame for that?

For several days we were entertained with depositions about boats "smelling a bar." Why did the Afton then, after she had come up smelling so close to the long pier sheer off so strangely? When she got to the centre of the very nose she was smelling, she seems suddenly to have lost her sense of smell and flanks over to the short pier.

Mr. Lincoln said there was no practicability in the project of building a tunnel under the river, for there is not a tunnel that is a successful project, in the world. A suspension bridge cannot be built so high, but that the chimneys of the boats will grow up till they cannot pass. The steamboatmen will take pains to make them grow. The cars of a railroad, cannot, without immense expense, rise high enough to get even with a suspension bridge, or go low enough to get down through a tunnel. Such expense is unreasonable.

The plaintiffs have to establish that the bridge is a material obstruction, and that they managed their boat with reasonable care and skill. As to the last point, high winds have nothing to do with it, for it was not a windy day. They must show "due skill and care." Difficulties going down stream, will not do, for they were going up stream. Difficulties with barges in tow, have nothing to do with it, for they had no barge. He said he had much more to say, many things he could suggest to the jury, but he would close to save time.

"House Divided" Speech
at Springfield, Illinois

The Speech, immediately succeeding, was delivered, June 16, 1858 at Springfield Illinois, at the close of the Republican State convention held at that time and place; and by which convention Mr. Lincoln had been named as their candidate for U. S. Senator.

Senator Douglas was not present.

MR. PRESIDENT and Gentlemen of the Convention.

If we could first know *where* we are, and *whither* we are tending, we could then better judge *what* to do, and *how* to do it.

We are now far into the *fifth* year, since a policy was initiated, with the *avowed* object, and *confident* promise, of putting an end to slavery agitation.

Under the operation of that policy, that agitation has not only, *not ceased*, but has *constantly augmented*.

In *my* opinion, it *will* not cease, until a *crisis* shall have been reached, and passed.

"A house divided against itself cannot stand."

I believe this government cannot endure, permanently half *slave* and half *free*.

I do not expect the Union to be *dissolved*—I do not expect the house to *fall*—but I *do* expect it will cease to be divided.

It will become *all* one thing, or *all* the other.

Either the *opponents* of slavery, will arrest the further spread of it, and place it where the public mind shall rest in the belief that it is in course of ultimate extinction; or its *advocates* will push it forward, till it shall become alike lawful in *all* the States, *old* as well as *new*—*North* as well as *South*.

Have we no *tendency* to the latter condition?

Let any one who doubts, carefully contemplate that now almost complete legal combination—piece of *machinery* so to speak—compounded of the Nebraska doctrine, and the Dred Scott decision. Let him consider not only *what work* the machinery is adapted to do, and *how well* adapted; but also, let him study the *history* of its construction, and trace, if he can, or rather *fail*, if he can, to trace the evidences of design, and concert of action, among its chief bosses, from the beginning.

The new year of 1854 found slavery excluded from more than half the States by State Constitutions, and from most of the national territory by Congressional prohibition.

Four days later, commenced the struggle, which ended in repealing that Congressional prohibition.

This opened all the national territory to slavery; and was the first point gained.

But, so far, *Congress* only, had acted; and an *indorsement* by the people, *real* or apparent, was indispensable, to *save* the point already gained, and give chance for more.

This necessity had not been overlooked; but had been provided for, as well as might be, in the notable argument of "*squatter sovereignty*," otherwise called "*sacred right of self government*," which latter phrase, though expressive of the only rightful basis of any government, was so perverted in this attempted use of it as to amount to just this: That if any *one* man, choose to enslave *another*, no *third* man shall be allowed to object.

That argument was incorporated into the Nebraska bill itself, in the language which follows: "*It being the true intent and meaning of this act not to legislate slavery into any Territory or state, nor to exclude it therefrom; but to leave the people thereof perfectly free to form and regulate their domestic institutions in their own way, subject only to the Constitution of the United States.*"

Then opened the roar of loose declamation in favor of "Squatter Sovereignty," and "Sacred right of self government."

"But," said opposition members, "let us be more *specific*—let us *amend* the bill so as to expressly declare that the people of the territory *may* exclude slavery." "Not we," said the friends of the measure; and down they voted the amendment.

While the Nebraska bill was passing through congress, a *law case*, involving the question of a negroe's freedom, by reason of his owner having voluntarily taken him first into a free state and then a territory covered by the congressional prohibition, and held him as a slave, for a long time in each, was passing through the U.S. Circuit Court for the District of Missouri; and both Nebraska bill and law suit were brought to a decision in the same month of May, 1854. The negroe's name was "Dred Scott," which name now designates the decision finally made in the case.

Before the *then* next Presidential election, the law case came *to*, and was argued *in* the Supreme Court of the United States; but the *decision* of it was deferred until *after* the election. Still, *before* the election, Senator Trumbull, on the floor of the Senate, requests the leading advocate of the Nebraska bill to state *his opinion* whether the people of a territory can constitutionally exclude slavery from their limits; and the latter answers, "That is a question for the Supreme Court."

The election came. Mr. Buchanan was elected, and the *indorsement*, such as it was, secured. That was the *second* point gained. The indorsement, however, fell short of a clear popular majority by nearly four hundred thousand votes, and so, perhaps, was not overwhelmingly reliable and satisfactory.

The *outgoing* President, in his last annual message, as impressively as possible *echoed back* upon the people the *weight* and *authority* of the indorsement.

The Supreme Court met again; *did not* announce their decision, but ordered a re-argument.

The Presidential inauguration came, and still no decision of the court; but the *incoming* President, in his inaugural address, fervently exhorted the people to abide by the forthcoming decision, *whatever it might be.*

Then, in a few days, came the decision.

The reputed author of the Nebraska bill finds an early occasion to make a speech at this capitol indorsing the Dred Scott Decision, and vehemently denouncing all opposition to it.

The new President, too, seizes the early occasion of the Silliman letter to *indorse* and strongly *construe* that decision, and to express his *astonishment* that any different view had ever been entertained.

At length a squabble springs up between the President and the author of the Nebraska bill, on the *mere* question of *fact*, whether the Lecompton constitution was or was not, in any just sense, made by the people of Kansas; and in that squabble the latter declares that all he wants is a fair vote for the people, and that he *cares* not whether slavery be voted *down* or voted *up*. I do not understand his declaration that he cares not whether slavery be voted down or voted up, to be intended by him other than as an *apt definition* of the *policy* he would impress upon the public mind— the *principle* for which he declares he has suffered much, and is ready to suffer to the end.

And well may he cling to that principle. If he has any parental feeling, well may he cling to it. That principle, is the only *shred* left of his original Nebraska doctrine. Under the Dred Scott decision, "squatter sovereignty" squatted out of existence, tumbled down like temporary scaffolding—like the mould at the foundry served through one blast and fell back into loose sand—helped to carry an election, and then was kicked to the winds. His late *joint* struggle with the Republicans, against the Lecompton Constitution, involves

nothing of the original Nebraska doctrine. That struggle
was made on a point, the right of a people to make their
own constitution, upon which he and the Republicans have
never differed.

The several points of the Dred Scott decision, in connection with Senator Douglas' "care not" policy, constitute the
piece of machinery, in its *present* state of advancement. This
was the third point gained.

The *working* points of that machinery are:

First, that no negro slave, imported as such from Africa,
and no descendant of such slave can ever be a *citizen* of any
State, in the sense of that term as used in the Constitution of
the United States.

This point is made in order to deprive the negro, in every
possible event, of the benefit of this provision of the United
States Constitution, which declares that—

"The citizens of each State shall be entitled to all privileges and immunities of citizens in the several States."

Secondly, that "subject to the Constitution of the United
States," neither *Congress* nor a *Territorial Legislature* can
exclude slavery from any United States territory.

This point is made in order that individual men may *fill
up* the territories with slaves, without danger of losing them
as property, and thus to enhance the chances of *permanency*
to the institution through all the future.

Thirdly, that whether the holding a negro in actual slavery
in a free State, makes him free, as against the holder, the
United States courts will not decide, but will leave to be
decided by the courts of any slave State the negro may be
forced into by the master.

This point is made, not to be pressed *immediately;* but,
if acquiesced in for a while, and apparently *indorsed* by the
people at an election, *then* to sustain the logical conclusion
that what Dred Scott's master might lawfully do with Dred
Scott, in the free State of Illinois, every other master may

lawfully do with any other *one*, or one *thousand* slaves, in Illinois, or in any other free State.

Auxiliary to all this, and working hand in hand with it, the Nebraska doctrine, or what is left of it, is to *educate* and *mould* public opinion, at least *Northern* public opinion, to not *care* whether slavery is voted *down* or voted *up*.

This shows exactly where we now *are;* and *partially* also, whither we are tending.

It will throw additional light on the latter, to go back, and run the mind over the string of historical facts already stated. Several things will *now* appear less *dark* and *mysterious* than they did *when* they were transpiring. The people were to be left "perfectly free" "subject only to the Constitution." What the *Constitution* had to do with it, outsiders could not *then* see. Plainly enough *now*, it was an exactly fitted *niche*, for the Dred Scott decision to afterwards come in, and declare the *perfect freedom* of the people, to be just no freedom at all.

Why was the amendment, expressly declaring the right of the people to exclude slavery, voted down? Plainly enough *now*, the adoption of it, would have spoiled the niche for the Dred Scott decision.

Why was the court decision held up? Why, even a Senator's individual opinion withheld, till *after* the Presidential election? Plainly enough *now*, the speaking out *then* would have damaged the *"perfectly free"* argument upon which the election was to be carried.

Why the *outgoing* President's felicitation on the indorsement? Why the delay of a reargument? Why the incoming President's *advance* exhortation in favor of the decision?

These things *look* like the cautious *patting* and *petting* a spirited horse, preparatory to mounting him, when it is dreaded that he may give the rider a fall.

And why the hasty after indorsements of the decision by the President and others?

We can not absolutely *know* that all these exact adaptations are the result of preconcert. But when we see a lot of framed timbers, different portions of which we know have been gotten out at different times and places and by different workmen—Stephen, Franklin, Roger and James, for instance—and when we see these timbers joined together, and see they exactly make the frame of a house or a mill, all the tenons and mortices exactly fitting, and all the lengths and proportions of the different pieces exactly adapted to their respective places, and not a piece too many or too few—not omitting even scaffolding—or, if a single piece be lacking, we can see the place in the frame exactly fitted and prepared to yet bring such piece in—in *such* a case, we find it impossible to not *believe* that Stephen and Franklin and Roger and James all understood one another from the beginning, and all worked upon a common *plan* or *draft* drawn up before the first lick was struck.

It should not be overlooked that, by the Nebraska bill, the people of a *State* as well as *Territory*, were to be left "*perfectly free*" "*subject only to the Constitution.*"

Why mention a *State*? They were legislating for *territories*, and not *for* or *about* States. Certainly the people of a State *are* and *ought to be* subject to the Constitution of the United States; but why is mention of this *lugged* into this merely *territorial* law? Why are the people of a *territory* and the people of a *state* therein *lumped* together, and their relation to the Constitution therein treated as being *precisely* the same?

While the opinion of *the Court*, by Chief Justice Taney, in the Dred Scott case, and the separate opinions of all the concurring Judges, expressly declare that the Constitution of the United States neither permits Congress nor a Territorial legislature to exclude slavery from any United States territory, they all *omit* to declare whether or not the same Constitution permits a *state*, or the people of a State, to exclude it.

Possibly, this was a mere *omission;* but who can be *quite* sure, if McLean or Curtis had sought to get into the opinion a declaration of unlimited power in the people of a *state* to exclude slavery from their limits, just as Chase and Macy sought to get such declaration, in behalf of the people of a territory, into the Nebraska bill—I ask, who can be quite *sure* that it would not have been voted down, in the one case, as it had been in the other.

The nearest approach to the point of declaring the power of a State over slavery, is made by Judge Nelson. He approaches it more than once, using the precise idea, and *almost* the language too, of the Nebraska act. On one occasion his exact language is, "except in cases where the power is restrained by the Constitution of the Unites States, the law of the State is supreme over the subject of slavery within its jurisdiction."

In what *cases* the power of the *states is* so restrained by the U.S. Constitution, is left an *open* question, precisely as the same question, as to the restraint on the power of the *territories* was left open in the Nebraska act. Put *that* and *that* together, and we have another nice little niche, which we may, ere long, see filled with another Supreme Court decision, declaring that the Constitution of the United States does not permit a *state* to exclude slavery from its limits.

And this may especially be expected if the doctrine of "care not whether slavery be voted *down* or voted *up*," shall gain upon the public mind sufficiently to give promise that such a decision can be maintained when made.

Such a decision is all that slavery now lacks of being alike lawful in all the States.

Welcome or unwelcome, such decision *is* probably coming, and will soon be upon us, unless the power of the present political dynasty shall be met and overthrown.

We shall *lie down* pleasantly dreaming that the people of *Missouri* are on the verge of making their State *free;* and we shall *awake* to the *reality*, instead, that the *Supreme* Court has made *Illinois* a *slave* State.

To meet and overthrow the power of that dynasty, is the work now before all those who would prevent that consummation.

That is *what* we have to do.

But *how* can we best do it?

There are those who denounce us *openly* to their *own* friends, and yet whisper *us softly*, that *Senator Douglas* is the *aptest* instrument there is, with which to effect that object. *They* do *not* tell us, nor has *he* told us, that he *wishes* any such object to be effected. They wish us to *infer* all, from the facts, that he now has a little quarrel with the present head of the dynasty; and that he has regularly voted with us, on a single point, upon which, he and we, have never differed.

They remind us that *he* is a very *great man*, and that the largest of *us* are very small ones. Let this be granted. But "a *living dog* is better than a *dead lion*." Judge Douglas, if not a *dead* lion *for this work*, is at least a *caged* and *toothless* one. How can he oppose the advances of slavery? He don't *care* anything about it. His avowed *mission is impressing* the "public heart" to *care* nothing about it.

A leading Douglas Democratic newspaper thinks Douglas' superior talent will be needed to resist the revival of the African slave trade.

Does Douglas believe an effort to revive that trade is approaching? He has not said so. Does he *really* think so? But if it is, how can he resist it? For years he has labored to prove it a *sacred right* of white men to take negro slaves into the new territories. Can he possibly show that it is *less* a sacred right to *buy* them where they can be bought cheapest? And, unquestionably they can be bought *cheaper in Africa* than in *Virginia*.

He has done all in his power to reduce the whole question of slavery to one of a mere *right of property;* and as such, how can *he* oppose the foreign slave trade—how can he refuse that trade in that "property" shall be "perfectly free"—unless he does it as a *protection* to the home production? And as the home *producers* will probably not *ask* the protection, he will be wholly without a ground of opposition.

Senator Douglas holds, we know, that a man may rightfully be *wiser to-day* than he was *yesterday*—that he may rightfully *change* when he finds himself wrong.

But, can we for that reason, run ahead, and *infer* that he *will* make any particular change, of which he, himself, has given no intimation? Can we *safely* base *our* action upon any such *vague* inference?

Now, as ever, I wish to not *misrepresent* Judge Douglas' *position*, question his *motives*, or do ought that can be personally offensive to him.

Whenever, *if ever*, he and we can come together on *principle* so that *our great cause* may have assistance from *his great ability*, I hope to have interposed no adventitious obstacle.

But clearly, he is not *now* with us—he does not *pretend* to be—he does not *promise* to *ever* be.

Our cause, then, must be intrusted to, and conducted by its own undoubted friends—those whose hands are free, whose hearts are in the work—who *do care* for the result.

Two years ago the Republicans of the nation mustered over thirteen hundred thousand strong.

We did this under the single impulse of resistance to a common danger, with every external circumstance against us.

Of *strange, discordant,* and even, *hostile* elements, we gathered from the four winds, and *formed* and fought the battle through, under the constant hot fire of a disciplined, proud, and pampered enemy.

Did we brave all *then,* to *falter* now?—*now*—when that same enemy is *wavering,* dissevered and belligerent?

The result is not doubtful. We shall not fail—if we stand firm, we shall not fail.

Wise councils may *accelerate* or *mistakes delay* it, but, sooner or later the victory is *sure* to come.

Fragment on the Struggle Against Slavery

I have never professed an indifference to the honors of official station; and were I to do so now, I should only make
myself ridiculous. Yet I have never failed—do not now
fail—to remember that in the republican cause there is a
higher aim than that of mere office. I have not allowed
myself to forget that the abolition of the Slave-trade by
Great Brittain, was agitated a hundred years before it was
a final success; that the measure had it's open fire-eating
opponents; it's stealthy "dont care" opponents; it's dollar
and cent opponents; it's inferior race opponents; its negro
equality opponents; and its religion and good order opponents; that all these opponents got offices, and their adversaries got none. But I have also remembered that though
they blazed, like tallow-candles for a century, at last they
flickered in the socket, died out, stank in the dark for a
brief season, and were remembered no more, even by the
smell. School-boys know that Wilbeforce, and Granville
Sharpe, helped that cause forward; but who can now name
a single man who labored to retard it? Remembering these
things I can not but regard it as possible that the higher
object of this contest may not be completely attained within
the term of my natural life.

c. July 1858

First Lincoln-Douglas Debate, Ottawa, Illinois

FIRST JOINT DEBATE:—AUGUST 21—1858, AT OTTAWA, ILLINOIS.

Mr. Lincoln's Reply, from the Press & Tribune

Mr. Lincoln then came forward and was greeted with loud and protracted cheers from fully two-thirds of the audience. This was admitted by the Douglas men on the platform. It was some minutes before he could make himself heard, even by those on the stand. At last he said:

MY FELLOW-CITIZENS: When a man hears himself somewhat misrepresented, it provokes him—at least, I find it so with myself; but when the misrepresentation becomes very gross and palpable, it is more apt to amuse him. [Laughter.] The first thing I see fit to notice, is the fact that Judge Douglas alleges, after running through the history of the old Democratic and the old Whig parties, that Judge Trumbull and myself made an arrangement in 1854, by which I was to have the place of Gen. Shields in the United States Senate, and Judge Trumbull was to have the place of Judge Douglas. Now all I have to say upon that subject is, that I think no man—not even Judge Douglas—can prove it, *because it is not true.* [Cheers.] I have no doubt he is "*conscientious*" in saying it. [Laughter.] As to those resolutions that he took such a length of time to read, as being the platform of the Republican party in 1854, I say I never had anything to do with them, and I think Trumbull never had. [Renewed laughter.] Judge Douglas cannot show that either one of us ever did have any thing to do with them. I believe *this* is true about those resolutions: There was a call for a Convention to form a Republican party at Springfield, and I think that my friend Mr. Lovejoy, who is here upon this stand, had a hand in it. I think this is true, and I think if he will remember accurately, he will be able to recollect that he tried to get me into it, and I would not go in. [Cheers and laughter.] I believe it is also true, that I went away from Springfield when the Convention was in session, to attend court in Tazewell County. It is true they did place my name, though without authority, upon the Committee, and afterwards wrote me to attend the meeting of the Committee, but I refused to do so, and I never had anything to do with that organization. This is the plain truth about all that matter of the resolutions.

Now, about this story that Judge Douglas tells of Trumbull bargaining to sell out the old Democratic party, and Lincoln agreeing to sell out the old Whig party, I have the means of *knowing* about that; [laughter] Judge Douglas cannot have; and I know there is no substance to it whatever. [Applause.] Yet I have no doubt he is *"conscientious"* about it. [Laughter.] I know that after Mr. Lovejoy got into the Legislature that winter, he complained of me that I had told all the old Whigs in his district that the old Whig party was good enough for them, and some of them voted against him because I told them so. Now I have no means of totally disproving such charges as this which the Judge makes. A man cannot prove a negative, but he has a right to claim that when a man makes an affirmative charge, he must offer some proof to show the truth of what he says. I certainly cannot introduce testimony to show the negative about things, but I have a right to claim that if a man says he *knows* a thing, then he must show *how* he knows it. I always have a right to claim this, and it is not satisfactory to me that he may be "conscientious" on the subject. [Cheers and Laughter.]

Now gentlemen, I hate to waste my time on such things, but in regard to that general abolition tilt that Judge Douglas makes, when he says that I was engaged at that time in selling out and abolitionizing the old Whig party—I hope you will permit me to read a part of a printed speech that I made then at Peoria, which will show altogether a different view of the position I took in that contest of 1854.

VOICE—Put on your specs.

MR. LINCOLN—Yes, sir, I am obliged to do so. I am no longer a young man. [Laughter.]

This is the *repeal* of the Missouri Compromise. The foregoing history may not be precisely accurate in every particular; but I am sure it is sufficiently so, for all the uses I shall attempt to make of it, and in it, we have before us, the chief materials enabling us to correctly judge whether the repeal of the Missouri Compromise is right or wrong.

I think, and shall try to show, that it is wrong; wrong in its direct effect, letting slavery into Kansas and Nebraska—and wrong in its prospective principle, allowing it to spread to every other part of the wide world, where men can be found inclined to take it.

This *declared* indifference, but as I must think, covert *real* zeal for the spread of slavery, I can not but hate. I hate it because of the monstrous injustice of slavery itself. I hate it because it deprives our republican example of its just influence in the world—enables the enemies of free institutions, with plausibility, to taunt us as hypocrites—causes the real friends of freedom to doubt our sincerity, and especially because it forces so many really good men amongst ourselves into an open war with the very fundamental principles of civil liberty—criticising the Declaration of Independence, and insisting that there is no right principle of action but *self-interest*.

Before proceeding, let me say I think I have no prejudice against the Southern people. They are just what we would be in their situation. If slavery did not now exist amongst them, they would not introduce it. If it did now exist amongst us, we should not instantly give it up. This I believe of the masses north and south. Doubtless there are individuals, on both sides, who would not hold slaves under any circumstances; and others who would gladly introduce slavery anew, if it were out of existence. We know that some southern men do free their slaves, go north, and become tip-top abolitionists; while some northern ones go south, and become most cruel slave-masters.

When southern people tell us they are no more responsible for the origin of slavery, than we; I acknowledge the fact. When it is said that the institution exists, and that it is very difficult to get rid of it, in any satisfactory way, I can understand and appreciate the saying. I surely will not blame them for not doing what I should not know how to do myself. If all earthly power were given me, I should not know what to do, as to the existing institution. My first impulse would be to free all the slaves, and send them to Liberia,—to their own native land. But a moment's reflection would convince me, that whatever of high hope, (as I think there is) there may be in this, in the long run, its sudden execution is impossible. If they were all landed there in a day, they would all perish in the next ten days; and there are not surplus shipping and surplus money enough in the world to carry them there in many times ten days. What then? Free them all, and keep them among us as underlings? Is it quite certain that this betters their condition? I think I would not hold one in slavery, at any rate; yet the point is not clear enough to me to denounce people upon. What next? Free them, and make them politically and socially, our equals? My own feelings will not admit of this; and if mine would, we well know that those of the great mass of white people will not. Whether this feeling accords with justice and sound judgment, is not the sole question, if indeed, it is any part of it. A universal feeling, whether well or ill-founded, can not be safely disregarded. We can not, then, make them equals. It does seem to me that systems of gradual emancipation might be adopted; but for their tardiness in this, I will not undertake to judge our brethren of the south.

When they remind us of their constitutional rights, I acknowledge them, not grudgingly, but fully, and fairly; and I would give them any legislation for the reclaiming of their fugitives, which should not, in its stringency, be more likely to carry a free man into slavery, than our ordinary criminal laws are to hang an innocent one.

But all this; to my judgment, furnishes no more excuse for

permitting slavery to go into our own free territory, than it would for reviving the African slave trade by law. The law which forbids the bringing of slaves *from* Africa; and that which has so long forbid the taking them *to* Nebraska, can hardly be distinguished on any moral principle; and the repeal of the former could find quite as plausible excuses as that of the latter.

I have reason to know that Judge Douglas *knows* that I said this. I think he has the answer here to one of the questions he put to me. I do not mean to allow him to catechise me unless he pays back for it in kind. I will not answer questions one after another unless he reciprocates, but as he made this inquiry and I have answered it before, he has got it without my getting anything in return. He has got my answer on the Fugitive Slave Law.

Now gentlemen, I don't want to read at any greater length, but this is the true complexion of all I have ever said in regard to the institution of slavery and the black race. This is the whole of it, and anything that argues me into his idea of perfect social and political equality with the negro, is but a specious and fantastic arrangement of words, by which a man can prove a horse chestnut to be a chestnut horse. [Laughter.] I will say here, while upon this subject, that I have no purpose directly or indirectly to interfere with the institution of slavery in the States where it exists. I believe I have no lawful right to do so, and I have no inclination to do so. I have no purpose to introduce political and social equality between the white and the black races. There is a physical difference between the two, which in my judgment will probably forever forbid their living together upon the footing of perfect equality, and inasmuch as it becomes a necessity that there must be a difference, I, as well as Judge Douglas, am in favor of the race to which I belong, having the superior position. I have never said anything to the contrary, but I hold that notwithstanding all this, there is no reason in the world why the negro is not entitled to all the natural rights enumerated in the Declaration of Independence, the right to life, liberty and the pursuit of happiness. [Loud cheers.] I hold that he is as much entitled to these as the white man. I agree with Judge Douglas he is not my equal in many respects—certainly not in color, perhaps not in moral or intellectual endowment. But in the right to eat the bread, without leave of anybody else, which his own hand earns, *he is my equal and the equal of Judge Douglas, and the equal of every living man.* [Great applause.]

Now I pass on to consider one or two more of these little follies. The Judge is wofully at fault about his early friend Lincoln being a "grocery keeper." [Laughter.] I don't know as it would be a great sin, if I had been, but he is mistaken. Lincoln never kept a grocery anywhere in the world. [Laughter.] It is true that Lincoln did work the latter part of one winter in a small still house, up at the head of a hollow. [Roars of laughter.] And so I think my friend, the Judge, is equally at fault when he charges me at the time when I was in Congress of having opposed our soldiers who were fighting in the Mexican war. The Judge did not make his charge very distinctly but I can tell you what he can prove by referring to the record. You remember I was an old Whig, and whenever the Democratic party tried to get me to vote that the war had been righteously begun by the President, I would not do it. But whenever they asked for any money, or land warrants, or anything to pay the soldiers there, during all that time, I gave the same votes that Judge Douglas did. [Loud applause.] You can think as you please as to whether that was consistent. Such is the truth; and the Judge has the right to make all he can out of it. But when he, by a general charge, conveys the idea that I withheld supplies from the soldiers who were fighting in the Mexican war, or did anything else to hinder the soldiers, he is, to say the least, grossly and altogether mistaken, as a consultation of the records will prove to him.

As I have not used up so much of my time as I had supposed, I will dwell a little longer upon one or two of these minor topics upon which the Judge has spoken. He has read from my speech in Springfield, in which I say that "a house divided against itself cannot stand." Does the Judge say it *can* stand? [Laughter.] I don't know whether he does or not. The Judge does not seem to be attending to me just now, but I would like to know if it is his opinion that a house divided against itself *can stand*. If he does, then there is a question of veracity, not between him and me, but between the Judge and an authority of a somewhat higher character. [Laughter and applause.]

Now, my friends, I ask your attention to this matter for the purpose of saying something seriously. I know that the Judge may readily enough agree with me that the maxim which was put forth by the Saviour is true, but he may allege that I misapply it; and the Judge has a right to urge that, in my application, I do misapply it, and then I have a right to show that I do *not* misapply it. When he undertakes to say that because I think this nation, so far as the question of Slavery is concerned, will all become one thing or all the other, I am in favor of bringing about a dead uniformity in the various States, in all their institutions, he argues erroneously. The great variety of the local institutions in the States, springing from differences in the soil, differences in the face of the country, and in the climate, are bonds of Union. They do not make "a house divided against itself," but they make a house united. If they produce in one section of the country what is called for by the wants of another section, and this other section can supply the wants of the first, they are not matters of discord but bonds of union, true bonds of union. But can this question of slavery be considered as among *these* varieties in the institutions of the country? I leave it to you to say whether, in the history of our government, this institution of slavery has not always failed to be a bond of union, and, on the con-

trary, been an apple of discord and an element of division
in the house. [Cries of "Yes, yes," and applause.] I ask
you to consider whether, so long as the moral constitution
of men's minds shall continue to be the same, after this
generation and assemblage shall sink into the grave, and
another race shall arise, with the same moral and intellectual
development we have—whether, if that institution is standing in the same irritating position in which it now is, it will
not continue an element of division? [Cries of "Yes, yes."]
If so, then I have a right to say that in regard to this
question, the Union is a house divided against itself, and
when the Judge reminds me that I have often said to him
that the institution of slavery has existed for eighty years in
some States, and yet it does not exist in some others, I
agree to the fact, and I account for it by looking at the
position in which our fathers originally placed it—restricting
it from the new Territories where it had not gone, and
legislating to cut off its source by the abrogation of the slave
trade, thus putting the seal of legislation *against its spread.*
The public mind *did* rest in the belief that it was in the
course of ultimate extinction. [Cries of "Yes, yes."] But
lately, I think—and in this I charge nothing on the Judge's
motives—lately, I think, that he, and those acting with him,
have placed that institution on a new basis, which looks to
the *perpetuity and nationalization of slavery.* [Loud cheers.]
And while it is placed upon this new basis, I say, and I
have said, that I believe we shall not have peace upon the
question until the opponents of slavery arrest the further
spread of it, and place it where the public mind shall rest
in the belief that it is in the course of ultimate extinction;
or, on the other hand, that its advocates will push it forward
until it shall become alike lawful in all the States, old as
well as new, North as well as South. Now, I believe if we
could arrest the spread, and place it where Washington,
and Jefferson, and Madison placed it, it *would be* in the
course of ultimate extinction, and the public mind *would*, as

for eighty years past, believe that it was in the course of ultimate extinction. The crisis would be past and the institution might be let alone for a hundred years, if it should live so long, in the States where it exists, yet it would be going out of existence in the way best for both the black and the white races. [Great cheering.]

A VOICE—Then do you repudiate Popular Sovereignty?

MR. LINCOLN—Well, then, let us talk about Popular Sovereignty! [Laughter.] What is Popular Sovereignty? [Cries of "A humbug," "a humbug."] Is it the right of the people to have Slavery or not have it, as they see fit, in the territories? I will state—and I have an able man to watch me—my understanding is that Popular Sovereignty, as now applied to the question of Slavery, does allow the people of a Territory to have Slavery if they want to, but does not allow them *not* to have it if they *do not* want it. [Applause and laughter.] I do not mean that if this vast concourse of people were in a Territory of the United States, any one of them would be obliged to have a slave if he did not want one; but I do say that, as I understand the Dred Scott decision, if any one man wants slaves, all the rest have no way of keeping that one man from holding them.

When I made my speech at Springfield, of which the Judge complains, and from which he quotes, I really was not thinking of the things which he ascribes to me at all. I had no thought in the world that I was doing anything to bring about a war between the free and slave States. I had no thought in the world that I was doing anything to bring about a political and social equality of the black and white races. It never occurred to me that I was doing anything or favoring anything to reduce to a dead uniformity all the local institutions of the various States. But I must say, in all fairness to him, if he thinks I am doing something which leads to these bad results, it is none the better that I did not mean it. It is just as fatal to the country, if I have any influence in producing it, whether I intend it or not. But can it be true, that placing this institution upon the original basis—the basis upon which our fathers placed it—can have any tendency to set the Northern and the Southern States at war with one another, or that it can have any tendency to make the people of Vermont raise sugar cane, because they raise it in Louisiana, or that it can compel the people of Illinois to cut pine logs on the Grand Prairie, where they will not grow, because they cut pine logs in Maine, where they do grow? [Laughter.] The Judge says this is a new principle started in regard to this question. Does the Judge claim that he is working on the plan of the founders of government? I think he says in some of his speeches—indeed I have one here now—that he saw evidence of a policy to allow slavery to be south of a certain line, while north of it should be excluded, and he saw an indisposition on the part of the country to stand upon that policy, and therefore he set about studying the subject upon *original principles*, and upon *original principles* he got up the Nebraska bill! I am fighting it upon these "original principles"—fighting it in the Jeffersonian, Washingtonian, and Madisonian fashion. [Laughter and applause.]

Now my friends I wish you to attend for a little while to one or two other things in that Springfield speech. My main object was to show, so far as my humble ability was capable of showing to the people of this country, what I believed was the truth—that there was a *tendency*, if not a conspiracy among those who have engineered this slavery question for the last four or five years, to make slavery perpetual and universal in this nation. Having made that speech principally for that object, after arranging the evidences that I thought tended to prove my proposition, I concluded with this bit of comment:

We cannot absolutely know that these exact adaptations are the result of pre-concert, but when we see a lot of framed timbers, different portions of which we know have been gotten out at different times and places, and by different workmen—Stephen, Franklin, Roger and James, for instance—and when we see these timbers joined together, and see they exactly make the frame of a house or a mill, all the tenons and mortices exactly fitting and all the lengths and proportions of the different pieces exactly adapted to their respective places and not a piece too many or too few— not omitting even the scaffolding—or if a single piece be lacking we see the place in the frame exactly fitted and prepared yet to bring such piece in—in such a case we feel it impossible not to believe that Stephen and Franklin, and Roger and James, all understood one another from the beginning, and all worked upon a common plan or draft drawn before the first blow was struck. [Great cheeers.]

When my friend, Judge Douglas, came to Chicago, on the 16th of July, this speech having been delivered on the 16th of June, he made an harangue there, in which he took hold of this speech of mine, showing that he had carefully read it; and while he paid no attention to *this* matter at all, but complimented me as being a "kind, amiable, and intelligent gentleman," notwithstanding I had said this; he goes on and eliminates, or draws out, from my speech this tendency of mine to set the States at war with one another, to make all the institutions uniform, and set the niggers and white people to marrying together. [Laughter.] Then, as the Judge had complimented me with these pleasant titles, (I must confess to my weakness,) I was a little "taken," [laughter] for it came from a great man. I was not very much accustomed to flattery, and it came the sweeter to me. I was rather like the Hoosier, with the gingerbread, when he said he reckoned he loved it better than any other man, and got less of it. [Roars of laughter.] As the Judge had so flattered me, I could not make up my mind that he meant to deal unfairly with me; so I went to work to show him that he misunderstood the whole scope of my speech, and that I really never intended to set the people at war with one another. As an illustration, the next time I met him, which was at Springfield, I used this expression, that I claimed no right under the Constitution, nor had I any inclination, to enter into the Slave States and interfere with the institutions of slavery. He says upon that: Lincoln will not enter into the Slave States, but will go to the banks of the Ohio, on this side, and shoot over! [Laughter.] He runs on, step by step, in the horse-chestnut style of argument, until in the Springfield speech, he says, "Unless he shall be successful in firing his batteries until he shall have extinguished slavery in all the States, the Union shall be dissolved." Now I don't think that was exactly the way to treat a kind, amiable, intelligent gentleman. [Roars of laughter.] I know if I had asked the Judge to show when or where it was I had said that, if I didn't succeed in firing into the Slave States until slavery should be extinguished, the Union should be dissolved, he could not have shown it. I understand what he would do. He would say, "I don't mean to quote from you, but this was the *result* of what you say." But I have the right to ask, and I do ask now, Did you not put it in such a form that an ordinary reader or listener would take it as an expression *from me*? [Laughter.]

In a speech at Springfield, on the night of the 17th, I thought I might as well attend to my own business a little, and I recalled his attention as well as I could to this charge of conspiracy to nationalize Slavery. I called his attention to the fact that he had acknowledged, in my hearing twice, that he had carefully read the speech, and, in the language of the lawyers, as he had twice read the speech, and still had put in no plea or answer, I took a default on him. I insisted that I had a right then to renew that charge of conspiracy. Ten days afterwards, I met the Judge at Clinton—that is to say, I was on the ground, but not in the discussion—and heard him make a speech. Then he comes in with his plea to this charge, for the first time, and his

plea when put in, as well as I can recollect it, amounted to
this: that he never had any talk with Judge Taney or the
President of the United States with regard to the Dred
Scott decision before it was made. I (Lincoln) ought to
know that the man who makes a charge without knowing it
to be true, falsifies as much as he who knowingly tells a
falsehood; and lastly, that he would pronounce the whole
thing a falsehood; but he would make no personal application of the charge of falsehood, not because of any regard
for the "kind, amiable, intelligent gentleman," but because
of his own personal self-respect! [Roars of laughter.] I have
understood since then, (but [turning to Judge Douglas] will
not hold the Judge to it if he is not willing) that he has
broken through the "self-respect," and has got to saying the
thing *out*. The Judge nods to me that it is so. [Laughter.]
It is fortunate for me that I can keep as good-humored as
I do, when the Judge acknowledges that he has been trying
to make a question of veracity with me. I know the Judge
is a great man, while I am only a small man, but *I feel that
I have got him*. [Tremendous cheering.] I demur to that
plea. I waive all objections that it was not filed till after
default was taken, and demur to it upon the merits. What
if Judge Douglas never did talk with Chief Justice Taney
and the President, before the Dred Scott decision was
made, does it follow that he could not have had as perfect
an understanding without talking, as with it? I am not disposed to stand upon my legal advantage. I am disposed to
take his denial as being like an answer in chancery, that he
neither had any knowledge, information or belief in the existence of such a conspiracy. I am disposed to take his answer
as being as broad as though he had put it in these words.
And now, I ask, even if he has done so, have not I a right
to *prove it on him*, and to offer the evidence of more than
two witnesses, by whom to prove it; and if the evidence
proves the existence of the conspiracy, does his broad an-

swer denying all knowledge, information, or belief, disturb
the fact? It can only show that he was *used* by conspirators,
and was not a *leader* of them. [Vociferous cheering.]

Now in regard to his reminding me of the moral rule that
persons who tell what they do not know to be true, falsify
as much as those who knowingly tell falsehoods. I remember
the rule, and it must be borne in mind that in what I have
read to you, I do not say that I *know* such a conspiracy to
exist. To that, I reply *I believe it.* If the Judge says that I
do *not* believe it, then *he* says what *he* does not know, and
falls within his own rule, that he who asserts a thing which
he does not know to be true, falsifies as much as he who
knowingly tells a falsehood. I want to call your attention to
a little discussion on that branch of the case, and the evidence which brought my mind to the conclusion which I
expressed as my *belief.* If, in arraying that evidence, I had
stated anything which was false or erroneous, it needed but
that Judge Douglas should point it out, and I would have
taken it back with all the kindness in the world. I do not
deal in that way. If I have brought forward anything not a
fact, if he will point it out, it will not even ruffle me to take
it back. But if he will not point out anything erroneous in
the evidence, is it not rather for him to show, by a compari-
son of the evidence that I have *reasoned* falsely, than to call
the "kind, amiable, intelligent gentleman," a liar? [Cheers
and laughter.] If I have reasoned to a false conclusion, it is
the vocation of an able debater to show by argument that
I have wandered to an erroneous conclusion. I want to ask
your attention to a portion of the Nebraska Bill, which
Judge Douglas has quoted: "It being the true intent and
meaning of this act, not to legislate slavery into any Territory or State, nor to exclude it therefrom, but to leave the
people thereof perfectly free to form and regulate their domestic institutions in their own way, subject only to the
Constitution of the United States." Thereupon Judge Douglas and others began to argue in favor of "Popular Sover-

eignty"—the right of the people to have slaves if they wanted them, and to exclude slavery if they did not want them. "But," said, in substance, a Senator from Ohio, (Mr. Chase, I believe,) "we more than suspect that you do not mean to allow the people to exclude slavery if they wish to, and if you do mean it, accept an amendment which I propose expressly authorizing the people to exclude slavery." I believe I have the amendment here before me, which was offered, and under which the people of the Territory, through their proper representatives, might if they saw fit, prohibit the existence of slavery therein. And now I state it as a *fact*, to be taken back if there is any mistake about it, that Judge Douglas and those acting with him, *voted that amendment down*. [Tremendous applause.] I now think that those men who voted it down, had a *real reason* for doing so. They know what that reason was. It looks to us, since we have seen the Dred Scott decision pronounced holding that "under the Constitution" the people cannot exclude slavery—I say it looks to outsiders, poor, simple, "amiable, intelligent gentlemen," [great laughter,] as though the niche was left as a place to put that Dred Scott decision in— [laughter and cheers]—a niche which would have been spoiled by adopting the amendment. And now, I say again, if *this* was not the reason, it will avail the Judge much more to calmly and good-humoredly point out to these people what that *other* reason was for voting the amendment down, than, swelling himself up, to vociferate that he may be provoked to call somebody a liar. [Tremendous applause.]

Again: there is in that same quotation from the Nebraska bill this clause—"It being the true intent and meaning of this bill not to legislate slavery into any Territory or *State*." I have always been puzzled to know what business the word "State" had in that connection. Judge Douglas knows. *He put it there*. He knows what he put it there for. We outsiders cannot say what he put it there for. The law they were passing was not about States, and was not making provisions for States. What was it placed there for? After seeing the Dred Scott decision, which holds that the people cannot exclude slavery from a *Territory*, if another Dred Scott decision shall come, holding that they cannot exclude it from a *State*, we shall discover that when the word was originally put there, it was in view of something which was to come in due time, we shall see that it was the *other half* of something. [Applause.] I now say again, if there is any different reason for putting it there, Judge Douglas, in a good-humored way, without calling anybody a liar, *can tell what the reason was*. [Renewed cheers.]

When the Judge spoke at Clinton, he came very near making a charge of falsehood against me. He used, as I found it printed in a newspaper, which I remember was very nearly like the real speech, the following language:

I did not answer the charge [of conspiracy] before, for the reason that I did not suppose there was a man in America with a heart so corrupt as to believe such a charge could be true. I have too much respect for Mr. Lincoln to suppose he is serious in making the charge.

I confess this is rather a curious view, that out of respect for me he should consider I was making what I deemed rather a grave charge in fun. [Laughter.] I confess it strikes me rather strangely. But I let it pass. As the Judge did not for a moment believe that there was a man in America whose heart was so "corrupt" as to make such a charge, and as he places me among the "men in America" who have hearts base enough to make such a charge, I hope he will excuse me if I hunt out another charge very like this; and if it should turn out that in hunting I should find that other, and it should turn out to be Judge Douglas himself who made it, I hope he will reconsider this question of the deep corruption of heart he has thought fit to ascribe to me. [Great applause and laughter.] In Judge Douglas' speech of March 22d, 1858, which I hold in my hand, he says:

In this connection there is another topic to which I desire to allude. I seldom refer to the course of newspapers, or notice the articles which they publish in regard to myself; but the course of the Washington *Union* has been so extraordinary, for the last two or three months, that I think it well enough to make some allusion to it. It has read me out of the Democratic party every other day, at least for two or three months, and keeps reading me out, (laughter;) and, as if it had not succeeded still continues to read me out, using such terms as "traitor," "renegade," "deserter," and other kind and polite epithets of that nature. Sir, I have no vindication to make of my democracy against the Washington *Union*, or any other newspapers. I am willing to allow my history and action for the last twenty years to speak for themselves as to my political principles, and my fidelity to political obligations. The Washington *Union* has a personal grievance. When its editor was nominated for Public Printer I declined to vote for him, and stated that at some time I might give my reasons for doing so. Since I declined to give that vote, this scurrilous abuse, these vindictive and constant attacks have been repeated almost daily on me. Will my friend from Michigan read the article to which I allude.

This is a part of the speech. You must excuse me from reading the entire article of the Washington *Union*, as Mr. Stuart read it for Mr. Douglas. The Judge goes on and sums up, as I think correctly:

Mr. President, you here find several distinct propositions advanced boldly by the Washington *Union* editorially and apparently *authoritatively*, and every man who questions any of them is denounced as an Abolitionist, a Free-Soiler, a fanatic. The propositions are, first, that the primary object of all government at its original institution is the protection of person and property; second, that the Constitution of the United States declares that the citizens of each State shall be entitled to all the privileges and immunities of citizens in the several States; and that, therefore, thirdly, all State laws, whether organic or otherwise, which prohibit the citizens of one State from settling in another with their slave property, and especially declaring it forfeited, are direct violations of the original intention of the Government and Constitution of the

United States; and fourth, that the emancipation of the slaves of the northern States was a gross outrage on the rights of property, inasmuch as it was involuntarily done on the part of the owner.

Remember that this article was published in the *Union* on the 17th of November, and on the 18th appeared the first article giving the adhesion of the *Union* to the Lecompton constitution. It was in these words:

"KANSAS AND HER CONSTITUTION.—The vexed question is settled. The problem is solved. The dread point of danger is passed. All serious trouble to Kansas affairs is over and gone."

And a column, nearly of the same sort. Then, when you come to look into the Lecompton Constitution, you find the same doctrine incorporated in it which was put forth editorially in the *Union*. What is it?

"ARTICLE 7, *Section* 1. The right of property is before and higher than any constitutional sanction; and the right of the owner of a slave to such slave and its increase is the same and as inviolable as the right of the owner of any property whatever."

Then in the schedule is a provision that the Constitution may be amended after 1864 by a two-thirds vote.

"But no alteration shall be made to affect the right of property in the ownership of slaves."

It will be seen by these clauses in the Lecompton Constitution that they are identical in spirit with this *authoritative* article in the Washington *Union* of the day previous to its indorsement of this Constitution.

I pass over some portions of the speech, and I hope that any one who feels interested in this matter will read the entire section of the speech, and see whether I do the Judge injustice. He proceeds:

When I saw that article in the *Union* of the 17th of November, followed by the glorification of the Lecompton Constitution on the 18th of November, and this clause in the Constitution asserting the doctrine that a State has no right to prohibit slavery within its limits, I saw that there was a *fatal blow* being struck at the sovereignty of the States of this Union.

I stop the quotation there, again requesting that it may all be read. I have read all of the portion I desire to comment upon. What is this charge that the Judge thinks I must have a very corrupt heart to make? It was a purpose on the part of certain high functionaries to make it impossible for the people of one State to prohibit the people of any other State from entering it with their "property," so called, and making it a slave State. In other words, it was a charge implying a design to make the institution of slavery national. And now I ask your attention to what Judge Douglas has himself done here. I know he made that part of the speech as a reason why he had refused to vote for a certain man for public printer, but when we get at it, the charge itself is the very one I made against him, that he thinks I am so corrupt for uttering. Now whom does he make that charge against? Does he make it against that newspaper editor merely? No; he says it is identical in spirit with the Lecompton Constitution, and so the framers of that Constitution are brought in with the editor of the newspaper in that "fatal blow being struck." He did not call it a "conspiracy." In his language it is a "fatal blow being struck." And if the words carry the meaning better when changed from a "conspiracy" into a "fatal blow being struck," I will change *my* expression and call it "fatal blow being struck." [Cheers and laughter.] We see the charge made not merely against the editor of the *Union* but all the framers of the Lecompton Constitution; and not only so, but the article was an *authoritative* article. By whose authority? Is there any question but he means it was by the authority of the President, and his Cabinet—the Administration?

Is there any sort of question but he means to make that charge? Then there are the editors of the *Union*, the framers of the Lecompton Constitution, the President of the United States and his Cabinet, and all the supporters of the Lecompton Constitution in Congress and out of Congress, who are all involved in this "fatal blow being struck." I commend to

Judge Douglas' consideration the question of *how corrupt a man's heart must be to make such a charge!* [Vociferous cheering.]

Now my friends, I have but one branch of the subject, in the little time I have left, to which to call your attention, and as I shall come to a close at the end of that branch, it is probable that I shall not occupy quite all the time allotted to me. Although on these questions I would like to talk twice as long as I have, I could not enter upon another head and discuss it properly without running over my time. I ask the attention of the people here assembled and elsewhere, to the course that Judge Douglas is pursuing every day as bearing upon this question of making slavery national. Not going back to the records but taking the speeches he makes, the speeches he made yesterday and day before and makes constantly all over the country—I ask your attention to them. In the first place what is necessary to make the institution national? Not war. There is no danger that the people of Kentucky will shoulder their muskets and with a young nigger stuck on every bayonet march into Illinois and force them upon us. There is no danger of our going over there and making war upon them. Then what is necessary for the nationalization of slavery? It is simply the next Dred Scott decision. It is merely for the Supreme Court to decide that no *State* under the Constitution can exclude it, just as they have already decided that under the Constitution neither Congress nor the Territorial Legislature can do it. When that is decided and acquiesced in, the whole thing is done. This being true, and this being the way as I think that slavery is to be made national, let us consider what Judge Douglas is doing every day to that end. In the first place, let us see what influence he is exerting on public sentiment. In this and like communities, public sentiment is everything. With public sentiment, nothing can fail; without it nothing can succeed. Consequently he who moulds public sentiment, goes deeper than he who enacts statutes or pronounces decisions. He makes statutes and decisions possible or impossible to be executed. This must be borne in mind, as also the additional fact that Judge Douglas is a man of vast influence, so great that it is enough for many men to profess to believe anything, when they once find out that Judge Douglas professes to believe it. Consider also the attitude he occupies at the head of a large party—a party which he claims has a majority of all the voters in the country. This man sticks to a decision which forbids the people of a Territory from excluding slavery, and he does so not because he says it is right in itself—he does not give any opinion on that—but because it has been *decided by the court*, and being decided by the court, he is, and you are bound to take it in your political action as *law*—not that he judges at all of its merits, but because a decision of the court is to him a *"Thus saith the Lord."* [Applause.] He places it on that ground alone, and you will bear in mind that thus committing himself unreservedly to this decision, *commits him to the next one* just as firmly as to this. He did not commit himself on account of the merit or demerit of the decision, but it is a *Thus saith the Lord.* The next decision, as much as this, will be a *thus saith the Lord.* There is nothing that can divert or turn him away from this decision. It is nothing that I point out to him that his great prototype, Gen. Jackson, did not believe in the binding force of decisions. It is nothing to him that Jefferson did not so believe. I have said that I have often heard him approve of Jackson's course in disregarding the decision of the Supreme Court pronouncing a National Bank constitutional. He says, I did not hear him say so. He denies the accuracy of my recollection. I say he ought to know better than I, but I will make no question about this thing, though it still seems to me that I heard him say it twenty times. [Applause and laughter.] I will tell him though, that he now claims to stand on the Cincinnati platform, which affirms that Congress *cannot* charter a National Bank, in the teeth of that old standing

decision that Congress *can* charter a bank. [Loud applause.]
And I remind him of another piece of history on the question
of respect for judicial decisions, and it is a piece of Illinois
history, belonging to a time when the large party to which
Judge Douglas belonged, were displeased with a decision
of the Supreme Court of Illinois, because they had decided
that a Governor could not remove a Secretary of State.
You will find the whole story in Ford's History of Illinois,
and I know that Judge Douglas will not deny that he was
then in favor of over-slaughing that decision by the mode of
adding five new Judges, so as to vote down the four old
ones. Not only so, but it ended in *the Judge's sitting down
on that very bench as one of the five new Judges to break
down the four old ones.* [Cheers and laughter.] It was in
this way precisely that he got his title of Judge. Now, when
the Judge tells me that men appointed conditionally to sit
as members of a court, will have to be catechised beforehand
upon some subject, I say "You know Judge; you have tried
it." [Laughter.] When he says a court of this kind will lose
the confidence of all men, will be prostituted and disgraced
by such a proceeding, I say, "You know best, Judge; you
have been through the mill." [Great laughter.] But I cannot
shake Judge Douglas' teeth loose from the Dred Scott decision. Like some obstinate animal (I mean no disrespect,)
that will hang on when he has once got his teeth fixed, you
may cut off a leg, or you may tear away an arm, still he
will not relax his hold. And so I may point out to the
Judge, and say that he is bespattered all over, from the
beginning of his political life to the present time, with attacks
upon judicial decisions—I may cut off limb after limb of his
public record, and strive to wrench him from a single dictum
of the Court—yet I cannot divert him from it. He hangs to
the last, to the Dred Scott decision. [Loud cheers.] These
things show there is a purpose *strong as death and eternity*
for which he adheres to this decision, and for which he will

adhere to *all other decisions* of the same Court. [Vociferous applause.]

A HIBERNIAN.—Give us something besides Dred Scott.

MR. LINCOLN.—Yes; no doubt you want to hear something that don't hurt. [Laughter and applause.] Now, having spoken of the Dred Scott decision, one more word and I am done. Henry Clay, my beau ideal of a statesman, the man for whom I fought all my humble life—Henry Clay once said of a class of men who would repress all tendencies to liberty and ultimate emancipation, that they must, if they would do this, go back to the era of our Independence, and muzzle the cannon which thunders its annual joyous return; they must blow out the moral lights around us; they must penetrate the human soul, and eradicate there the love of liberty; and then and not till then, could they perpetuate slavery in this country! [Loud cheers.] To my thinking, Judge Douglas is, by his example and vast influence, doing that very thing in this community, [cheers,] when he says that the negro has nothing in the Declaration of Independence. Henry Clay plainly understood the contrary. Judge Douglas is going back to the era of our Revolution, and to the extent of his ability, muzzling the cannon which thunders its annual joyous return. When he invites any people willing to have slavery, to establish it, he is blowing out the moral lights around us. [Cheers.] When he says he "cares not whether slavery is voted down or voted up,"—that it is a sacred right of self government—he is in my judgment penetrating the human soul and eradicating the light of reason and the love of liberty in this American people. [Enthusiastic and continued applause.] And now I will only say that when, by all these means and appliances, Judge Douglas shall succeed in bringing public sentiment to an exact accordance with his own views—when these vast assemblages shall echo back all these sentiments—when they shall come to repeat his views and to avow his principles, and to say all that he says on these mighty questions—then it needs only the formality of the second Dred Scott decision, which he endorses in advance, to make Slavery alike lawful in all the States—old as well as new, North as well as South.

My friends, that ends the chapter. The Judge can take his half-hour.

Lecture on Discoveries and Inventions, Jacksonville, Illinois

We have all heard of Young America. He is the most *current* youth of the age. Some think him conceited, and arrogant; but has he not reason to entertain a rather extensive opinion of himself? Is he not the inventor and owner of the *present*, and sole hope of the *future*? Men, and things, everywhere, are ministering unto him. Look at his apparel, and you shall see cotten fabrics from Manchester and Lowell; flax-linen from Ireland; wool-cloth from Spain; silk from France; furs from the Arctic regions, with a buffalo-robe from the Rocky Mountains, as a general out-sider. At his table, besides plain bread and meat made at home, are sugar from Louisiana; coffee and fruits from the tropics; salt from Turk's Island; fish from New-foundland; tea from China, and spices from the Indies. The whale of the Pacific furnishes his candle-light; he has a diamond-ring from Brazil; a gold-watch from California, and a spanish cigar from Havanna. He not only has a present supply of all these, and much more; but thousands of hands are engaged in producing fresh supplies, and other thousands, in bringing them to him. The iron horse is panting, and impatient, to carry him everywhere, in no time; and the lightening stands ready harnessed to take and bring his tidings in a trifle less than no time. He owns a large part of the world, by right of possessing it; and all the rest by right of *wanting* it, and *intending* to have it. As Plato had for the immortality of the soul, so Young America has "a pleasing hope—a fond desire—a longing after" teritory. He has a great passion— a perfect rage—for the *"new"*; particularly new men for office, and the new earth mentioned in the revelations, in which, being no more sea, there must be about three times as much land as in the present. He is a great friend of humanity; and his desire for land is not selfish, but merely an impulse to extend the area of freedom. He is very anxious to fight for the liberation of enslaved nations and colonies, provided, always, they *have* land, and have *not* any liking for his interference. As to those who have no land, and would be glad of help from any quarter, he considers *they* can afford to wait a few hundred years longer. In knowledge he is particularly rich. He knows all that can possibly be known; inclines to believe in spiritual rappings, and is the unquestioned inventor of *"Manifest Destiny."* His horror is for all that is old, particularly "Old Fogy"; and if there be any thing old which he can endure, it is only old whiskey and old tobacco.

If the said Young America really is, as he claims to be, the owner of all present, it must be admitted that he has considerable advantage of Old Fogy. Take, for instance, the first of all fogies, father Adam. There he stood, a very perfect physical man, as poets and painters inform us; but he must have been very ignorant, and simple in his habits. He had had no sufficient time to learn much by observation; and he had no near neighbors to teach him anything. No part of his breakfast had been brought from the other side of the world; and it is quite probable, he had no conception of the world having any other side. In all of these things, it is very plain, he was no equal of Young America; the most that can be said is, that *according to his chance* he may have been quite as much of a man as his very self-complaisant descendant. Little as was what he knew, let the Youngster discard all he has learned from others, and then show, if he can, any advantage on his side. In the way of *land,* and *live stock,* Adam was quite in the ascendant. He had dominion over all the earth, and all the living things upon, and round about it. The land has been sadly divided out since; but never fret, Young America will *re-annex* it.

The great difference between Young America and Old Fogy, is the result of *Discoveries, Inventions,* and *Improvements.* These, in turn, are the result of *observation, reflection* and *experiment.* For instance, it is quite certain that ever since water has been boiled in covered vessels, men have seen the lids of the vessels rise and fall a little, with a sort of fluttering motion, by force of the steam; but so long as this was not specially observed, and reflected and experimented upon, it came to nothing. At length however, after many thousand years, some man observes this long-known effect of hot water lifting a pot-lid, and begins a train of reflection upon it. He says "Why, to be sure, the force that lifts the pot-lid, will lift any thing else, which is no heavier than the pot-lid." "And, as man has much hard lifting to do, can not this hot-water power be made to help him?" He has become a little excited on the subject, and he fancies he hears a voice answering "Try me" He does try it; and the *observation, reflection,* and *trial* gives to the world the control of that tremendous, and now well known agent, called steam-power. This is not the actual history in detail, but the general principle.

But was this first inventor of the application of steam, wiser or more ingenious than those who had gone before him? Not at all. Had he not learned much of them, he never would have succeeded—probably, never would have thought of making the attempt. To be fruitful in invention, it is indispensable to have a *habit* of observation and reflection; and this *habit,* our steam friend acquired, no doubt, from those who, to him, were old fogies. But for the difference in *habit* of observation, why did yankees, almost instantly, discover gold in California, which had been trodden upon, and overlooked by indians and Mexican greasers, for centuries? Goldmines are not the only mines overlooked in the same way. There are more mines above the Earth's surface than below it. All nature—the whole world, material, moral, and intellectual,—is a mine; and, in Adam's day, it was a wholly unexplored mine. Now, it was the destined work of Adam's race to develope, by discoveries, inventions, and improvements, the hidden treasures of this mine. But Adam had nothing to turn his attention to the work. If he should do anything in the way of invention, he had first to invent the art of invention—the *instance* at least, if not the *habit* of observation and reflection. As might be expected he seems not to have been a very observing man at first; for it appears he went about naked a considerable length of time, before he even noticed that obvious fact. But when he did observe it, the observation was not lost upon him; for it immediately led to the first of all inventions, of which we have any direct account—*the fig-leaf apron*.

The inclination to exchange thoughts with one another is probably an original impulse of our nature. If I be in pain I wish to let you know it, and to ask your sympathy and assistance; and my pleasurable emotions also, I wish to communicate to, and share with you. But to carry on such communication, some *instrumentality* is indispensable. Accordingly speech—articulate sounds rattled off from the tongue—was used by our first parents, and even by Adam, before the creation of Eve. He gave names to the animals while she was still a bone in his side; and he broke out quite volubly when she first stood before him, the best present of his maker. From this it would appear that speech was not an invention of man, but rather the direct gift of his Creator. But whether Divine gift, or invention, it is still plain that if a mode of communication had been left to invention, *speech* must have been the first, from the superior adaptation to the end, of the organs of speech, over every other means within the whole range of nature. Of the organs of speech the tongue is the principal; and if we shall test it, we shall find the capacities of the tongue, in the utterance of articulate sounds, absolutely wonderful. You can count from one to one hundred, quite distinctly in about forty seconds. In doing this two hundred and eighty three distinct sounds or syllables are uttered, being seven to each second; and yet there shall be enough difference between every two, to be easily recognized by the ear of the hearer. What other *signs* to represent *things* could possibly be produced so rapidly? or, even, if ready made, could be *arranged* so rapidly to express the sense? *Motions* with the hands, are no adequate substitute. *Marks* for the recognition of the eye—*writing*— although a wonderful auxiliary for speech, is no worthy substitute for it. In addition to the more slow and laborious process of getting up a communication in writing, the materials—pen, ink, and paper—are not always at hand. But one always has his tongue with him, and the breath of his life is the ever-ready material with which it works. Speech, then, by enabling different individuals to interchange thoughts, and thereby to combine their powers of observation and reflection, greatly facilitates useful discoveries and inventions. What one observes, and would himself infer nothing from, he tells to another, and that other at once sees a valuable hint in it. A result is thus reached which neither *alone* would have arrived at.

And this reminds me of what I passed unnoticed before, that the very first invention was a joint operation, Eve having shared with Adam in the getting up of the apron. And, indeed, judging from the fact that sewing has come down to our times as "woman's work" it is very probable she took the leading part; he, perhaps, doing no more than to stand by and thread the needle. That proceeding may be reckoned as the mother of all "Sewing societies"; and the first and most perfect "world's fair" all inventions and all inventors then in the world, being on the spot.

But speech alone, valuable as it ever has been, and is, has not advanced the condition of the world much. This is abundantly evident when we look at the degraded condition of all those tribes of human creatures who have no considerable additional means of communicating thoughts. *Writing*— the art of communicating thoughts to the mind, through the eye—is the great invention of the world. Great in the astonishing range of analysis and combination which necessarily underlies the most crude and general conception of it—great, very great in enabling us to converse with the dead, the absent, and the unborn, at all distances of time and of space; and great, not only in its direct benefits, but greatest help, to all other inventions. Suppose the art, with all conception of it, were this day lost to the world, how long, think you, would it be, before even Young America could get up the letter A, with any adequate notion of using it to advantage? The precise period at which writing was invented, is not known; but it certainly was as early as the time of Moses; from which we may safely infer that it's inventors were very old fogies.

Webster, at the time of writing his Dictionary, speaks of the English Language as then consisting of seventy or eighty thousand words. If so, the language in which the five books of Moses were written must, at that time, now thirtythree or four hundred years ago, have consisted of at least one quarter as many, or, twenty thousand. When we remember that words are *sounds* merely, we shall conclude that the idea of representing those sounds by *marks*, so that whoever should at any time after see the marks, would understand what sounds they meant, was a bold and ingenius conception, not likely to occur to one man of a million, in the run of a thousand years. And, when it did occur, a distinct mark for each word, giving twenty thousand different marks first to be learned, and afterwards remembered, would follow as the second thought, and would present such a difficulty as would lead to the conclusion that the whole thing was impracticable. But the *necessity* still would exist; and we may readily suppose that the idea was conceived, and lost, and reproduced, and dropped, and taken up again and again, until at last, the thought of dividing sounds into parts, and making a mark, not to represent a whole sound, but only a part of one, and then of combining these marks, not very many in number, upon the principles of permutation, so as to represent any and all of the whole twenty thousand words, and even any additional number was somehow conceived and pushed into practice. This was the invention of *phoenetic* writing, as distinguished from the clumsy picture writing of some of the nations. That it was difficult of conception and execution, is apparant, as well by the foregoing reflections, as by the fact that so many tribes of men have come down from Adam's time to ours without ever having possessed it. It's utility may be conceived, by the reflection that, to *it* we owe everything which distinguishes us from savages. Take it from us, and the Bible, all history, all science, all government, all commerce, and nearly all social intercourse go with it.

The great activity of the tongue, in articulating sounds, has already been mentioned; and it may be of some passing interest to notice the wonderful powers of the *eye*, in conveying ideas to the mind from writing. Take the same example of the numbers from *one* to *one hundred*, written down, and you can run your eye over the list, and be assured that every number is in it, in about one half the time it would require to pronounce the words with the voice; and not only so, but you can, in the same short time, determine whether every word is spelled correctly, by which it is evident that every separate letter, amounting to eight hundred and sixty four, has been recognized, and reported to the mind, within the incredibly short space of twenty seconds, or one third of a minute.

I have already intimated my opinion that in the world's history, certain inventions and discoveries occurred, of peculiar value, on account of their great efficiency in facilitating all other inventions and discoveries. Of these were the arts of writing and of printing—the discovery of America, and the introduction of Patent-laws. The date of the first, as already stated, is unknown; but it certainly was as much as fifteen hundred years before the Christian era; the second—printing—came in 1436, or nearly three thousand years after the first. The others followed more rapidly—the discovery of America in 1492, and the first patent laws in 1624. Though not apposite to my present purpose, it is but justice to the fruitfulness of that period, to mention two other important events—the Lutheran Reformation in 1517, and, still earlier, the invention of negroes, or, of the present mode of using them, in 1434. But, to return to the consideration of printing, it is plain that it is but the *other* half—and in real utility, the *better* half—of writing; and that both together are but the assistants of speech in the communication of thoughts between man and man. When man was possessed of speech alone, the chances of invention, discovery, and improvement, were very limited; but by the introduction of each of these, they were greatly multiplied. When writing was invented, any important observation, likely to lead to a discovery, had at least a chance of being written down, and consequently, a better chance of never being forgotten; and of being seen, and reflected upon, by a much greater number of persons; and thereby the chances of a valuable hint being caught, proportionably augmented. By this means the observation of a single individual might lead to an important invention, years, and even centuries after he was dead. In one word, by means of writing, the seeds of invention were more permanently preserved, and more widely sown.

And yet, for the three thousand years during which printing remained undiscovered after writing was in use, it was only a small portion of the people who could write, or read writing; and consequently the field of invention, though much extended, still continued very limited. At length printing came. It gave ten thousand copies of any written matter, quite as cheaply as ten were given before; and consequently a thousand minds were brought into the field where there was but one before. This was a great *gain;* and history shows a great *change* corresponding to it, in point of time. I will venture to consider *i,* the true termination of that period called "the dark ages." Discoveries, inventions, and improvements followed rapidly, and have been increasing their rapidity ever since. The effects could not come, all at once. It required time to bring them out; and they are still coming. The *capacity* to read, could not be multiplied as fast as the *means* of reading. Spelling-books just began to go into the hands of the children; but the teachers were not very numerous, or very competent; so that it is safe to infer they did not advance so speedily as they do now-a-days. It is very probable—almost certain—that the great mass of men, at that time, were utterly unconscious, that their *conditions*, or their *minds* were capable of improvement. They not only looked upon the educated few as superior beings; but they supposed themselves to be naturally incapable of rising to equality. To immancipate the mind from this false and under estimate of itself, is the great task which printing came into the world to perform. It is difficult for us, *now* and *here*, to conceive how strong this slavery of the mind was; and how long it did, of necessity, take, to break it's shackles, and to get a habit of freedom of thought, established. It is, in this connection, a curious fact that a new country is most favorable—almost necessary—to the immancipation of thought, and the consequent advancement of civilization and the arts. The human family originated as is thought, somewhere in Asia, and have worked their way principally Westward. Just now, in civilization, and the arts, the people of Asia are entirely behind those of Europe; those of the East of Europe behind those of the West of it; while we, here in America, *think* we discover, and invent, and improve, faster than any of them. *They* may think this is arrogance; but they can not deny that Russia has called on us to show her how to build steam-boats and railroads—while in the older parts of Asia, they scarcely know that such things as S.Bs & RR.s. exist. In anciently inhabited countries, the dust of ages—a real downright old-fogyism—seems to settle upon, and smother the intellects and energies of man. It is in this view that I have mentioned the discovery of America as an event greatly favoring and facilitating useful discoveries and inventions.

Next came the Patent laws. These began in England in 1624; and, in this country, with the adoption of our constitution. Before then, any man might instantly use what another had invented; so that the inventor had no special advantage from his own invention. The patent system changed this; secured to the inventor, for a limited time, the exclusive use of his invention; and thereby added the fuel of *interest* to the *fire* of genius, in the discovery and production of new and useful things.

February 11, 1859

To Jesse W. Fell,
Enclosing Autobiography

J. W. Fell, Esq   Springfield,
My dear Sir: Dec. 20. 1859

Herewith is a little sketch, as you requested. There is not much of it, for the reason, I suppose, that there is not much of me.

If any thing be made out of it, I wish it to be modest, and not to go beyond the materials. If it were thought necessary to incorporate any thing from any of my speeches, I suppose there would be no objection. Of course it must not appear to have been written by myself. Yours very truly

I was born Feb. 12, 1809, in Hardin County, Kentucky. My parents were both born in Virginia, of undistinguished families—second families, perhaps I should say. My mother, who died in my tenth year, was of a family of the name of Hanks, some of whom now reside in Adams, and others in Macon counties, Illinois. My paternal grandfather, Abraham Lincoln, emigrated from Rockingham County, Virginia, to Kentucky, about 1781 or 2, where, a year or two later, he was killed by indians, not in battle, but by stealth, when he was laboring to open a farm in the forest. His ancestors, who were quakers, went to Virginia from Berks County, Pennsylvania. An effort to identify them with the New-England family of the same name ended in nothing more definite, than a similarity of Christian names in both families, such as Enoch, Levi, Mordecai, Solomon, Abraham, and the like.

My father, at the death of his father, was but six years of age; and he grew up, litterally without education. He removed from Kentucky to what is now Spencer county, Indiana, in my eighth year. We reached our new home about the time the State came into the Union. It was a wild region, with many bears and other wild animals still in the woods. There I grew up. There were some schools, so called; but no qualification was ever required of a teacher, beyond *"readin, writin, and cipherin,"* to the Rule of Three. If a straggler supposed to understand latin, happened to sojourn in the neighborhood, he was looked upon as a wizzard. There was absolutely nothing to excite ambition for education. Of course when I came of age I did not know much. Still somehow, I could read, write, and cipher to the Rule of Three; but that was all. I have not been to school since. The little advance I now have upon this store of education, I have picked up from time to time under the pressure of necessity.

I was raised to farm work, which I continued till I was twenty two. At twenty one I came to Illinois, and passed the first year in Macon county. Then I got to New-Salem (at that time in Sangamon, now in Menard county, where I remained a year as a sort of Clerk in a store. Then came the Black-Hawk war; and I was elected a Captain of Volunteers—a success which gave me more pleasure than any I have had since. I went the campaign, was elated, ran for the Legislature the same year (1832) and was beaten— the only time I ever have been beaten by the people. The next, and three succeeding biennial elections, I was elected to the Legislature. I was not a candidate afterwards. During this Legislative period I had studied law, and removed to Springfield to practice it. In 1846 I was once elected to the lower House of Congress. Was not a candidate for re-election. From 1849 to 1854, both inclusive, practiced law more assiduously than ever before. Always a whig in politics, and generally on the whig electoral tickets, making active canvasses. I was losing interest in politics, when the repeal of the Missouri Compromise aroused me again. What I have done since then is pretty well known.

If any personal description of me is thought desirable, it may be said, I am, in height, six feet, four inches, nearly; lean in flesh, weighing, on an average, one hundred and eighty pounds; dark complexion, with coarse black hair, and grey eyes—no other marks or brands recollected. Yours very truly

Address at Cooper Institute,
New York City

MR. PRESIDENT AND FELLOW-CITIZENS OF NEW-YORK:—The facts with which I shall deal this evening are mainly old and familiar; nor is there anything new in the general use I shall make of them. If there shall be any novelty, it will be in the mode of presenting the facts, and the inferences and observations following that presentation.

In his speech last autumn, at Columbus, Ohio, as reported in "The New-York Times," Senator Douglas said:

"Our fathers, when they framed the Government under which we live, understood this question just as well, and even better, than we do now."

I fully indorse this, and I adopt it as a text for this discourse. I so adopt it because it furnishes a precise and an agreed starting point for a discussion between Republicans and that wing of the Democracy headed by Senator Douglas. It simply leaves the inquiry: *"What was the understanding those fathers had of the question mentioned?"*

What is the frame of Government under which we live?

The answer must be: "The Constitution of the United States." That Constitution consists of the original, framed in 1787, (and under which the present government first went into operation,) and twelve subsequently framed amendments, the first ten of which were framed in 1789.

Who were our fathers that framed the Constitution? I suppose the "thirty-nine" who signed the original instrument may be fairly called our fathers who framed that part of the present Government. It is almost exactly true to say they framed it, and it is altogether true to say they fairly represented the opinion and sentiment of the whole nation at that time. Their names, being familiar to nearly all, and accessible to quite all, need not now be repeated.

I take these "thirty-nine" for the present, as being "our fathers who framed the Government under which we live."

What is the question which, according to the text, those fathers understood "just as well, and even better than we do now?"

It is this: Does the proper division of local from federal authority, or anything in the Constitution, forbid *our Federal Government* to control as to slavery in *our Federal Territories?*

Upon this, Senator Douglas holds the affirmative, and Republicans the negative. This affirmation and denial form an issue; and this issue—this question—is precisely what the text declares our fathers understood "better than we."

Let us now inquire whether the "thirty-nine," or any of them, ever acted upon this question; and if they did, how they acted upon it—how they expressed that better understanding?

In 1784, three years before the Constitution—the United States then owning the Northwestern Territory, and no other, the Congress of the Confederation had before them the question of prohibiting slavery in that Territory; and four of the "thirty-nine," who afterward framed the Constitution, were in that Congress, and voted on that question. Of these, Roger Sherman, Thomas Mifflin, and Hugh Williamson voted for the prohibition, thus showing that, in their understanding, no line dividing local from federal authority, nor anything else, properly forbade the Federal Government to control as to slavery in federal territory. The other of the four—James M'Henry—voted against the prohibition, showing that, for some cause, he thought it improper to vote for it.

In 1787, still before the Constitution, but while the Convention was in session framing it, and while the Northwestern Territory still was the only territory owned by the United States, the same question of prohibiting slavery in the territory again came before the Congress of the Confederation; and two more of the "thirty-nine" who afterward signed the Constitution, were in that Congress, and voted on the question. They were William Blount and William Few; and they both voted for the prohibition—thus showing that, in their understanding, no line dividing local from federal authority, nor anything else, properly forbade the Federal Government to control as to slavery in federal territory. This time the prohibition became a law, being part of what is now well known as the Ordinance of '87.

The question of federal control of slavery in the territories, seems not to have been directly before the Convention which framed the original Constitution; and hence it is not recorded that the "thirty-nine," or any of them, while engaged on that instrument, expressed any opinion of that precise question.

In 1789, by the first Congress which sat under the Constitution, an act was passed to enforce the Ordinance of '87, including the prohibition of slavery in the Northwestern Territory. The bill for this act was reported by one of the "thirty-nine," Thomas Fitzsimmons, then a member of the House of Representatives from Pennsylvania. It went through all its stages without a word of opposition, and finally passed both branches without yeas and nays, which is equivalent to an unanimous passage. In this Congress there were sixteen of the thirty-nine fathers who framed the original Constitution. They were John Langdon, Nicholas Gilman, Wm. S. Johnson, Roger Sherman, Robert Morris, Thos. Fitzsimmons, William Few, Abraham Baldwin, Rufus King, William Paterson, George Clymer, Richard Bassett, George Read, Pierce Butler, Daniel Carroll, James Madison.

This shows that, in their understanding, no line dividing local from federal authority, nor anything in the Constitution, properly forbade Congress to prohibit slavery in the federal territory; else both their fidelity to correct principle, and their oath to support the Constitution, would have constrained them to oppose the prohibition.

Again, George Washington, another of the "thirty-nine," was then President of the United States, and, as such, approved and signed the bill; thus completing its validity as a law, and thus showing that, in his understanding, no line dividing local from federal authority, nor anything in the Constitution, forbade the Federal Government, to control as to slavery in federal territory.

No great while after the adoption of the original Constitution, North Carolina ceded to the Federal Government the country now constituting the State of Tennessee; and a few years later Georgia ceded that which now constitutes the States of Mississippi and Alabama. In both deeds of cession it was made a condition by the ceding States that the Federal Government should not prohibit slavery in the ceded country. Besides this, slavery was then actually in the ceded country. Under these circumstances, Congress, on taking charge of these countries, did not absolutely prohibit slavery within them. But they did interfere with it—take control of it—even there, to a certain extent. In 1798, Congress organized the Territory of Mississippi. In the act of organization, they prohibited the bringing of slaves into the Territory, from any place without the United States, by fine, and giving freedom to slaves so brought. This act passed both branches of Congress without yeas and nays. In that Congress were three of the "thirty-nine" who framed the original Constitution. They were John Langdon, George Read and Abraham Baldwin. They all, probably, voted for it. Certainly they would have placed their opposition to it upon record, if, in their understanding, any line dividing local from federal authority, or anything in the Constitution, properly forbade the Federal Government to control as to slavery in federal territory.

In 1803, the Federal Government purchased the Louisiana country. Our former territorial acquisitions came from certain of our own States; but this Louisiana country was acquired from a foreign nation. In 1804, Congress gave a territorial organization to that part of it which now constitutes the State of Louisiana. New Orleans, lying within that part, was an old and comparatively large city. There were other considerable towns and settlements, and slavery was extensively and thoroughly intermingled with the people. Congress did not, in the Territorial Act, prohibit slavery; but they did interfere with it—take control of it—in a more marked and extensive way than they did in the case of Mississippi. The substance of the provision therein made, in relation to slaves, was:

First. That no slave should be imported into the territory from foreign parts.

Second. That no slave should be carried into it who had been imported into the United States since the first day of May, 1798.

Third. That no slave should be carried into it, except by the owner, and for his own use as a settler; the penalty in all the cases being a fine upon the violator of the law, and freedom to the slave.

This act also was passed without yeas and nays. In the Congress which passed it, there were two of the "thirty-nine." They were Abraham Baldwin and Jonathan Dayton. As stated in the case of Mississippi, it is probable they both voted for it. They would not have allowed it to pass without recording their opposition to it, if, in their understanding, it violated either the line properly dividing local from federal authority, or any provision of the Constitution.

In 1819–20, came and passed the Missouri question. Many votes were taken, by yeas and nays, in both branches of Congress, upon the various phases of the general question. Two of the "thirty-nine"—Rufus King and Charles Pinckney—were members of that Congress. Mr. King steadily voted for slavery prohibition and against all compromises, while Mr. Pinckney as steadily voted against slavery prohibition and against all compromises. By this, Mr. King showed that, in his understanding, no line dividing local from federal authority, nor anything in the Constitution, was violated by Congress prohibiting slavery in federal territory; while Mr. Pinckney, by his votes, showed that, in his understanding, there was some sufficient reason for opposing such prohibition in that case.

The cases I have mentioned are the only acts of the "thirty-nine," or of any of them, upon the direct issue, which I have been able to discover.

To enumerate the persons who thus acted, as being four in 1784, two in 1787, seventeen in 1789, three in 1798, two in 1804, and two in 1819–20—there would be thirty of them. But this would be counting John Langdon, Roger Sherman, William Few, Rufus King, and George Read, each twice, and Abraham Baldwin, three times. The true number of those of the "thirty-nine" whom I have shown to have acted upon the question, which, by the text, they understood better than we, is twenty-three, leaving sixteen not shown to have acted upon it in any way.

Here, then, we have twenty-three out of our thirty-nine fathers "who framed the Government under which we live," who have, upon their official responsibility and their corporal oaths, acted upon the very question which the text affirms they "understood just as well, and even better than we do now;" and twenty-one of them—a clear majority of the whole "thirty-nine"—so acting upon it as to make them guilty of gross political impropriety and wilful perjury, if, in their understanding, any proper division between local and federal authority, or anything in the Constitution they had made themselves, and sworn to support, forbade the Federal Government to control as to slavery in the federal territories. Thus the twenty-one acted; and, as actions speak louder than words, so actions, under such responsibility, speak still louder.

Two of the twenty-three voted against Congressional prohibition of slavery in the federal territories, in the instances in which they acted upon the question. But for what reasons they so voted is not known. They may have done so because they thought a proper division of local from federal authority, or some provision or principle of the Constitution, stood in the way; or they may, without any such question, have voted against the prohibition, on what appeared to them to be sufficient grounds of expediency. No one who has sworn to support the Constitution, can conscientiously vote for what he understands to be an unconstitutional measure, however expedient he may think it; but one may and ought to vote against a measure which he deems constitutional, if, at the same time, he deems it inexpedient. It, therefore, would be unsafe to set down even the two who voted against the prohibition, as having done so because, in their understanding, any proper division of local from federal authority, or anything in the Constitution, forbade the Federal Government to control as to slavery in federal territory.

The remaining sixteen of the "thirty-nine," so far as I have discovered, have left no record of their understanding upon the direct question of federal control of slavery in the federal territories. But there is much reason to believe that their understanding upon that question would not have appeared different from that of their twenty-three compeers, had it been manifested at all.

For the purpose of adhering rigidly to the text, I have purposely omitted whatever understanding may have been manifested by any person, however distinguished, other than the thirty-nine fathers who framed the original Constitution; and, for the same reason, I have also omitted whatever understanding may have been manifested by any of the "thirty-nine" even, on any other phase of the general question of slavery. If we should look into their acts and declarations on those other phases, as the foreign slave trade, and the morality and policy of slavery generally, it would appear to us that on the direct question of federal control of slavery in federal territories, the sixteen, if they had acted at all, would probably have acted just as the twenty-three did. Among that sixteen were several of the most noted anti-slavery men of those times—as Dr. Franklin, Alexander Hamilton and Gouverneur Morris—while there was not one now known to have been otherwise, unless it may be John Rutledge, of South Carolina.

The sum of the whole is, that of our thirty-nine fathers who framed the original Constitution, twenty-one—a clear majority of the whole—certainly understood that no proper division of local from federal authority, nor any part of the Constitution, forbade the Federal Government to control slavery in the federal territories; while all the rest probably had the same understanding. Such, unquestionably, was the understanding of our fathers who framed the original Constitution; and the text affirms that they understood the question "better than we."

But, so far, I have been considering the understanding of the question manifested by the framers of the original Constitution. In and by the original instrument, a mode was provided for amending it; and, as I have already stated, the present frame of "the Government under which we live" consists of that original, and twelve amendatory articles framed and adopted since. Those who now insist that federal control of slavery in federal territories violates the Constitution, point us to the provisions which they suppose it thus violates; and, as I understand, they all fix upon provisions in these amendatory articles, and not in the original instrument. The Supreme Court, in the Dred Scott case, plant themselves upon the fifth amendment, which provides that no person shall be deprived of "life, liberty or property without due process of law;" while Senator Douglas and his peculiar adherents plant themselves upon the tenth amendment, providing that "the powers not delegated to the United States by the Constitution," "are reserved to the States respectively, or to the people."

Now, it so happens that these amendments were framed by the first Congress which sat under the Constitution—the identical Congress which passed the act already mentioned, enforcing the prohibition of slavery in the Northwestern Territory. Not only was it the same Congress, but they were the identical, same individual men who, at the same session, and at the same time within the session, had under consideration, and in progress toward maturity, these Constitutional amendments, and this act prohibiting slavery in all the territory the nation then owned. The Constitutional amendments were introduced before, and passed after the act enforcing the Ordinance of '87; so that, during the whole pendency of the act to enforce the Ordinance, the Constitutional amendments were also pending.

The seventy-six members of that Congress, including sixteen of the framers of the original Constitution, as before stated, were preeminently our fathers who framed that part of "the Government under which we live," which is now claimed as forbidding the Federal Government to control slavery in the federal territories.

Is it not a little presumptuous in any one at this day to affirm that the two things which that Congress deliberately framed, and carried to maturity at the same time, are absolutely inconsistent with each other? And does not such affirmation become impudently absurd when coupled with the other affirmation from the same mouth, that those who did the two things, alleged to be inconsistent, understood whether they really were inconsistent better than we—better than he who affirms that they are inconsistent?

It is surely safe to assume that the thirty-nine framers of the original Constitution, and the seventy-six members of the Congress which framed the amendments thereto, taken together, do certainly include those who may be fairly called "our fathers who framed the Government under which we live." And so assuming, I defy any man to show that any one of them ever, in his whole life, declared that, in his understanding, any proper division of local from federal authority, or any part of the Constitution, forbade the Federal Government to control as to slavery in the federal territories. I go a step further. I defy any one to show that any living man in the whole world ever did, prior to the beginning of the present century, (and I might almost say prior to the beginning of the last half of the present century,) declare that, in his understanding, any proper division of local from federal authority, or any part of the Constitution, forbade the Federal Government to control as to slavery in the federal territories. To those who now so declare, I give, not only "our fathers who framed the Government under which we live," but with them all other living men within the century in which it was framed, among whom to search, and they shall not be able to find the evidence of a single man agreeing with them.

Now, and here, let me guard a little against being misunderstood. I do not mean to say we are bound to follow implicitly in whatever our fathers did. To do so, would be to discard all the lights of current experience—to reject all progress—all improvement. What I do say is, that if we would supplant the opinions and policy of our fathers in any case, we should do so upon evidence so conclusive, and argument so clear, that even their great authority, fairly considered and weighed, cannot stand; and most surely not in a case whereof we ourselves declare they understood the question better than we.

If any man at this day sincerely believes that a proper division of local from federal authority, or any part of the Constitution, forbids the Federal Government to control as to slavery in the federal territories, he is right to say so, and to enforce his position by all truthful evidence and fair argument which he can. But he has no right to mislead others, who have less access to history, and less leisure to study it, into the false belief that "our fathers, who framed the Government under which we live," were of the same

opinion—thus substituting falsehood and deception for truthful evidence and fair argument. If any man at this day
sincerely believes "our fathers who framed the Government
under which we live," used and applied principles, in other
cases, which ought to have led them to understand that a
proper division of local from federal authority or some part
of the Constitution, forbids the Federal Government to control as to slavery in the federal territories, he is right to say
so. But he should, at the same time, brave the responsibility
of declaring that, in his opinion, he understands their principles better than they did themselves; and especially should
he not shirk that responsibility by asserting that they "understood the question just as well, and even better, than we
do now."

But enough! *Let all who believe that "our fathers, who
framed the Government under which we live, understood this
question just as well, and even better, than we do now,"
speak as they spoke, and act as they acted upon it. This is
all Republicans ask—all Republicans desire—in relation to
slavery. As those fathers marked it, so let it be again marked,
as an evil not to be extended, but to be tolerated and protected
only because of and so far as its actual presence among us
makes that toleration and protection a necessity. Let all the
guaranties those fathers gave it, be, not grudgingly, but fully
and fairly maintained.* For this Republicans contend, and
with this, so far as I know or believe, they will be content.

And now, if they would listen—as I suppose they will
not—I would address a few words to the Southern people.

I would say to them:—You consider yourselves a reasonable and a just people; and I consider that in the general
qualities of reason and justice you are not inferior to any
other people. Still, when you speak of us Republicans, you
do so only to denounce us as reptiles, or, at the best, as
no better than outlaws. You will grant a hearing to pirates
or murderers, but nothing like it to "Black Republicans."
In all your contentions with one another, each of you deems

an unconditional condemnation of "Black Republicanism" as the first thing to be attended to. Indeed, such condemnation of us seems to be an indispensable prerequisite—license, so to speak—among you to be admitted or permitted to speak at all. Now, can you, or not, be prevailed upon to pause and to consider whether this is quite just to us, or even to yourselves? Bring forward your charges and specifications, and then be patient long enough to hear us deny or justify.

You say we are sectional. We deny it. That makes an issue; and the burden of proof is upon you. You produce your proof; and what is it? Why, that our party has no existence in your section—gets no votes in your section. The fact is substantially true; but does it prove the issue? If it does, then in case we should, without change of principle, begin to get votes in your section, we should thereby cease to be sectional. You cannot escape this conclusion; and yet, are you willing to abide by it? If you are, you will probably soon find that we have ceased to be sectional, for we shall get votes in your section this very year. You will then begin to discover, as the truth plainly is, that your proof does not touch the issue. The fact that we get no votes in your section, is a fact of your making, and not of ours. And if there be fault in that fact, that fault is primarily yours, and remains so until you show that we repel you by some wrong principle or practice. If we do repel you by any wrong principle or practice, the fault is ours; but this brings you to where you ought to have started—to a discussion of the right or wrong of our principle. If our principle, put in practice, would wrong your section for the benefit of ours, or for any other object, then our principle, and we with it, are sectional, and are justly opposed and denounced as such. Meet us, then, on the question of whether our principle, put in practice, would wrong your section; and so meet us as if it were possible that something may be said on our side. Do you accept the challenge? No! Then you really believe that the principle which "our fathers who framed the Government under which we live" thought so clearly right as to adopt it, and indorse it again and again, upon their official oaths, is in fact so clearly wrong as to demand your condemnation without a moment's consideration.

Some of you delight to flaunt in our faces the warning against sectional parties given by Washington in his Farewell Address. Less than eight years before Washington gave that warning, he had, as President of the United States, approved and signed an act of Congress, enforcing the prohibition of slavery in the Northwestern Territory, which act embodied the policy of the Government upon that subject up to and at the very moment he penned that warning; and about one year after he penned it, he wrote La Fayette that he considered that prohibition a wise measure, expressing in the same connection his hope that we should at some time have a confederacy of free States.

Bearing this in mind, and seeing that sectionalism has since arisen upon this same subject, is that warning a weapon in your hands against us, or in our hands against you? Could Washington himself speak, would he cast the blame of that sectionalism upon us, who sustain his policy, or upon you who repudiate it? We respect that warning of Washington, and we commend it to you, together with his example pointing to the right application of it.

But you say you are conservative—eminently conservative—while we are revolutionary, destructive, or something of the sort. What is conservatism? Is it not adherence to the old and tried, against the new and untried? We stick to, contend for, the identical old policy on the point in controversy which was adopted by "our fathers who framed the Government under which we live;" while you with one accord reject, and scout, and spit upon that old policy, and insist upon substituting something new. True, you disagree among yourselves as to what that substitute shall be. You are divided on new propositions and plans, but you are unanimous in rejecting and denouncing the old policy of the fathers. Some of you are for reviving the foreign trade; some for a Congressional Slave-Code for the Territories; some for Congress forbidding the Territories to prohibit Slavery within their limits; some for maintaining Slavery in the Territories through the judiciary; some for the "gur-reat pur-rinciple" that "if one man would enslave another, no third man should object," fantastically called "Popular Sovereignty;" but never a man among you in favor of federal prohibition of slavery in federal territories, according to the practice of "our fathers who framed the Government under which we live." Not one of all your various plans can show a precedent or an advocate in the century within which our Government originated. Consider, then, whether your claim of conservatism for yourselves, and your charge of destructiveness against us, are based on the most clear and stable foundations.

Again, you say we have made the slavery question more prominent than it formerly was. We deny it. We admit that it is more prominent, but we deny that we made it so. It was not we, but you, who discarded the old policy of the fathers. We resisted, and still resist, your innovation; and thence comes the greater prominence of the question. Would you have that question reduced to its former proportions? Go back to that old policy. What has been will be again, under the same conditions. If you would have the peace of the old times, readopt the precepts and policy of the old times.

You charge that we stir up insurrections among your slaves. We deny it; and what is your proof? Harper's Ferry! John Brown!! John Brown was no Republican; and you have failed to implicate a single Republican in his Harper's Ferry enterprise. If any member of our party is guilty in that matter, you know it or you do not know it. If you do know it, you are inexcusable for not designating the man and proving the fact. If you do not know it, you are inexcus-

able for asserting it, and especially for persisting in the
assertion after you have tried and failed to make the proof.
You need not be told that persisting in a charge which one
does not know to be true, is simply malicious slander.

Some of you admit that no Republican designedly aided
or encouraged the Harper's Ferry affair; but still insist that
our doctrines and declarations necessarily lead to such results. We do not believe it. We know we hold to no doctrine, and make no declaration, which were not held to and
made by "our fathers who framed the Government under
which we live." You never dealt fairly by us in relation to
this affair. When it occurred, some important State elections
were near at hand, and you were in evident glee with the
belief that, by charging the blame upon us, you could get
an advantage of us in those elections. The elections came,
and your expectations were not quite fulfilled. Every Republican man knew that, as to himself at least, your charge
was a slander, and he was not much inclined by it to cast
his vote in your favor. Republican doctrines and declarations are accompanied with a continual protest against any
interference whatever with your slaves, or with you about
your slaves. Surely, this does not encourage them to revolt.
True, we do, in common with "our fathers, who framed
the Government under which we live," declare our belief
that slavery is wrong; but the slaves do not hear us declare
even this. For anything we say or do, the slaves would
scarcely know there is a Republican party. I believe they
would not, in fact, generally know it but for your misrepre-
sentations of us, in their hearing. In your political contests
among yourselves, each faction charges the other with sympathy with Black Republicanism; and then, to give point
to the charge, defines Black Republicanism to simply be
insurrection, blood and thunder among the slaves.

Slave insurrections are no more common now than they
were before the Republican party was organized. What

induced the Southampton insurrection, twenty-eight years ago, in which, at least, three times as many lives were lost as at Harper's Ferry? You can scarcely stretch your very elastic fancy to the conclusion that Southampton was "got up by Black Republicanism." In the present state of things in the United States, I do not think a general, or even a very extensive slave insurrection, is possible. The indispensable concert of action cannot be attained. The slaves have no means of rapid communication; nor can incendiary freemen, black or white, supply it. The explosive materials are everywhere in parcels; but there neither are, nor can be supplied, the indispensable connecting trains.

Much is said by Southern people about the affection of slaves for their masters and mistresses; and a part of it, at least, is true. A plot for an uprising could scarcely be devised and communicated to twenty individuals before some one of them, to save the life of a favorite master or mistress, would divulge it. This is the rule; and the slave revolution in Hayti was not an exception to it, but a case occurring under peculiar circumstances. The gunpowder plot of British history, though not connected with slaves, was more in point. In that case, only about twenty were admitted to the secret; and yet one of them, in his anxiety to save a friend, betrayed the plot to that friend, and, by consequence, averted the calamity. Occasional poisonings from the kitchen, and open or stealthy assassinations in the field, and local revolts extending to a score or so, will continue to occur as the natural results of slavery; but no general insurrection of slaves, as I think, can happen in this country for a long time. Whoever much fears, or much hopes for such an event, will be alike disappointed.

In the language of Mr. Jefferson, uttered many years ago, "It is still in our power to direct the process of emancipation, and deportation, peaceably, and in such slow degrees, as that the evil will wear off insensibly; and their places be, *pari passu*, filled up by free white laborers. If, on the contrary, it is left to force itself on, human nature must shudder at the prospect held up."

Mr. Jefferson did not mean to say, nor do I, that the power of emancipation is in the Federal Government. He spoke of Virginia; and, as to the power of emancipation, I speak of the slaveholding States only. The Federal Government, however, as we insist, has the power of restraining the extension of the institution—the power to insure that a slave insurrection shall never occur on any American soil which is now free from slavery.

John Brown's effort was peculiar. It was not a slave insurrection. It was an attempt by white men to get up a revolt among slaves, in which the slaves refused to participate. In fact, it was so absurd that the slaves, with all their ignorance, saw plainly enough it could not succeed. That affair, in its philosophy, corresponds with the many attempts, related in history, at the assassination of kings and emperors. An enthusiast broods over the oppression of a people till he fancies himself commissioned by Heaven to liberate them. He ventures the attempt, which ends in little else than his own execution. Orsini's attempt on Louis Napoleon, and John Brown's attempt at Harper's Ferry were, in their philosophy, precisely the same. The eagerness to cast blame on old England in the one case, and on New England in the other, does not disprove the sameness of the two things.

And how much would it avail you, if you could, by the use of John Brown, Helper's Book, and the like, break up the Republican organization? Human action can be modified to some extent, but human nature cannot be changed. There is a judgment and a feeling against slavery in this nation, which cast at least a million and a half of votes. You cannot destroy that judgment and feeling—that sentiment—by breaking up the political organization which rallies around it. You can scarcely scatter and disperse an army which has been formed into order in the face of your heaviest fire; but if you could, how much would you gain by forcing the sentiment which created it out of the peaceful channel of the ballot-box, into some other channel? What would that other channel probably be? Would the number of John Browns be lessened or enlarged by the operation?

But you will break up the Union rather than submit to a denial of your Constitutional rights.

That has a somewhat reckless sound; but it would be palliated, if not fully justified, were we proposing, by the mere force of numbers, to deprive you of some right, plainly written down in the Constitution. But we are proposing no such thing.

When you make these declarations, you have a specific and well-understood allusion to an assumed Constitutional right of yours, to take slaves into the federal territories, and to hold them there as property. But no such right is specifically written in the Constitution. That instrument is literally silent about any such right. We, on the contrary, deny that such a right has any existence in the Constitution, even by implication.

Your purpose, then, plainly stated, is, that you will destroy the Government, unless you be allowed to construe and enforce the Constitution as you please, on all points in dispute between you and us. You will rule or ruin in all events.

This, plainly stated, is your language. Perhaps you will say the Supreme Court has decided the disputed Constitutional question in your favor. Not quite so. But waiving the lawyer's distinction between dictum and decision, the Court have decided the question for you in a sort of way. The Court have substantially said, it is your Constitutional right to take slaves into the federal territories, and to hold them there as property. When I say the decision was made in a sort of way, I mean it was made in a divided Court, by a bare majority of the Judges, and they not quite agreeing with one another in the reasons for making it; that it is so made as that its avowed supporters disagree with one another about its meaning, and that it was mainly based upon a mistaken statement of fact—the statement in the opinion that "the right of property in a slave is distinctly and expressly affirmed in the Constitution."

An inspection of the Constitution will show that the right of property in a slave is not "*distinctly* and *expressly* affirmed" in it. Bear in mind, the Judges do not pledge their judicial opinion that such right is *impliedly* affirmed in the Constitution; but they pledge their veracity that it is "*distinctly* and *expressly*" affirmed there—"distinctly," that is, not mingled with anything else—"expressly," that is, in words meaning just that, without the aid of any inference, and susceptible of no other meaning.

If they had only pledged their judicial opinion that such right is affirmed in the instrument by implication, it would be open to others to show that neither the word "slave" nor "slavery" is to be found in the Constitution, nor the word "property" even, in any connection with language alluding to the things slave, or slavery, and that wherever in that instrument the slave is alluded to, he is called a "person;"—and wherever his master's legal right in relation to him is alluded to, it is spoken of as "service or labor which may be due,"—as a debt payable in service or labor. Also, it would be open to show, by contemporaneous history, that this mode of alluding to slaves and slavery, instead of speaking of them, was employed on purpose to exclude from the Constitution the idea that there could be property in man.

To show all this, is easy and certain.

When this obvious mistake of the Judges shall be brought to their notice, is it not reasonable to expect that they will withdraw the mistaken statement, and reconsider the conclusion based upon it?

And then it is to be remembered that "our fathers, who framed the Government under which we live"—the men who made the Constitution—decided this same Constitutional question in our favor, long ago—decided it without division among themselves, when making the decision; without division among themselves about the meaning of it after it was made, and, so far as any evidence is left, without basing it upon any mistaken statement of facts.

Under all these circumstances, do you really feel yourselves justified to break up this Government, unless such a court decision as yours is, shall be at once submitted to as a conclusive and final rule of political action? But you will not abide the election of a Republican President! In that supposed event, you say, you will destroy the Union; and then, you say, the great crime of having destroyed it will be upon us! That is cool. A highwayman holds a pistol to my ear, and mutters through his teeth, "Stand and deliver, or I shall kill you, and then you will be a murderer!"

To be sure, what the robber demanded of me—my money—was my own; and I had a clear right to keep it; but it was no more my own than my vote is my own; and the threat of death to me, to extort my money, and the threat of destruction to the Union, to extort my vote, can scarcely be distinguished in principle.

A few words now to Republicans. *It is exceedingly desirable that all parts of this great Confederacy shall be at peace, and in harmony, one with another. Let us Republicans do our part to have it so. Even though much provoked, let us do nothing through passion and ill temper. Even though the southern people will not so much as listen to us, let us calmly consider their demands, and yield to them if, in our deliberate view of our duty, we possibly can. Judging by all they say and do, and by the subject and nature of their controversy with us, let us determine, if we can, what will satisfy them.*

Will they be satisfied if the Territories be unconditionally surrendered to them? We know they will not. In all their present complaints against us, the Territories are scarcely mentioned. Invasions and insurrections are the rage now.

Will it satisfy them, if, in the future, we have nothing to do with invasions and insurrections? We know it will not. We so know, because we know we never had anything to do with invasions and insurrections; and yet this total abstaining does not exempt us from the charge and the denunciation.

The question recurs, what will satisfy them? Simply this: We must not only let them alone, but we must, somehow, convince them that we do let them alone. This, we know by experience, is no easy task. We have been so trying to convince them from the very beginning of our organization, but with no success. In all our platforms and speeches we have constantly protested our purpose to let them alone; but this has had no tendency to convince them. Alike unavailing to convince them, is the fact that they have never detected a man of us in any attempt to disturb them.

These natural, and apparently adequate means all failing, what will convince them? This, and this only: cease to call slavery *wrong*, and join them in calling it *right*. And this must be done thoroughly—done in *acts* as well as in *words*. Silence will not be tolerated—we must place ourselves avowedly with them. Senator Douglas's new sedition law must be enacted and enforced, suppressing all declarations that slavery is wrong, whether made in politics, in presses, in pulpits, or in private. We must arrest and return their fugitive slaves with greedy pleasure. We must pull down our Free State constitutions. The whole atmosphere must be disinfected from all taint of opposition to slavery, before they will cease to believe that all their troubles proceed from us.

I am quite aware they do not state their case precisely in this way. Most of them would probably say to us, "Let us alone, *do* nothing to us, and *say* what you please about slavery." But we do let them alone—have never disturbed them—so that, after all, it is what we say, which dissatisfies them. They will continue to accuse us of doing, until we cease saying.

I am also aware they have not, as yet, in terms, demanded the overthrow of our Free-State Constitutions. Yet those Constitutions declare the wrong of slavery, with more solemn emphasis, than do all other sayings against it; and when all these other sayings shall have been silenced, the overthrow of these Constitutions will be demanded, and nothing be left to resist the demand. It is nothing to the contrary, that they do not demand the whole of this just now. Demanding what they do, and for the reason they do, they can voluntarily stop nowhere short of this consummation. Holding, as they do, that slavery is morally right, and socially elevating, they cannot cease to demand a full national recognition of it, as a legal right, and a social blessing.

Nor can we justifiably withhold this, on any ground save our conviction that slavery is wrong. If slavery is right, all words, acts, laws, and constitutions against it, are themselves wrong, and should be silenced, and swept away. If it is right, we cannot justly object to its nationality—its universality; if it is wrong, they cannot justly insist upon its extension—its enlargement. All they ask, we could readily grant, if we thought slavery right; all we ask, they could as readily grant, if they thought it wrong. Their thinking it right, and our thinking it wrong, is the precise fact upon which depends the whole controversy. Thinking it right, as they do, they are not to blame for desiring its full recognition, as being right; but, thinking it wrong, as we do, can we yield to them? Can we cast our votes with their view, and against our own? In view of our moral, social, and political responsibilities, can we do this?

Wrong as we think slavery is, we can yet afford to let it alone where it is, because that much is due to the necessity arising from its actual presence in the nation; but can we, while our votes will prevent it, allow it to spread into the

National Territories, and to overrun us here in these Free States? If our sense of duty forbids this, then let us stand by our duty, fearlessly and effectively. Let us be diverted by none of those sophistical contrivances wherewith we are so industriously plied and belabored—contrivances such as groping for some middle ground between the right and the wrong, vain as the search for a man who should be neither a living man nor a dead man—such as a policy of "don't care" on a question about which all true men do care—such as Union appeals beseeching true Union men to yield to Disunionists, reversing the divine rule, and calling, not the sinners, but the righteous to repentance—such as invocations to Washington, imploring men to unsay what Washington said, and undo what Washington did.

Neither let us be slandered from our duty by false accusations against us, nor frightened from it by menaces of destruction to the Government nor of dungeons to ourselves. LET US HAVE FAITH THAT RIGHT MAKES MIGHT, AND IN THAT FAITH, LET US, TO THE END, DARE TO DO OUR DUTY AS WE UNDERSTAND IT.

February 27, 1860

To Mary Todd Lincoln

Dear Wife: Exeter, N. H. March 4. 1860

When I wrote you before I was just starting on a little speech-making tour, taking the boys with me. On Thursday they went with me to Concord, where I spoke in day-light, and back to Manchester where I spoke at night. Friday we came down to Lawrence—the place of the Pemberton Mill tragedy—where we remained four hours awaiting the train back to Exeter. When it came, we went upon it to Exeter where the boys got off, and I went on to Dover and spoke there Friday evening. Saturday I came back to Exeter, reaching here about noon, and finding the boys all right, having caught up with their lessons. Bob had a letter from you saying Willie and Taddy were very sick the Saturday night after I left. Having no despatch from you, and having one from Springfield, of Wednesday, from Mr. Fitzhugh, saying nothing about our family, I trust the dear little fellows are well again.

This is Sunday morning; and according to Bob's orders, I am to go to church once to-day. Tomorrow I bid farewell to the boys, go to Hartford, Conn. and speak there in the evening; Tuesday at Meriden, Wednesday at New-Haven—and Thursday at Woonsocket R. I. Then I start home, and think I will not stop. I may be delayed in New-York City an hour or two. I have been unable to escape this toil. If I had foreseen it I think I would not have come East at all. The speech at New-York, being within my calculation before I started, went off passably well, and gave me no trouble whatever. The difficulty was to make nine others, before reading audiences, who have already seen all my ideas in print.

If the trains do not lie over Sunday, of which I do not know, I hope to be home to-morrow week. Once started I shall come as quick as possible.

Kiss the dear boys for Father.

Affectionately

Autobiography Written for Campaign

Abraham Lincoln was born Feb. 12, 1809, then in Hardin, now in the more recently formed county of Larue, Kentucky. His father, Thomas, & grand-father, Abraham,

were born in Rockingham county Virginia, whither their
ancestors had come from Berks county Pennsylvania. His
lineage has been traced no farther back than this. The family
were originally quakers, though in later times they have
fallen away from the peculiar habits of that people. The
grand-father Abraham, had four brothers—Isaac, Jacob,
John & Thomas. So far as known, the descendants of Jacob
and John are still in Virginia. Isaac went to a place near
where Virginia, North Carolina, and Tennessee, join; and
his decendants are in that region. Thomas came to Kentucky, and after many years, died there, whence his decendants went to Missouri. Abraham, grandfather of the
subject of this sketch, came to Kentucky, and was killed by
indians about the year 1784. He left a widow, three sons
and two daughters. The eldest son, Mordecai, remained in
Kentucky till late in life, when he removed to Hancock
county, Illinois, where soon after he died, and where several
of his descendants still reside. The second son, Josiah, removed at an early day to a place on Blue River, now
within Harrison county, Indiana; but no recent information
of him, or his family, has been obtained. The eldest sister,
Mary, married Ralph Crume and some of her descendants
are now known to be in Breckenridge county Kentucky.
The second sister, Nancy, married William Brumfield, and
her family are not known to have left Kentucky, but there
is no recent information from them. Thomas, the youngest
son, and father of the present subject, by the early death
of his father, and very narrow circumstances of his mother,
even in childhood was a wandering laboring boy, and grew
up litterally without education. He never did more in the
way of writing than to bunglingly sign his own name. Before
he was grown, he passed one year as a hired hand with his
uncle Isaac on Wataga, a branch of the Holsteen River.
Getting back into Kentucky, and having reached his 28th.
year, he married Nancy Hanks—mother of the present subject—in the year 1806. She also was born in Virginia; and

relatives of hers of the name of Hanks, and of other names, now reside in Coles, in Macon, and in Adams counties, Illinois, and also in Iowa. The present subject has no brother or sister of the whole or half blood. He had a sister, older than himself, who was grown and married, but died many years ago, leaving no child. Also a brother, younger than himself, who died in infancy. Before leaving Kentucky he and his sister were sent for short periods, to A.B.C. schools, the first kept by Zachariah Riney, and the second by Caleb Hazel.

At this time his father resided on Knob-creek, on the road from Bardstown Ky. to Nashville Tenn. at a point three, or three and a half miles South or South-West of Atherton's ferry on the Rolling Fork. From this place he removed to what is now Spencer county Indiana, in the autumn of 1816, A. then being in his eigth year. This removal was partly on account of slavery; but chiefly on account of the difficulty in land titles in Ky. He settled in an unbroken forest; and the clearing away of surplus wood was the great task a head. A. though very young, was large of his age, and had an axe put into his hands at once; and from that till within his twentythird year, he was almost constantly handling that most useful instrument—less, of course, in plowing and harvesting seasons. At this place A. took an early start as a hunter, which was never much improved afterwards. (A few days before the completion of his eigth year, in the absence of his father, a flock of wild turkeys approached the new log-cabin, and A. with a rifle gun, standing inside, shot through a crack, and killed one of them. He has never since pulled a trigger on any larger game.) In the autumn of 1818 his mother died; and a year afterwards his father married Mrs. Sally Johnston, at Elizabeth-Town, Ky—a widow, with three children of her first marriage. She proved a good and kind mother to A. and is still living in Coles Co. Illinois. There were no children of this second marriage. His father's residence continued at the same place in Indiana, till 1830. While here A. went to A.B.C. schools by littles, kept successively by Andrew Crawford,——Sweeney, and Azel W. Dorsey. He does not remember any other. The family of Mr. Dorsey now reside in Schuyler Co. Illinois. A. now thinks that the agregate of all his schooling did not amount to one year. He was never in a college or Academy as a student; and never inside of a college or academy building till since he had a law-license. What he has in the way of education, he has picked up. After he was twentythree, and had separated from his father, he studied English grammar, imperfectly of course, but so as to speak and write as well as he now does. He studied and nearly mastered the Six-books of Euclid, since he was a member of Congress. He regrets his want of education, and does what he can to supply the want. In his tenth year he was kicked by a horse, and apparently killed for a time. When he was nineteen, still residing in Indiana, he made his first trip upon a flat-boat to New-Orleans. He was a hired hand merely; and he and a son of the owner, without other assistance, made the trip. The nature of part of the cargo-load, as it was called—made it necessary for them to linger and trade along the Sugar coast—and one night they were attacked by seven negroes with intent to kill and rob them. They were hurt some in the melee, but succeeded in driving the negroes from the boat, and then "cut cable" "weighed anchor" and left.

March 1st. 1830—A. having just completed his 21st. year, his father and family, with the families of the two daughters and sons-in-law, of his step-mother, left the old homestead in Indiana, and came to Illinois. Their mode of conveyance was waggons drawn by ox-teams, or A. drove one of the teams. They reached the county of Macon, and stopped there some time within the same month of March. His father and family settled a new place on the North side of the Sangamon river, at the junction of the timber-land and prairie, about ten miles Westerly from Decatur. Here they built a log-cabin, into which they removed, and made sufficient of rails to fence ten acres of ground, fenced and broke the ground, and raised a crop of sown corn upon it the same year. These are, or are supposed to be, the rails about which so much is being said just now, though they are far from being the first, or only rails ever made by A.

The sons-in-law, were temporarily settled at other places in the county. In the autumn all hands were greatly afflicted with augue and fever, to which they had not been used, and by which they were greatly discouraged—so much so that they determined on leaving the county. They remained however, through the succeeding winter, which was the winter of the very celebrated "deep snow" of Illinois. During that winter, A. together with his step-mother's son, John D. Johnston, and John Hanks, yet residing in Macon county, hired themselves to one Denton Offutt, to take a flat boat from Beardstown Illinois to New-Orleans; and for that purpose, were to join him—Offut—at Springfield, Ills so soon as the snow should go off. When it did go off which was about the 1st. of March 1831—the county was so flooded, as to make traveling by land impracticable; to obviate which difficulty they purchased a large canoe and came down the Sangamon river in it. This is the time and the manner of A's first entrance into Sangamon County. They found Offutt at Springfield, but learned from him that he had failed in getting a boat at Beardstown. This lead to their hiring themselves to him at $12 per month, each; and getting the timber out of the trees and building a boat at old Sangamon Town on the Sangamon river, seven miles N.W. of Springfield, which boat they took to New-Orleans, substantially upon the old contract. It was in connection with this boat that occurred the ludicrous incident of sewing up the hogs eyes. Offutt bought thirty odd large fat live hogs, but found difficulty in driving them from where he purchased them to the boat, and thereupon conceived the whim that he could sew up their eyes and drive them where he pleased. No sooner thought of than decided, he put his hands, including A. at the job, which they completed—all but the driving. In their blind condition they could not be driven out of the lot or field they were in. This expedient failing, they were tied and hauled on carts to the boat. It was near the Sangamon River, within what is now Menard county.

During this boat enterprize acquaintance with Offutt, who was previously an entire stranger, he conceved a liking for A. and believing he could turn him to account, he contracted with him to act as clerk for him, on his return from New-Orleans, in charge of a store and Mill at New-Salem, then in Sangamon, now in Menard county. Hanks had not gone to New-Orleans, but having a family, and being likely to be detained from home longer than at first expected, had turned back from St. Louis. He is the same John Hanks who now engineers the "rail enterprize" at Decatur; and is a first cousin to A's mother. A's father, with his own family & others mentioned, had, in pursuance of their intention, removed from Macon to Coles county. John D. Johnston, the step-mother's son, went to them; and A. stopped indefinitely, and, for the first time, as it were, by himself at New-Salem, before mentioned. This was in July 1831. Here he rapidly made acquaintances and friends. In less than a year Offutt's business was failing—had almost failed,—when the Black-Hawk war of 1832—broke out. A. joined a volunteer company, and to his own surprize, was elected captain of it. He says he has not since had any success in life which gave him so much satisfaction. He went the campaign, served near three months, met the ordinary hardships of such an expedition, but was in no battle. He now owns in Iowa, the land upon which his own warrants for this service, were located. Returning from the campaign, and encouraged by his great popularity among his immediate neighbors, he, the same year, ran for the Legislature and was beaten—his own precinct, however, casting it's votes

277 for and 7, against him. And this too while he was an
avowed Clay man, and the precinct the autumn afterwards,
giving a majority of 115 to Genl. Jackson over Mr. Clay.
This was the only time A. was ever beaten on a direct vote
of the people. He was now without means and out of business, but was anxious to remain with his friends who had
treated him with so much generosity, especially as he had
nothing elsewhere to go to. He studied what he should do—
thought of learning the black-smith trade—thought of trying
to study law—rather thought he could not succeed at that
without a better education. Before long, strangely enough,
a man offered to sell and did sell, to A. and another as
poor as himself, an old stock of goods, upon credit. They
opened as merchants; and he says that was *the* store. Of
course they did nothing but get deeper and deeper in debt.
He was appointed Postmaster at New-Salem—the office
being too insignificant, to make his politics an objection.
The store winked out. The Surveyor of Sangamon, offered
to depute to A. that portion of his work which was within
his part of the county. He accepted, procured a compass
and chain, studied Flint, and Gibson a little, and went at
it. This procured bread, and kept soul and body together.
The election of 1834 came, and he was then elected to the
Legislature by the highest vote cast for any candidate.
Major John T. Stuart, then in full practice of the law, was
also elected. During the canvass, in a private conversation
he encouraged A. to study law. After the election he borrowed books of Stuart, took them home with him, and went
at it in good earnest. He studied with nobody. He still
mixed in the surveying to pay board and clothing bills.
When the Legislature met, the law books were dropped,
but were taken up again at the end of the session. He was
re-elected in 1836, 1838, and 1840. In the autumn of
1836 he obtained a law licence, and on April 15, 1837
removed to Springfield, and commenced the practice, his
old friend, Stuart taking him into partnership. March 3rd.

1837, by a protest entered upon the Ills. House Journal of that date, at pages 817, 818, A. with Dan Stone, another representative of Sangamon, briefly defined his position on the slavery question; and so far as it goes, it was then the same that it is now. The protest is as follows—(Here insert it) In 1838, & 1840 Mr. L's party in the Legislature voted for him as Speaker; but being in the minority, he was not elected. After 1840 he declined a re-election to the Legislature. He was on the Harrison electoral ticket in 1840, and on that of Clay in 1844, and spent much time and labor in both those canvasses. In Nov. 1842 he was married to Mary, daughter of Robert S. Todd, of Lexington, Kentucky. They have three living children, all sons—one born in 1843, one in 1850, and one in 1853. They lost one, who was born in 1846. In 1846, he was elected to the lower House of Congress, and served one term only, commencing in Dec. 1847 and ending with the inauguration of Gen. Taylor, in March 1849. All the battles of the Mexican war had been fought before Mr. L. took his seat in congress, but the American army was still in Mexico, and the treaty of peace was not fully and formally ratified till the June afterwards. Much has been said of his course in Congress in regard to this war. A careful examination of the Journals and Congressional Globe shows, that he voted for all the supply measures which came up, and for all the measures in any way favorable to the officers, soldiers, and their families, who conducted the war through; with this exception that some of these measures passed without yeas and nays, leaving no record as to how particular men voted. The Journals and Globe also show him voting that the war was unnecessarily and unconstitutionally begun by the President of the United States. This is the language of Mr. Ashmun's amendment, for which Mr. L. and nearly or quite all, other whigs of the H. R. voted.

Mr. L's reasons for the opinion expressed by this vote

were briefly that the President had sent Genl. Taylor into an inhabited part of the country belonging to Mexico, and not to the U.S. and thereby had provoked the first act of hostility—in fact the commencement of the war; that the place, being the country bordering on the East bank of the Rio Grande, was inhabited by native Mexicans, born there under the Mexican government; and had never submitted to, nor been conquered by Texas, or the U.S. nor transferred to either by treaty—that although Texas claimed the Rio Grande as her boundary, Mexico had never recognized it, the people on the ground had never recognized it, and neither Texas nor the U.S. had ever enforced it—that there was a broad desert between that, and the country over which Texas had actual control—that the country where hostilities commenced, having once belonged to Mexico, must remain so, until it was somehow legally transferred, which had never been done.

Mr. L. thought the act of sending an armed force among the Mexicans, was *unnecessary*, inasmuch as Mexico was in no way molesting, or menacing the U.S. or the people thereof; and that it was *unconstitutional*, because the power of levying war is vested in Congress, and not in the President. He thought the principal motive for the act, was to divert public attention from the surrender of "Fifty-four, forty, or fight" to Great Brittain, on the Oregon boundary question.

Mr. L. was not a candidate for re-election. This was determined upon, and declared before he went to Washington, in accordance with an understanding among whig friends, by which Col. Hardin, and Col. Baker had each previously served a single term in the same District.

In 1848, during his term in congress, he advocated Gen. Taylor's nomination for the Presidency, in opposition to all others, and also took an active part for his election, after his nomination—speaking a few times in Maryland, near

Washington, several times in Massachusetts, and canvassing quite fully his own district in Illinois, which was followed by a majority in the district of over 1500 for Gen. Taylor.

Upon his return from Congress he went to the practice of the law with greater earnestness than ever before. In 1852 he was upon the Scott electoral ticket, and did something in the way of canvassing, but owing to the hopelessness of the cause in Illinois, he did less than in previous presidential canvasses.

In 1854, his profession had almost superseded the thought of politics in his mind, when the repeal of the Missouri compromise aroused him as he had never been before.

In the autumn of that year he took the stump with no broader practical aim or object than to secure, if possible, the re-election of Hon Richard Yates to congress. His speeches at once attracted a more marked attention than they had ever before done. As the canvass proceeded, he was drawn to different parts of the state, outside of Mr. Yates' district. He did not abandon the law, but gave his attention, by turns, to that and politics. The State agricultural fair was at Springfield that year, and Douglas was announced to speak there.

In the canvass of 1856, Mr. L. made over fifty speeches, no one of which, so far as he remembers, was put in print. One of them was made at Galena, but Mr. L. has no recollection of any part of it being printed; nor does he remember whether in that speech he said anything about a Supreme court decision. He may have spoken upon that subject; and some of the newspapers may have reported him as saying what is now ascribed to him; but he thinks he could not have expressed himself as represented.

c. June 1860

To Grace Bedell

Private

Miss. Grace Bedell   Springfield, Ills.
My dear little Miss.   Oct 19. 1860

Your very agreeable letter of the 15th. is received.

I regret the necessity of saying I have no daughters. I have three sons—one seventeen, one nine, and one seven, years of age. They, with their mother, constitute my whole family.

As to the whiskers, having never worn any, do you not think people would call it a piece of silly affection if I were to begin it now? Your very sincere well-wisher

Farewell Address at Springfield, Illinois

My friends—No one, not in my situation, can appreciate my feeling of sadness at this parting. To this place, and the kindness of these people, I owe every thing. Here I have lived a quarter of a century, and have passed from a young to an old man. Here my children have been born, and one is buried. I now leave, not knowing when, or whether ever, I may return, with a task before me greater than that which rested upon Washington. Without the assistance of that Divine Being, who ever attended him, I cannot succeed. With that assistance I cannot fail. Trusting in Him, who can go with me, and remain with you and be every where for good, let us confidently hope that all will yet be well. To His care commending you, as I hope in your prayers you will commend me, I bid you an affectionate farewell

February 11, 1861

2.

THE COMMANDING PRESIDENT

First Inaugural Address

Fellow citizens of the United States:

In compliance with a custom as old as the government itself, I appear before you to address you briefly, and to take, in your presence, the oath prescribed by the Constitution of the United States, to be taken by the President "before he enters on the execution of his office."

I do not consider it necessary, at present, for me to discuss those matters of administration about which there is no special anxiety, or excitement.

Apprehension seems to exist among the people of the Southern States, that by the accession of a Republican Administration, their property, and their peace, and personal security, are to be endangered. There has never been any reasonable cause for such apprehension. Indeed, the most ample evidence to the contrary has all the while existed, and been open to their inspection. It is found in nearly all the published speeches of him who now addresses you. I do but quote from one of those speeches when I declare that "I have no purpose, directly or indirectly, to interfere with the institution of slavery in the States where it exists. I believe I have no lawful right to do so, and I have no inclination to do so." Those who nominated and elected me did so with full knowledge that I had made this, and many similar declarations, and had never recanted them. And more than this, they placed in the platform, for my acceptance, and as a law to themselves, and to me, the clear and emphatic resolution which I now read:

"*Resolved*, That the maintenance inviolate of the rights of the States, and especially the right of each State to order and control its own domestic institutions according to its own judgment exclusively, is essential to that balance of power on which the perfection and endurance of our political fabric depend; and we denounce the lawless invasion by armed force of the soil of any State or Territory, no matter under what pretext, as among the gravest of crimes."

I now reiterate these sentiments: and in doing so, I only press upon the public attention the most conclusive evidence of which the case is susceptible, that the property, peace and security of no section are to be in anywise endangered by the now incoming Administration. I add too, that all the protection which, consistently with the Constitution and the laws, can be given, will be cheerfully given to all the States when lawfully demanded, for whatever cause—as cheerfully to one section, as to another.

There is much controversy about the delivering up of fugitives from service or labor. The clause I now read is as plainly written in the Constitution as any other of its provisions:

"No person held to service or labor in one State, under the laws thereof, escaping into another, shall, in consequence of any law or regulation therein, be discharged from such service or labor, but shall be delivered up on claim of the party to whom such service or labor may be due."

It is scarcely questioned that this provision was intended by those who made it, for the reclaiming of what we call fugitive slaves; and the intention of the law-giver is the law. All members of Congress swear their support to the whole Constitution—to this provision as much as to any other. To the proposition, then, that slaves whose cases come within the terms of this clause, "shall be delivered up," their oaths are unanimous. Now, if they would make the effort in good temper, could they not, with nearly equal unanimity, frame and pass a law, by means of which to keep good that unanimous oath?

There is some difference of opinion whether this clause should be enforced by national or by state authority; but surely that difference is not a very material one. If the slave is to be surrendered, it can be of but little consequence to him, or to others, by which authority it is done. And should any one, in any case, be content that his oath shall go unkept, on a merely unsubstantial controversy as to *how* it shall be kept?

Again, in any law upon this subject, ought not all the safeguards of liberty known in civilized and humane jurisprudence to be introduced, so that a free man be not, in any case, surrendered as a slave? And might it not be well, at the same time, to provide by law for the enforcement of that clause in the Constitution which guarranties that "The citizens of each State shall be entitled to all previleges and immunities of citizens in the several States?"

I take the official oath to-day, with no mental reservations, and with no purpose to construe the Constitution or laws, by any hypercritical rules. And while I do not choose now to specify particular acts of Congress as proper to be enforced, I do suggest, that it will be much safer for all, both in official and private stations, to conform to, and abide by, all those acts which stand unrepealed, than to violate any of them, trusting to find impunity in having them held to be unconstitutional.

It is seventy-two years since the first inauguration of a President under our national Constitution. During that period fifteen different and greatly distinguished citizens, have, in succession, administered the executive branch of the government. They have conducted it through many perils; and, generally, with great success. Yet, with all this scope for precedent, I now enter upon the same task for the brief constitutional term of four years, under great and peculiar difficulty. A disruption of the Federal Union heretofore only menaced, is now formidably attempted.

I hold, that in contemplation of universal law, and of the Constitution, the Union of these States is perpetual. Perpetuity is implied, if not expressed, in the fundamental law of all national governments. It is safe to assert that no government proper, ever had a provision in its organic law for its own termination. Continue to execute all the express provisions of our national Constitution, and the Union will endure forever—it being impossible to destroy it, except by some action not provided for in the instrument itself.

Again, if the United States be not a government proper, but an association of States in the nature of contract merely, can it, as a contract, be peaceably unmade, by less than all the parties who made it? One party to a contract may violate it—break it, so to speak; but does it not require all to lawfully rescind it?

Descending from these general principles, we find the proposition that, in legal contemplation, the Union is perpetual, confirmed by the history of the Union itself. The Union is much older than the Constitution. It was formed in fact, by the Articles of Association in 1774. It was matured and continued by the Declaration of Independence in 1776. It was further matured and the faith of all the then thirteen States expressly plighted and engaged that it should be perpetual, by the Articles of Confederation in 1778. And finally, in 1787, one of the declared objects for ordaining and establishing the Constitution, was *"to form a more perfect union."*

But if destruction of the Union, by one, or by a part only, of the States, be lawfully possible, the Union is *less* perfect than before the Constitution, having lost the vital element of perpetuity.

It follows from these views that no State, upon its own mere motion, can lawfully get out of the Union,—that *resolves* and *ordinances* to that effect are legally void; and that acts of violence, within any State or States, against the authority of the United States, are insurrectionary or revolutionary, according to circumstances.

I therefore consider that, in view of the Constitution and the laws, the Union is unbroken; and, to the extent of my ability, I shall take care, as the Constitution itself expressly enjoins upon me, that the laws of the Union be faithfully executed in all the States. Doing this I deem to be only a simple duty on my part; and I shall perform it, so far as practicable, unless my rightful masters, the American people, shall withhold the requisite means, or, in some authoritative manner, direct the contrary. I trust this will not be regarded as a menace, but only as the declared purpose of the Union that it *will* constitutionally defend, and maintain itself.

In doing this there needs to be no bloodshed or violence; and there shall be none, unless it be forced upon the national authority. The power confided to me, will be used to hold, occupy, and possess the property, and places belonging to the government, and to collect the duties and imposts; but beyond what may be necessary for these objects, there will be no invasion—no using of force against, or among the people anywhere. Where hostility to the United States, in any interior locality, shall be so great and so universal, as to prevent competent resident citizens from holding the Federal offices, there will be no attempt to force obnoxious strangers among the people for that object. While the strict legal right may exist in the government to enforce the exercise of these offices, the attempt to do so would be so irritating, and so nearly impracticable with all, that I deem it better to forego, for the time, the uses of such offices.

The mails, unless repelled, will continue to be furnished in all parts of the Union. So far as possible, the people everywhere shall have that sense of perfect security which is most favorable to calm thought and reflection. The course here indicated will be followed, unless current events, and experience, shall show a modification, or change, to be proper; and in every case and exigency, my best discretion will be exercised, according to circumstances actually existing, and with a view and a hope of a peaceful solution of the national troubles, and the restoration of fraternal sympathies and affections.

That there are persons in one section, or another who seek to destroy the Union at all events, and are glad of any pretext to do it, I will neither affirm or deny; but if there be such, I need address no word to them. To those, however, who really love the Union, may I not speak?

Before entering upon so grave a matter as the destruction of our national fabric, with all its benefits, its memories, and its hopes, would it not be wise to ascertain precisely why we do it? Will you hazard so desperate a step, while there is any possibility that any portion of the ills you fly from, have no real existence? Will you, while the certain ills you fly to, are greater than all the real ones you fly from? Will you risk the commission of so fearful a mistake?

All profess to be content in the Union, if all constitutional rights can be maintained. Is it true, then, that any right, plainly written in the Constitution, has been denied? I think not. Happily the human mind is so constituted, that no party can reach to the audacity of doing this. Think, if you can, of a single instance in which a plainly written provision of the Constitution has ever been denied. If, by the mere force of numbers, a majority should deprive a minority of any clearly written constitutional right, it might, in a moral point of view, justify revolution—certainly would, if such right were a vital one. But such is not our case. All the vital rights of minorities, and of individuals, are so plainly assured to them, by affirmations and negations, guarranties and prohibitions, in the Constitution, that controversies never arise concerning them. But no organic law can ever be framed with a provision specifically applicable to every question which may occur in practical administration. No foresight can anticipate, nor any document of reasonable length contain express provisions for all possible questions. Shall fugitives from labor be surrendered by national or by State authority? The Constitution does not expressly say. *May* Congress prohibit slavery in the territories? The Constitution does not expressly say. *Must* Congress protect slavery in the territories? The Constitution does not expressly say.

From questions of this class spring all our constitutional controversies, and we divide upon them into majorities and minorities. If the minority will not acquiesce, the majority must, or the government must cease. There is no other alternative; for continuing the government, is acquiescence on one side or the other. If a minority, in such case, will secede rather than acquiesce, they make a precedent which, in turn, will divide and ruin them; for a minority of their own will secede from them, whenever a majority refuses to be controlled by such minority. For instance, why may not any portion of a new confederacy, a year or two hence, arbitrarily secede again, precisely as portions of the present Union now claim to secede from it. All who cherish disunion sentiments, are now being educated to the exact temper of doing this. Is there such perfect identity of interests among the States to compose a new Union, as to produce harmony only, and prevent renewed secession?

Plainly, the central idea of secession, is the essence of anarchy. A majority, held in restraint by constitutional checks, and limitations, and always changing easily, with deliberate changes of popular opinions and sentiments, is the only true sovereign of a free people. Whoever rejects it, does, of necessity, fly to anarchy or to despotism. Unanimity is impossible; the rule of a minority, as a permanent arrangement, is wholly inadmissable; so that, rejecting the majority principle, anarchy, or despotism in some form, is all that is left.

I do not forget the position assumed by some, that constitutional questions are to be decided by the Supreme Court; nor do I deny that such decisions must be binding in any case, upon the parties to a suit, as to the object of that suit, while they are also entitled to very high respect and consideration, in all paralel cases, by all other departments of the government. And while it is obviously possible that

may be erroneous in any given case, still the
lowing it, being limited to that particular case,
ce that it may be over-ruled, and never become
a precedent for other cases, can better be borne than could
the evils of a different practice. At the same time the candid
citizen must confess that if the policy of the government,
upon vital questions, affecting the whole people, is to be
irrevocably fixed by decisions of the Supreme Court, the
instant they are made, in ordinary litigation between parties,
in personal actions, the people will have ceased, to be their
own rulers, having, to that extent, practically resigned their
government, into the hands of that eminent tribunal. Nor is
there, in this view, any assault upon the court, or the judges.
It is a duty, from which they may not shrink, to decide cases
properly brought before them; and it is no fault of theirs, if
others seek to turn their decisions to political purposes.

One section of our country believes slavery is *right*, and
ought to be extended, while the other believes it is *wrong*,
and ought not to be extended. This is the only substantial
dispute. The fugitive slave clause of the Constitution, and
the law for the suppression of the foreign slave trade, are
each as well enforced, perhaps, as any law can ever be in
a community where the moral sense of the people imperfectly
supports the law itself. The great body of the people abide
by the dry legal obligation in both cases, and a few break
over in each. This, I think, cannot be perfectly cured; and
it would be worse in both cases *after* the separation of the
sections, than before. The foreign slave trade, now imperfectly suppressed, would be ultimately revived without restriction, in one section; while fugitive slaves, now only
partially surrendered, would not be surrendered at all, by
the other.

Physically speaking, we cannot separate. We cannot remove our respective sections from each other, nor build an
impassable wall between them. A husband and wife may
be divorced, and go out of the presence, and beyond the

reach of each other; but the different parts of our country cannot do this. They cannot but remain face to face; and intercourse, either amicable or hostile, must continue between them. Is it possible then to make that intercourse more advantageous, or more satisfactory, *after* separation than *before*? Can aliens make treaties easier than friends can make laws? Can treaties be more faithfully enforced between aliens, than laws can among friends? Suppose you go to war, you cannot fight always; and when, after much loss on both sides, and no gain on either, you cease fighting, the identical old questions, as to terms of intercourse, are again upon you.

This country, with its institutions, belongs to the people who inhabit it. Whenever they shall grow weary of the existing government, they can exercise their *constitutional* right of amending it, or their *revolutionary* right to dismember, or overthrow it. I can not be ignorant of the fact that many worthy, and patriotic citizens are desirous of having the national constitution amended. While I make no recommendation of amendments, I fully recognize the rightful authority of the people over the whole subject, to be exercised in either of the modes prescribed in the instrument itself; and I should, under existing circumstances, favor, rather than oppose, a fair oppertunity being afforded the people to act upon it.

I will venture to add that, to me, the convention mode seems preferable, in that it allows amendments to originate with the people themselves, instead of only permitting them to take, or reject, propositions, originated by others, not especially chosen for the purpose, and which might not be precisely such, as they would wish to either accept or refuse. I understand a proposed amendment to the Constitution— which amendment, however, I have not seen, has passed Congress, to the effect that the federal government, shall never interfere with the domestic institutions of the States, including that of persons held to service. To avoid misconstruction of what I have said, I depart from my purpose not to speak of particular amendments, so far as to say that, holding such a provision to now be implied constitutional law, I have no objection to its being made express, and irrevocable.

The Chief Magistrate derives all his authority from the people, and they have conferred none upon him to fix terms for the separation of the States. The people themselves can do this also if they choose; but the executive, as such, has nothing to do with it. His duty is to administer the present government, as it came to his hands, and to transmit it, unimpaired by him, to his successor.

Why should there not be a patient confidence in the ultimate justice of the people? Is there any better, or equal hope, in the world? In our present differences, is either party without faith of being in the right? If the Almighty Ruler of nations, with his eternal truth and justice, be on your side of the North, or on yours of the South, that truth, and that justice, will surely prevail, by the judgment of this great tribunal, the American people.

By the frame of the government under which we live, this same people have wisely given their public servants but little power for mischief; and have, with equal wisdom, provided for the return of that little to their own hands at very short intervals.

While the people retain their virtue, and vigilence, no administration, by any extreme of wickedness or folly, can very seriously injure the government, in the short space of four years.

My countrymen, one and all, think calmly and *well*, upon this whole subject. Nothing valuable can be lost by taking time. If there be an object to *hurry* any of you, in hot haste, to a step which you would never take *deliberately*, that object will be frustrated by taking time; but no good object can be frustrated by it. Such of you as are now dissatisfied, still have the old Constitution unimpaired, and, on the sensitive point, the laws of your own framing under it; while the new administration will have no immediate power, if it would, to change either. If it were admitted that you who are dissatisfied, hold the right side in the dispute, there still is no single good reason for precipitate action. Intelligence, patriotism, Christianity, and a firm reliance on Him, who has never yet forsaken this favored land, are still competent to adjust, in the best way, all our present difficulty.

In *your* hands, my dissatisfied fellow countrymen, and not in *mine*, is the momentous issue of civil war. The government will not assail *you*. You can have no conflict, without being yourselves the aggressors. *You* have no oath registered in Heaven to destroy the government, while *I* shall have the most solemn one to "preserve, protect and defend" it.

I am loth to close. We are not enemies, but friends. We must not be enemies. Though passion may have strained, it must not break our bonds of affection. The mystic chords of memory, streching from every battle-field, and patriot grave, to every living heart and hearthstone, all over this broad land, will yet swell the chorus of the Union, when again touched, as surely they will be, by the better angels of our nature.

March 4, 1861

To Winfield Scott

Executive Mansion, March 9, 1861.

Lieutenant General Scott:

My dear Sir: On the 5th inst. I received from the Hon. Joseph Holt, the then faithful and vigilant Secretary of War, a letter of that date, inclosing a letter and accompanying documents received by him on the 4th inst. from Major Robert Anderson commanding at Fort Sumpter,

South Carolina; and copies of all which I now transmit. Immediately on the receipt of them by me, I transmitted the whole to you for your consideration; and the same day you returned the package to me with your opinion endorsed upon it, a copy of which opinion I now also transmit to you. Learning from you verbally that since then you have given the subject a more full and thorough consideration, you will much oblige me by giving answers, in writing, to the following interrogatories:

1st To what point of time can Major Anderson maintain his position at Fort Sumpter, without fresh supplies or reinforcement?

2d. Can you, with all the means now in your control, supply or re-inforce Fort Sumpter within that time?

3d If not, what amount of means and of what description, in addition to that already at your control, would enable you to supply and reinforce that fortress within the time?

Please answer these, adding such statements, information, and counsel as your great skill and experience may suggest. Your obedient Servant

Proclamation of Blockade

BY THE PRESIDENT
OF THE UNITED STATES OF AMERICA:
A PROCLAMATION.

Whereas an insurrection against the Government of the United States has broken out in the States of South Carolina, Georgia, Alabama, Florida, Mississippi, Louisiana, and Texas, and the laws of the United States for the collection of the revenue cannot be effectually executed therein comformably to that provision of the Constitution which requires duties to be uniform throughout the United States:

And whereas a combination of persons engaged in such insurrection, have threatened to grant pretended letters of marque to authorize the bearers thereof to commit assaults on the lives, vessels, and property of good citizens of the country lawfully engaged in commerce on the high seas, and in waters of the United States: And whereas an Executive Proclamation has been already issued, requiring the persons engaged in these disorderly proceedings to desist therefrom, calling out a militia force for the purpose of repressing the same, and convening Congress in extraordinary session, to deliberate and determine thereon:

Now, therefore, I, Abraham Lincoln, President of the United States, with a view to the same purposes before mentioned, and to the protection of the public peace, and the lives and property of quiet and orderly citizens pursuing their lawful occupations, until Congress shall have assembled and deliberated on the said unlawful proceedings, or until the same shall have ceased, have further deemed it advisable to set on foot a blockade of the ports within the States aforesaid, in pursuance of the laws of the United States, and of the law of Nations, in such case provided. For this purpose a competent force will be posted so as to prevent entrance and exit of vessels from the ports aforesaid. If, therefore, with a view to violate such blockade, a vessel shall approach, or shall attempt to leave either of the said ports, she will be duly warned by the Commander of one of the blockading vessels, who will endorse on her register the fact and date of such warning, and if the same vessel shall again attempt to enter or leave the blockaded port, she will be captured and sent to the nearest convenient port, for such proceedings against her and her cargo as prize, as may be deemed advisable.

And I hereby proclaim and declare that if any person, under the pretended authority of the said States, or under any other pretense, shall molest a vessel of the United States, or the persons or cargo on board of her, such person will be held amenable to the laws of the United States for the prevention and punishment of piracy.

In witness whereof, I have hereunto set my hand, and caused the seal of the United States to be affixed.

Done at the City of Washington, this nineteenth day of April, in the year of our Lord one thousand eight hundred and sixty-one, and of the Independence of the United States the eighty-fifth.

ABRAHAM LINCOLN

By the President:
    WILLIAM H. SEWARD, Secretary of State

Message to Congress in Special Session

Fellow-citizens of the Senate and House of Representatives:

Having been convened on an extraordinary occasion, as authorized by the Constitution, your attention is not called to any ordinary subject of legislation.

At the beginning of the present Presidential term, four months ago, the functions of the Federal Government were found to be generally suspended within the several States of South Carolina, Georgia, Alabama, Mississippi, Louisiana, and Florida, excepting only those of the Post Office Department.

Within these States, all the Forts, Arsenals, Dock-yards, Custom-houses, and the like, including the movable and stationary property in, and about them, had been seized, and were held in open hostility to this Government, excepting only Forts Pickens, Taylor, and Jefferson, on, and near the Florida coast, and Fort Sumter, in Charleston harbor, South Carolina. The Forts thus seized had been put in improved condition; new ones had been built; and armed forces had been organized, and were organizing, all avowedly with the same hostile purpose.

The Forts remaining in the possession of the Federal government, in, and near, these States, were either besieged or menaced by warlike preparations; and especially Fort Sumter was nearly surrounded by well-protected hostile batteries, with guns equal in quality to the best of its own, and out-numbering the latter as perhaps ten to one. A disproportionate share, of the Federal muskets and rifles, had somehow found their way into these States, and had been seized, to be used against the government. Accumulations of the public revenue, lying within them, had been seized for the same object. The Navy was scattered in distant seas; leaving but a very small part of it within the immediate reach of the government. Officers of the Federal Army and Navy, had resigned in great numbers; and, of those resigning, a large proportion had taken up arms against the government. Simultaneously, and in connection, with all this, the purpose to sever the Federal Union, was openly avowed. In accordance with this purpose, an ordinance had been adopted in each of these States, declaring the States, respectively, to be separated from the National Union. A formula for instituting a combined government of these states had been promulgated; and this illegal organization, in the character of confederate States was already invoking recognition, aid, and intervention, from Foreign Powers.

Finding this condition of things, and believing it to be an imperative duty upon the incoming Executive, to prevent, if possible, the consummation of such attempt to destroy the Federal Union, a choice of means to that end became indispensable. This choice was made; and was declared in the Inaugural address. The policy chosen looked to the exhaustion of all peaceful measures, before a resort to any stronger ones. It sought only to hold the public places and property, not already wrested from the Government, and to collect the revenue; relying for the rest, on time, discussion, and the ballot-box. It promised a continuance of the mails, at government expense, to the very people who were resisting the government; and it gave repeated pledges against any disturbance to any of the people, or any of their rights. Of all that which a president might constitutionally, and justifiably, do in such a case, everything was foreborne, without which, it was believed possible to keep the government on foot.

On the 5th of March, (the present incumbent's first full day in office) a letter of Major Anderson, commanding at Fort Sumter, written on the 28th of February, and received at the War Department on the 4th of March, was, by that Department, placed in his hands. This letter expressed the professional opinion of the writer, that re-inforcements could not be thrown into that Fort within the time for his relief, rendered necessary by the limited supply of provisions, and with a view of holding possession of the same, with a force of less than twenty thousand good, and well-disciplined men. This opinion was concurred in by all the officers of his command; and their *memoranda* on the subject, were made enclosures of Major Anderson's letter. The whole was immediately laid before Lieutenant General Scott, who at once concurred with Major Anderson in opinion. On reflection, however, he took full time, consulting with other officers, both of the Army and the Navy; and, at the end of four days, came reluctantly, but decidedly, to the same conclusion as before. He also stated at the same time that no such sufficient force was then at the control of the Government, or could be raised, and brought to the ground, within the time when the provisions in the Fort would be exhausted. In a purely military point of view, this reduced the duty of the administration, in the case, to the mere matter of getting the garrison safely out of the Fort.

It was believed, however, that to so abandon that position, under the circumstances, would be utterly ruinous; that the *necessity* under which it was to be done, would not be fully understood—that, by many, it would be construed as a part of a *voluntary* policy—that, at home, it would discourage the friends of the Union, embolden its adversaries, and go far to insure to the latter, a recognition abroad—that, in fact, it would be our national destruction consummated. This could not be allowed. Starvation was not yet upon the garrison; and ere it would be reached, *Fort Pickens* might be reinforced. This last, would be a clear indication of *policy*, and would better enable the country to accept the evacuation of Fort Sumter, as a military *necessity*. An order was at once directed to be sent for the landing of the troops from the Steamship Brooklyn, into Fort Pickens. This order could not go by land, but must take the longer, and slower route by sea. The first return news from the order was received just one week before the fall of Fort Sumter. The news itself was, that the officer commanding the Sabine, to which vessel the troops had been transferred from the Brooklyn, acting upon some *quasi* armistice of the late administration, (and of the existence of which, the present administration, up to the time the order was despatched, had only too vague and uncertain rumors, to fix attention) had refused to land the troops. To now re-inforce Fort Pickens, before a crisis would be reached at Fort Sumter was impossible—rendered so by the near exhaustion of provisions in the latter-named Fort. In precaution against such a conjuncture, the government had, a few days before, commenced preparing an expedition, as well adapted as might be, to relieve Fort Sumter, which expedition was intended to be ultimately used, or not, according to circumstances. The strongest anticipated case, for using it, was now presented; and it was resolved to send it forward. As had been intended, in this contingency, it was also resolved to notify the Governor of South Carolina, that he might expect an attempt would be made to provision the Fort; and that, if the attempt should not be resisted, there would be no

effort to throw in men, arms, or ammunition, without further
notice, or in case of an attack upon the Fort. This notice
was accordingly given; whereupon the Fort was attacked,
and bombarded to its fall, without even awaiting the arrival
of the provisioning expedition.

It is thus seen that the assault upon, and reduction of,
Fort Sumter, was, in no sense, a matter of self defence on
the part of the assailants. They well knew that the garrison
in the Fort could, by no possibility, commit aggression upon
them. They knew—they were expressly notified—that the
giving of bread to the few brave and hungry men of the
garrison, was all which would on that occasion be attempted, unless themselves, by resisting so much, should
provoke more. They knew that this Government desired to
keep the garrison in the Fort, not to assail them, but merely
to maintain visible possession, and thus to preserve the
Union from actual, and immediate dissolution—trusting, as
herein-before stated, to time, discussion, and the ballot-box,
for final adjustment; and they assailed, and reduced the
Fort, for precisely the reverse object—to drive out the visible authority of the Federal Union, and thus force it to
immediate dissolution.

That this was their object, the Executive well understood;
and having said to them in the inaugural address, "You can
have no conflict without being yourselves the aggressors,"
he took pains, not only to keep this declaration good, but
also to keep the case so free from the power of ingenious
sophistry, as that the world should not be able to misunder-
stand it. By the affair at Fort Sumter, with its surrounding
circumstances, that point was reached. Then, and thereby,
the assailants of the Government, began the conflict of
arms, without a gun in sight, or in expectancy, to return their
fire, save only the few in the Fort, sent to that harbor, years
before, for their own protection, and still ready to give that
protection, in whatever was lawful. In this act, discarding

all else, they have forced upon the country, the distinct issue: "Immediate dissolution, or blood."

And this issue embraces more than the fate of these United States. It presents to the whole family of man, the question, whether a constitutional republic, or a democracy—a government of the people, by the same people—can, or cannot, maintain its territorial integrity, against its own domestic foes. It presents the question, whether discontented individuals, too few in numbers to control administration, according to organic law, in any case, can always, upon the pretences made in this case, or on any other pretences, or arbitrarily, without any pretence, break up their Government, and thus practically put an end to free government upon the earth. It forces us to ask: "Is there, in all republics, this inherent, and fatal weakness?" "Must a government, of necessity, be too *strong* for the liberties of its own people, or too *weak* to maintain its own existence?"

So viewing the issue, no choice was left but to call out the war power of the Government; and so to resist force, employed for its destruction, by force, for its preservation.

The call was made; and the response of the country was most gratifying; surpassing, in unanimity and spirit, the most sanguine expectation. Yet none of the States commonly called Slave-states, except Delaware, gave a Regiment through regular State organization. A few regiments have been organized within some others of those states, by individual enterprise, and received into the government service. Of course the seceded States, so called, (and to which Texas had been joined about the time of the inauguration,) gave no troops to the cause of the Union. The border States, so called, were not uniform in their actions; some of them being almost *for* the Union, while in others—as Virginia, North Carolina, Tennessee, and Arkansas—the Union sentiment was nearly repressed, and silenced. The course taken in Virginia was the most remarkable—perhaps the most important. A convention, elected by the people of that State, to consider this very question of disrupting the Federal Union, was in session at the capital of Virginia when Fort Sumter fell. To this body the people had chosen a large majority of *professed* Union men. Almost immediately after the fall of Sumter, many members of that majority went over to the original disunion minority, and, with them, adopted an ordinance for withdrawing the State from the Union. Whether this change was wrought by their great approval of the assault upon Sumter, or their great resentment at the government's resistance to that assault, is not definitely known. Although they submitted the ordinance, for ratification, to a vote of the people, to be taken on a day then somewhat more than a month distant, the convention, and the Legislature, (which was also in session at the same time and place) with leading men of the State, not members of either, immediately commenced acting, as if the State were already out of the Union. They pushed military preparations vigorously forward all over the state. They seized the United States Armory at Harper's Ferry, and the Navy-yard at Gosport, near Norfolk. They received—perhaps invited—into their state, large bodies of troops, with their warlike appointments, from the so-called seceded States. They formally entered into a treaty of temporary alliance, and co-operation with the so-called "Confederate States," and sent members to their Congress at Montgomery. And, finally, they permitted the insurrectionary government to be transferred to their capital at Richmond.

The people of Virginia have thus allowed this giant insurrection to make its nest within her borders; and this government has no choice left but to deal with it, *where* it finds it. And it has the less regret, as the loyal citizens have, in due form, claimed its protection. Those loyal citizens, this government is bound to recognize, and protect, as being Virginia.

In the border States, so called—in fact, the middle

states—there are those who favor a policy which they call "armed neutrality"—that is, an arming of those states to prevent the Union forces passing one way, or the disunion, the other, over their soil. This would be disunion completed. Figuratively speaking, it would be the building of an impassable wall along the line of separation. And yet, not quite an impassable one; for, under the guise of neutrality, it would tie the hands of the Union men, and freely pass supplies from among them, to the insurrectionists, which it could not do as an open enemy. At a stroke, it would take all the trouble off the hands of secession, except only what proceeds from the external blockade. It would do for the disunionists that which, of all things, they most desire—feed them well, and give them disunion without a struggle of their own. It recognizes no fidelity to the Constitution, no obligation to maintain the Union; and while very many who have favored it are, doubtless, loyal citizens, it is, nevertheless, treason in effect.

Recurring to the action of the government, it may be stated that, at first, a call was made for seventy-five thousand militia; and rapidly following this, a proclamation was issued for closing the ports of the insurrectionary districts by proceedings in the nature of Blockade. So far all was believed to be strictly legal. At this point the insurrectionists announced their purpose to enter upon the practice of privateering.

Other calls were made for volunteers, to serve three years, unless sooner discharged; and also for large additions to the regular Army and Navy. These measures, whether strictly legal or not, were ventured upon, under what appeared to be a popular demand, and a public necessity; trusting, then as now, that Congress would readily ratify them. It is believed that nothing has been done beyond the constitutional competency of Congress.

Soon after the first call for militia, it was considered a duty to authorize the Commanding General, in proper cases, according to his discretion, to suspend the privilege of the writ of habeas corpus; or, in other words, to arrest, and detain, without resort to the ordinary processes and forms of law, such individuals as he might deem dangerous to the public safety. This authority has purposely been exercised but very sparingly. Nevertheless, the legality and propriety of what has been done under it, are questioned; and the attention of the country has been called to the proposition that one who is sworn to "take care that the laws be faithfully executed," should not himself violate them. Of course some consideration was given to the questions of power, and propriety, before this matter was acted upon. The whole of the laws which were required to be faithfully executed, were being resisted, and failing of execution, in nearly one-third of the States. Must they be allowed to finally fail of execution, even had it been perfectly clear, that by the use of the means necessary to their execution, some single law, made in such extreme tenderness of the citizen's liberty, that practically, it relieves more of the guilty, than of the innocent, should, to a very limited extent, be violated? To state the question more directly, are all the laws, *but one*, to go unexecuted, and the government itself go to pieces, lest that one be violated? Even in such a case, would not the official oath be broken, if the government should be overthrown, when it was believed that disregarding the single law, would tend to preserve it? But it was not believed that this question was presented. It was not believed that any law was violated. The provision of the Constitution that "The privilege of the writ of habeas corpus, shall not be suspended unless when, in cases of rebellion or invasion, the public safety may require it," is equivalent to a provision—is a provision—that such privilege may be suspended when, in cases of rebellion, or invasion, the public safety *does* require it. It was decided that we have a case of rebellion, and that the public safety does require the qualified suspension of the privilege of the writ which was authorized to be made. Now it is insisted that Congress, and not the Executive, is vested with this power. But the Constitution itself, is silent as to which, or who, is to exercise the power; and as the provision was plainly made for a dangerous emergency, it cannot be believed the framers of the instrument intended, that in every case, the danger should run its course, until Congress could be called together; the very assembling of which might be prevented, as was intended in this case, by the rebellion.

No more extended argument is now offered; as an opinion, at some length, will probably be presented by the Attorney General. Whether there shall be any legislation upon the subject, and if any, what, is submitted entirely to the better judgment of Congress.

The forbearance of this government had been so extraordinary, and so long continued, as to lead some foreign nations to shape their action as if they supposed the early destruction of our national Union was probable. While this, on discovery, gave the Executive some concern, he is now happy to say that the sovereignty, and rights of the United States, are now everywhere practically respected by foreign powers; and a general sympathy with the country is manifested throughout the world.

The reports of the Secretaries of the Treasury, War, and the Navy, will give the information in detail deemed necessary, and convenient for your deliberation, and action; while the Executive, and all the Departments, will stand ready to supply omissions, or to communicate new facts, considered important for you to know.

It is now recommended that you give the legal means for making this contest a short, and a decisive one; that you place at the control of the government, for the work, at least four hundred thousand men, and four hundred millions of dollars. That number of men is about one tenth of those of proper ages within the regions where, apparently, *all* are willing to engage; and the sum is less than a twentythird part of the money value owned by the men who seem ready to devote the whole. A debt of six hundred millions of dollars *now*, is a less sum per head, than was the debt of our revolution, when we came out of that struggle; and the money value in the country now, bears even a greater proportion to what it was *then*, than does the population. Surely each man has as strong a motive *now*, to *preserve* our liberties, as each had *then*, to *establish* them.

A right result, at this time, will be worth more to the world, than ten times the men, and ten times the money. The evidence reaching us from the country, leaves no doubt, that the material for the work is abundant; and that it needs only the hand of legislation to give it legal sanction, and the hand of the Executive to give it practical shape and efficiency. One of the greatest perplexities of the government, is to avoid receiving troops faster than it can provide for them. In a word, the people will save their government, if the government itself, will do its part, only indifferently well.

It might seem, at first thought, to be of little difference whether the present movement at the South be called "secession" or "rebellion." The movers, however, well understand the difference. At the beginning, they knew they could never raise their treason to any respectable magnitude, by any name which implies *violation* of law. They knew their people possessed as much of moral sense, as much of devotion to law and order, and as much pride in, and reverence for, the history, and government, of their common country, as any other civilized, and patriotic people. They knew they could make no advancement directly in the teeth of these strong and noble sentiments. Accordingly they commenced by an insidious debauching of the public mind. They invented an ingenious sophism, which, if conceded, was followed by perfectly logical steps, through all the incidents, to the complete destruction of the Union. The sophism itself is, that any state of the Union may, *consistently* with the national Constitution, and therefore *lawfully*, and *peacefully*, withdraw from the Union, without the consent of the Union, or of any other state. The little disguise that the supposed right is to be exercised only for just cause, themselves to be the sole judge of its justice, is too thin to merit any notice.

With rebellion thus sugar-coated, they have been drugging the public mind of their section for more than thirty years; and, until at length, they have brought many good men to a willingness to take up arms against the government the day *after* some assemblage of men have enacted the farcical pretence of taking their State out of the Union, who could have been brought to no such thing the day *before*.

This sophism derives much—perhaps the whole—of its currency, from the assumption, that there is some omnipotent, and sacred supremacy, pertaining to a *State*—to each State of our Federal Union. Our States have neither more, nor less power, than that reserved to them, in the Union, by the Constitution—no one of them ever having been a State *out* of the Union. The original ones passed into the Union even *before* they cast off their British colonial dependence; and the new ones each came into the Union directly from a condition of dependence, excepting Texas. And even Texas, in its temporary independence, was never designated a State. The new ones only took the designation of States, on coming into the Union, while that name was first adopted for the old ones, in, and by, the Declaration of Independence. Therein the "United Colonies" were declared to be "Free and Independent States"; but, even then, the object plainly was not to declare their independence of *one another*, or of the *Union;* but directly the contrary, as their mutual pledge, and their mutual action, before, at the time, and afterwards, abundantly show. The express plighting of faith, by each and all of the original thirteen, in the Articles of Confederation, two years later, that the Union shall be perpetual, is most conclusive. Having never been States, either in substance, or in name, *outside* of the Union, whence this magical omnipotence of "State rights," asserting a claim of power to lawfully destroy the Union itself? Much is said about the "sovereignty" of the States; but the word, even, is not in the national Constitution; nor, as is believed, in any of the State constitutions. What is a "sovereignty," in the political sense of the term? Would it be far wrong to define it "A political community, without a political superior"? Tested by this, no one of our States, except Texas, ever was a sovereignty. And even Texas gave up the character on coming into the Union; by which act, she acknowledged the Constitution of the United States, and the laws and treaties of the United States made in pursuance of the Constitution, to be, for her, the supreme law of the land. The States have their *status* IN the Union, and they have no other *legal status*. If they break from this, they can only do so against law, and by revolution. The Union, and not themselves separately, procured their independence, and their liberty. By conquest, or purchase, the Union gave each of them, whatever of independence, and liberty, it has. The Union is older than any of the States; and, in fact, it created them as States. Originally, some dependent colonies made the Union; and, in turn, the Union threw off their old dependence, for them, and made them States, such as they are. Not one of them ever had a State constitution, independent of the Union. Of course, it is not forgotten that all the new States framed their constitutions, before they entered the Union; nevertheless, dependent upon, and preparatory to, coming into the Union.

Unquestionably the States have the powers, and rights, reserved to them in, and by the National Constitution; but among these, surely, are not included all conceivable powers, however mischievous, or destructive; but, at most, such only, as were known in the world, at the time, as governmental powers; and certainly, a power to destroy the government itself, had never been known as a governmental—as a merely administrative power. This relative matter of National power, and State rights, as a principle, is no other than the principle of *generality*, and *locality*.

Whatever concerns the whole, should be confided to the whole—to the general government; while, whatever concerns *only* the State, should be left exclusively, to the State. This is all there is of original principle about it. Whether the National Constitution, in defining boundaries between the two, has applied the principle with exact accuracy, is not to be questioned. We are all bound by that defining, without question.

What is now combatted, is the position that secession is *consistent* with the Constitution—is *lawful*, and *peaceful*. It is not contended that there is any express law for it; and nothing should ever be implied as law, which leads to unjust, or absurd consequences. The nation purchased, with money, the countries out of which several of these States were formed. Is it just that they shall go off without leave, and without refunding? The nation paid very large sums, (in the aggregate, I believe, nearly a hundred millions) to relieve Florida of the aboriginal tribes. Is it just that she shall now be off without consent, or without making any return? The nation is now in debt for money applied to the benefit of these so-called seceding States, in common with the rest. Is it just, either that creditors shall go unpaid, or the remaining States pay the whole? A part of the present national debt was contracted to pay the old debts of Texas. Is it just that she shall leave, and pay no part of this herself?

Again, if one State may secede, so may another; and when all shall have seceded, none is left to pay the debts. Is this quite just to creditors? Did we notify them of this sage view of ours, when we borrowed their money? If we now recognize this doctrine, by allowing the seceders to go in peace, it is difficult to see what we can do, if others choose to go, or to extort terms upon which they will promise to remain.

The seceders insist that our Constitution admits of secession. They have assumed to make a National Constitution of their own, in which, of necessity, they have either *discarded*, or *retained*, the right of secession, as they insist, it exists in ours. If they have discarded it, they thereby admit that, on principle, it ought not to be in ours. If they have retained it, by their own construction of ours they show that to be consistent they must secede from one another, whenever they shall find it the easiest way of settling their debts, or effecting any other selfish, or unjust object. The principle itself is one of disintegration, and upon which no government can possibly endure.

If all the States, save one, should assert the power to *drive* that one out of the Union, it is presumed the whole class of seceder politicians would at once deny the power, and denounce the act as the greatest outrage upon State rights. But suppose that precisely the same act, instead of being called "driving the one out," should be called "the seceding of the others from that one," it would be exactly what the seceders claim to do; unless, indeed, they make the point, that the one, because it is a minority, may rightfully do, what the others, because they are a majority, may not rightfully do. These politicians are subtle, and profound, on the rights of minorities. They are not partial to that power which made the Constitution, and speaks from the preamble, calling itself "We, the People."

It may well be questioned whether there is, to-day, a majority of the legally qualified voters of any State, except perhaps South Carolina, in favor of disunion. There is much reason to believe that the Union men are the majority in many, if not in every other one, of the so-called seceded States. The contrary has not been demonstrated in any one of them. It is ventured to affirm this, even of Virginia and Tennessee; for the result of an election, held in military camps, where the bayonets are all on one side of the question voted upon, can scarcely be considered as demonstrating popular sentiment. At such an election, all that large class who are, at once, *for* the Union, and *against* coercion, would be coerced to vote against the Union.

It may be affirmed, without extravagance, that the free

institutions we enjoy, have developed the powers, and improved the condition, of our whole people, beyond any example in the world. Of this we now have a striking, and an impressive illustration. So large an army as the government has now on foot, was never before known, without a soldier in it, but who had taken his place there, of his own free choice. But more than this: there are many single Regiments whose members, one and another, possess full practical knowledge of all the arts, sciences, professions, and whatever else, whether useful or elegant, is known in the world; and there is scarcely one, from which there could not be selected, a President, a Cabinet, a Congress, and perhaps a Court, abundantly competent to administer the government itself. Nor do I say this is not true, also, in the army of our late friends, now adversaries, in this contest; but if it is, so much better the reason why the government, which has conferred such benefits on both them and us, should not be broken up. Whoever, in any section, proposes to abandon such a government, would do well to consider, in deference to what principle it is, that he does it—what better he is likely to get in its stead—whether the substitute will give, or be intended to give, so much of good to the people. There are some fore shadowings on this subject. Our adversaries have adopted some Declarations of Independence; in which, unlike the good old one, penned by Jefferson, they omit the words "all men are created equal." Why? They have adopted a temporary national constitution, in the preamble of which, unlike our good old one, signed by Washington, they omit "We, the People," and substitute "We, the deputies of the sovereign and independent States." Why? Why this deliberate pressing out of view, the rights of men, and the authority of the people?

This is essentially a People's contest. On the side of the Union, it is a struggle for maintaining in the world, that form, and substance of government, whose leading object is, to elevate the condition of men—to lift artificial weights from all shoulders—to clear the paths of laudable pursuit for all—to afford all, an unfettered start, and a fair chance, in the race of life. Yielding to partial, and temporary departures, from necessity, this is the leading object of the government for whose existence we contend.

I am most happy to believe that the plain people understand, and appreciate this. It is worthy of note, that while in this, the government's hour of trial, large numbers of those in the Army and Navy, who have been favored with the offices, have resigned, and proved false to the hand which had pampered them, not one common soldier, or common sailor is known to have deserted his flag.

Great honor is due to those officers who remain true, despite the example of their treacherous associates; but the greatest honor, and most important fact of all, is the unanimous firmness of the common soldiers, and common sailors. To the last man, so far as known, they have successfully resisted the traitorous efforts of those, whose commands, but an hour before, they obeyed as absolute law. This is the patriotic instinct of the plain people. They understand, without an argument, that destroying the government, which was made by Washington, means no good to them.

Our popular government has often been called an experiment. Two points in it, our people have already settled—the successful *establishing*, and the successful *administering* of it. One still remains—its successful *maintenance* against a formidable internal attempt to overthrow it. It is now for them to demonstrate to the world, that those who can fairly carry an election, can also suppress a rebellion—that ballots are the rightful, and peaceful, successors of bullets; and that when ballots have fairly, and constitutionally, decided, there can be no successful appeal, back to bullets; that there can be no successful appeal, except to ballots themselves, at succeeding elections. Such will be a great lesson of peace; teaching men that what they cannot take by an election, neither can they take it by a war—teaching all, the folly of being the beginners of a war.

Lest there be some uneasiness in the minds of candid men, as to what is to be the course of the government, towards the Southern States, *after* the rebellion shall have been suppressed, the Executive deems it proper to say, it will be his purpose then, as ever, to be guided by the Constitution, and the laws; and that he probably will have no different understanding of the powers, and duties of the Federal government, relatively to the rights of the States, and the people, under the Constitution, than that expressed in the inaugural address.

He desires to preserve the government, that it may be administered for all, as it was administered by the men who made it. Loyal citizens everywhere, have the right to claim this of their government; and the government has no right to withhold, or neglect it. It is not perceived that, in giving it, there is any coercion, any conquest, or any subjugation, in any just sense of those terms.

The Constitution provides, and all the States have accepted the provision, that "The United States shall guarantee to every State in this Union a republican form of government." But, if a State may lawfully go out of the Union, having done so, it may also discard the republican form of government; so that to prevent its going out, is an indispensable *means*, to the *end*, of maintaining the guaranty mentioned; and when an end is lawful and obligatory, the indispensable means to it, are also lawful, and obligatory.

It was with the deepest regret that the Executive found the duty of employing the war-power, in defence of the government, forced upon him. He could but perform this duty, or surrender the existence of the government. No compromise, by public servants, could, in this case, be a cure; not that compromises are not often proper, but that no popular government can long survive a marked precedent, that those who carry an election, can only save the government from immediate destruction, by giving up the main point, upon which the people gave the election. The people themselves, and not their servants, can safely reverse their own deliberate decisions. As a private citizen, the Executive could not have consented that these institutions shall perish; much less could he, in betrayal of so vast, and so sacred a trust, as these free people had confided to him. He felt that he had no moral right to shrink; nor even to count the chances of his own life, in what might follow. In full view of his great responsibility, he has, so far, done what he has deemed his duty. You will now, according to your own judgment, perform yours. He sincerely hopes that your views, and your action, may so accord with his, as to assure all faithful citizens, who have been disturbed in their rights, of a certain, and speedy restoration to them, under the Constitution, and the laws.

And having thus chosen our course, without guile, and with pure purpose, let us renew our trust in God, and go forward without fear, and with manly hearts.

July 4, 1861.

Memoranda on Military Policy

July 23. 1861.

1. Let the plan for making the Blockade effective be pushed forward with all possible despatch.

2. Let the volunteer forces at Fort-Monroe & vicinity— under Genl. Butler—be constantly drilled, disciplined, and instructed without more for the present.

3. Let Baltimore be held, as now, with a gentle, but firm, and certain hand.

4. Let the force now under Patterson, or Banks, be strengthened, and made secure in it's position.

5. Let the forces in Western Virginia act, till further orders, according to instructions, or orders from Gen. McClellan.

6. Gen. Fremont push forward his organization, and operations in the West as rapidly as possible, giving rather special attention to Missouri.

7. Let the forces late before Manassas, except the three months men, be reorganized as rapidly as possible, in their camps here and about Arlington.

8. Let the three months forces, who decline to enter the longer service, be discharged as rapidly as circumstances will permit.

9. Let the new volunteer forces be brought forward as fast as possible; and especially into the camps on the two sides of the river here.

July 27, 1861

When the foregoing shall have been substantially attended to—

1. Let Manassas junction, (or some point on one or other of the railroads near it;); and Strasburg, be seized, and permanently held, with an open line from Washington to Manassas; and an open line from Harper's Ferry to Strasburg—the military men to find the way of doing these.

2. This done, a joint movement from Cairo on Memphis; and from Cincinnati on East Tennessee.

To John C. Frémont

Private and confidential.

Washington D. C. Sept. 2, 1861.

Major General Fremont:

My dear Sir: Two points in your proclamation of August 30th give me some anxiety. First, should you shoot a man, according to the proclamation, the Confederates would very certainly shoot our best man in their hands in retaliation; and so, man for man, indefinitely. It is therefore my order that you allow no man to be shot, under the proclamation, without first having my approbation or consent.

Secondly, I think there is great danger that the closing paragraph, in relation to the confiscation of property, and the liberating slaves of traiterous owners, will alarm our Southern Union friends, and turn them against us—perhaps ruin our rather fair prospect for Kentucky. Allow me therefore to ask, that you will as of your own motion, modify that paragraph so as to conform to the *first* and *fourth* sections of the act of Congress, entitled, "An act to confiscate property used for insurrectionary purposes," approved August, 6th, 1861, and a copy of which act I herewith send you. This letter is written in a spirit of caution and not of censure.

I send it by a special messenger, in order that it may certainly and speedily reach you. Yours very truly

Copy of letter sent to Gen. Fremont, by special messenger leaving Washington Sep. 3. 1861.

Drafts of Bill for Compensated Emancipation in Delaware

Be it enacted by the State of Delaware, that on condition the United States of America will, at the present session of Congress, engage by law to pay, and thereafter faithfully pay to the said State of Delaware, in the six per cent bonds of said United States, the sum of seven hundred and nineteen thousand and two hundred dollars, in five equal annual instalments, there shall be neither slavery nor involuntary servitude, at any time after the first day of January in the year of our Lord one thousand, eight hundred and sixtyseven, within the said State of Delaware, except in the punishment of crime, whereof the party shall have been duly convicted: *Provided*, that said State shall, in good faith prevent, so far as possible, the carrying of any person out of said State, into involuntary servitude, beyond the limits of said State, at any time after the passage of this act; and shall also provide for one fifth of the adult slavery becoming free at the middle of the year one thousand eight hundred and sixtytwo; one fourth of the remainder of said adults, at the middle of the year one thousand eight hundred and sixtythree; one third of the remainder of said adults, at the middle of the year one thousand eight hundred and sixtyfour; one half the remainder of said adults at the middle of the year one thousand eight hundred and sixtyfive; and the entire remainder of adults, together with all minors, at the beginning of the year one thousand eight hundred and sixtyseven, as hereinbefore indicated. And *provided* also that said State may make provision of apprenticeship, not to extend beyond the age of twenty-one years for males, nor eighteen for females, for all minors whose mothers were not free, at the respective births of such minors.

Be it enacted by the State of Delaware that on condition the United States of America will, at the present session of Congress, engage by law to pay, and thereafter faithfully pay to the said State of Delaware, in the six per cent bonds of said United States, the sum of seven hundred and nineteen thousand, and two hundred dollars, in thirty one equal annual instalments, there shall be neither slavery nor involuntary servitude, at any time after the first day of January in the year of our Lord one thousand eight hundred and ninety three, within the said State of Delaware, except in the punishment of crime, whereof the party shall have been duly convicted; nor, except in the punishment of crime as aforesaid, shall any person who shall be born after the passage of this act, nor any person above the age of thirty five years, be held in slavery, or to involuntary servitude, within said State of Delaware, at any time after the passage of this act.

And be it further enacted that said State shall, in good faith prevent, so far as possible, the carrying of any person out of said state, into involuntary servitude, beyond the limits of said State, at any time after the passage of this act.

And be it further enacted that said State may make provision of apprenticeship, not to extend beyond the age of twentyone years for males, nor eighteen for females, for all minors whose mothers were not free at the respective births of such minors.

On reflection, I like No. 2 the better. By it the Nation would pay the State $23,200 per annum for thirtyone years—and

All born after the passage of the act would be born free—and

All slaves above the age of 35 years would become free on the passage of the act—and

All others would become free on arriving at the age of 35 years, until January 1893—when

All remaining of all ages would become free, subject to apprenticeship for minors born of slave mothers, up to the respective ages of 21 and 18.

If the State would desire to have the money sooner, let the bill be altered only in fixing the time of final emancipation earlier, and making the annual instalments correspondingly fewer in number, by which they would also be correspondingly larger in amount. For instance, strike out "1893," and insert "1872"; and strike out "thirtyone" annual instalments, and insert "ten" annual instalments. The instalments would then be $71,920 instead of $23,200 as now. In all other particulars let the bill stand precisely as it is.

c. late November 1861

Annual Message to Congress

Fellow Citizens of the Senate and House of Representatives:

In the midst of unprecedented political troubles, we have cause of great gratitude to God for unusual good health, and most abundant harvests.

You will not be surprised to learn that, in the peculiar exigencies of the times, our intercourse with foreign nations has been attended with profound solicitude, chiefly turning upon our own domestic affairs.

A disloyal portion of the American people have, during the whole year, been engaged in an attempt to divide and destroy the Union. A nation which endures factious domestic division, is exposed to disrespect abroad; and one party, if not both, is sure, sooner or later, to invoke foreign intervention.

Nations, thus tempted to interfere, are not always able to resist the counsels of seeming expediency, and ungenerous ambition, although measures adopted under such influences seldom fail to be unfortunate and injurious to those adopting them.

The disloyal citizens of the United States who have offered the ruin of our country, in return for the aid and comfort which they have invoked abroad, have received less patronage and encouragement than they probably expected. If it were just to suppose, as the insurgents have seemed to assume, that foreign nations, in this case, discarding all moral, social, and treaty obligations, would act solely, and selfishly, for the most speedy restoration of commerce, including, especially, the acquisition of cotton, those nations appear, as yet, not to have seen their way to their object more directly, or clearly, through the destruction, than through the preservation, of the Union. If we could dare to believe that foreign nations are actuated by no higher principle than this, I am quite sure a sound argument could be made to show them that they can reach their aim more readily, and easily, by aiding to crush this rebellion, than by giving encouragement to it.

The principal lever relied on by the insurgents for exciting foreign nations to hostility against us, as already intimated, is the embarrassment of commerce. Those nations, however, not improbably, saw from the first, that it was the Union which made as well our foreign, as our domestic, commerce. They can scarcely have failed to perceive that the effort for disunion produces the existing difficulty; and that one strong nation promises more durable peace, and a more extensive, valuable and reliable commerce, than can the same nation broken into hostile fragments.

It is not my purpose to review our discussions with foreign states, because whatever might be their wishes, or dispositions, the integrity of our country, and the stability of our government, mainly depend, not upon them, but on the loyalty, virtue, patriotism, and intelligence of the American people. The correspondence itself, with the usual reservations, is herewith submitted.

I venture to hope it will appear that we have practiced prudence, and liberality towards foreign powers, averting causes of irritation; and, with firmness, maintaining our own rights and honor.

Since, however, it is apparent that here, as in every other state, foreign dangers necessarily attend domestic difficulties, I recommend that adequate and ample measures be adopted for maintaining the public defences on every side. While, under this general recommendation, provision for defending our sea-coast line readily occurs to the mind, I also, in the same connexion, ask the attention of Congress to our great lakes and rivers. It is believed that some fortifications and depots of arms and munitions, with harbor and navigation improvements, all at well selected points upon these, would be of great importance to the national defence and preservation. I ask attention to the views of the Secretary of War, expressed in his report, upon the same general subject.

I deem it of importance that the loyal regions of East Tennessee and western North Carolina should be connected with Kentucky, and other faithful parts of the Union, by railroad. I therefore recommend, as a military measure, that Congress provide for the construction of such road, as speedily as possible. Kentucky, no doubt, will co-operate, and, through her legislature, make the most judicious selection of a line. The northern terminus must connect with some existing railroad; and whether the route shall be from Lexington, or Nicholasville, to the Cumberland Gap; or from Lebanon to the Tennessee line, in the direction of Knoxville; or on some still different line, can easily be determined. Kentucky and the general government co-operating, the work can be completed in a very short time; and when done, it will be not only of vast present usefulness, but also a valuable permanent improvement, worth its cost in all the future.

Some treaties, designed chiefly for the interests of commerce, and having no grave political importance, have been negotiated, and will be submitted to the Senate for their consideration.

Although we have failed to induce some of the commercial powers to adopt a desirable melioration of the rigor of maritime war, we have removed all obstructions from the way of this humane reform, except such as are merely of temporary and accidental occurrence.

I invite your attention to the correspondence between her Britannic Majesty's minister accredited to this government, and the Secretary of State, relative to the detention of the

British ship Perthshire in June last, by the United States
steamer Massachusetts, for a supposed breach of the blockade. As this detention was occasioned by an obvious misap-
prehension of the facts, and as justice requires that we
should commit no belligerent act not founded in strict right,
as sanctioned by public law, I recommend that an appropriation be made to satisfy the reasonable demand of the owners of the vessel for her detention.

I repeat the recommendation of my predecessor, in his
annual message to Congress in December last, in regard to
the disposition of the surplus which will probably remain
after satisfying the claims of American citizens against
China, pursuant to the awards of the commissioners under
the act of the 3rd of March, 1859. If, however, it should
not be deemed advisable to carry that recommendation into
effect, I would suggest that authority be given for investing
the principal, over the proceeds of the surplus referred to,
in good securities, with a view to the satisfaction of such
other just claims of our citizens against China as are not
unlikely to arise hereafter in the course of our extensive trade
with that Empire.

By the act of the 5th of August last, Congress authorized
the President to instruct the commanders of suitable vessels
to defend themselves against, and to capture pirates. This
authority has been exercised in a single instance only. For
the more effectual protection of our extensive and valuable
commerce, in the eastern seas especially, it seems to me that
it would also be advisable to authorize the commanders of
sailing vessels to re-capture any prizes which pirates might
make of United States vessels and their cargoes, and the
consular courts, now established by law in eastern countries,
to adjudicate the cases, in the event that this should not be
objected to by the local authorities.

If any good reason exists why we should persevere longer
in withholding our recognition of the independence and sovereignty of Hayti and Liberia, I am unable to discern it.

Unwilling, however, to inaugurate a novel policy in regard to them without the approbation of Congress, I submit for your consideration the expediency of an appropriation for maintaining a chargé d'affaires near each of those new states. It does not admit of doubt that important commercial advantages might be secured by favorable commercial treaties with them.

The operations of the treasury during the period which has elapsed since your adjournment have been conducted with signal success. The patriotism of the people has placed at the disposal of the government the large means demanded by the public exigencies. Much of the national loan has been taken by citizens of the industrial classes, whose confidence in their country's faith, and zeal for their country's deliverance from present peril, have induced them to contribute to the support of the government the whole of their limited acquisitions. This fact imposes peculiar obligations to economy in disbursement and energy in action.

The revenue from all sources, including loans, for the financial year ending on the 30th June, 1861, was eighty six million, eight hundred and thirty five thousand, nine hundred dollars, and twenty seven cents, ($86,835,900.27,) and the expenditures for the same period, including payments on account of the public debt, were eighty four million, five hundred and seventy eight thousand, eight hundred and thirty four dollars and forty seven cents, ($84,578,834.47;) leaving a balance in the treasury, on the 1st July, of two million, two hundred and fifty seven thousand, sixty five dollars and eighty cents, ($2,257,065.80.) For the first quarter of the financial year, ending on the 30th September, 1861, the receipts from all sources, including the balance of first of July, were $102,532,509.27, and the expenses $98,239,733.09; leaving a balance on the 1st of October, 1861, of $4,292,776.18.

Estimates for the remaining three quarters of the year, and for the financial year 1863, together with his views of

ways and means for meeting the demands contemplated by
them, will be submitted to Congress by the Secretary of the
Treasury. It is gratifying to know that the expenditures
made necessary by the rebellion are not beyond the resources
of the loyal people, and to believe that the same patriotism
which has thus far sustained the government will continue to
sustain it till Peace and Union shall again bless the land.

I respectfully refer to the report of the Secretary of War
for information respecting the numerical strength of the
army, and for recommendations having in view an increase
of its efficiency and the well being of the various branches
of the service intrusted to his care. It is gratifying to know
that the patriotism of the people has proved equal to the
occasion, and that the number of troops tendered greatly
exceeds the force which Congress authorized me to call into
the field.

I refer with pleasure to those portions of his report which
make allusion to the creditable degree of discipline already
attained by our troops, and to the excellent sanitary condition of the entire army.

The recommendation of the Secretary for an organization
of the militia upon a uniform basis, is a subject of vital
importance to the future safety of the country, and is com-
mended to the serious attention of Congress.

The large addition to the regular army, in connexion with
the defection that has so considerably diminished the number
of its officers, gives peculiar importance to his recommendation for increasing the corps of cadets to the greatest capacity of the Military Academy.

By mere omission, I presume, Congress has failed to
provide chaplains for hospitals occupied by volunteers. This
subject was brought to my notice, and I was induced to
draw up the form of a letter, one copy of which, properly
addressed, has been delivered to each of the persons, and
at the dates respectively named and stated, in a schedule,

containing also the form of the letter, marked A, and herewith transmitted.

These gentlemen, I understand, entered upon the duties designated, at the times respectively stated in the schedule, and have labored faithfully therein ever since. I therefore recommend that they be compensated at the same rate as chaplains in the army. I further suggest that general provision be made for chaplains to serve at hospitals, as well as with regiments.

The report of the Secretary of the Navy presents in detail the operations of that branch of the service, the activity and energy which have characterized its administration, and the results of measures to increase its efficiency and power. Such have been the additions, by construction and purchase, that it may almost be said a navy has been created and brought into service since our difficulties commenced.

Besides blockading our extensive coast, squadrons larger than ever before assembled under our flag have been put afloat and performed deeds which have increased our naval renown.

I would invite special attention to the recommendation of the Secretary for a more perfect organization of the navy by introducing additional grades in the service.

The present organization is defective and unsatisfactory, and the suggestions submitted by the department will, it is believed, if adopted, obviate the difficulties alluded to, promote harmony, and increase the efficiency of the navy.

There are three vacancies on the bench of the Supreme Court—two by the decease of Justices Daniel and McLean, and one by the resignation of Justice Campbell. I have so far forborne making nominations to fill these vacancies for reasons which I will now state. Two of the outgoing judges resided within the States now overrun by revolt; so that if successors were appointed in the same localities, they could not now serve upon their circuits; and many of the most competent men there, probably would not take the personal hazard of accepting to serve, even here, upon the supreme bench. I have been unwilling to throw all the appointments northward, thus disabling myself from doing justice to the south on the return of peace; although I may remark that to transfer to the north one which has heretofore been in the south, would not, with reference to territory and population, be unjust.

During the long and brilliant judicial career of Judge McLean his circuit grew into an empire—altogether too large for any one judge to give the courts therein more than a nominal attendance—rising in population from one million four hundred and seventy-thousand and eighteen, in 1830, to six million one hundred and fifty-one thousand four hundred and five, in 1860.

Besides this, the country generally has outgrown our present judicial system. If uniformity was at all intended, the system requires that all the States shall be accommodated with circuit courts, attended by supreme judges, while, in fact, Wisconsin, Minnesota, Iowa, Kansas, Florida, Texas, California, and Oregon, have never had any such courts. Nor can this well be remedied without a change of the system; because the adding of judges to the Supreme Court, enough for the accommodation of all parts of the country, with circuit courts, would create a court altogether too numerous for a judicial body of any sort. And the evil, if it be one, will increase as new States come into the Union. Circuit courts are useful, or they are not useful. If useful, no State should be denied them; if not useful, no State should have them. Let them be provided for all, or abolished as to all.

Three modifications occur to me, either of which, I think, would be an improvement upon our present system. Let the Supreme Court be of convenient number in every event. Then, first, let the whole country be divided into circuits of convenient size, the supreme judges to serve in a number of them corresponding to their own number, and independent circuit judges be provided for all the rest. Or, secondly, let the supreme judges be relieved from circuit duties, and circuit judges provided for all the circuits. Or, thirdly, dispense with circuit courts altogether, leaving the judicial functions wholly to the district courts and an independent Supreme Court.

I respectfully recommend to the consideration of Congress the present condition of the statute laws, with the hope that Congress will be able to find an easy remedy for many of the inconveniences and evils which constantly embarrass those engaged in the practical administration of them. Since the organization of the government, Congress has enacted some five thousand acts and joint resolutions, which fill more than six thousand closely printed pages, and are scattered through many volumes. Many of these acts have been drawn in haste and without sufficient caution, so that their provisions are often obscure in themselves, or in conflict with each other, or at least so doubtful as to render it very difficult for even the best informed persons to ascertain precisely what the statute law really is.

It seems to me very important that the statute laws should be made as plain and intelligible as possible, and be reduced to as small a compass as may consist with the fullness and precision of the will of the legislature and the perspicuity of its language. This, well done, would, I think, greatly facilitate the labors of those whose duty it is to assist in the administration of the laws, and would be a lasting benefit to the people, by placing before them, in a more accessible and intelligible form, the laws which so deeply concern their interests and their duties.

I am informed by some whose opinions I respect, that all the acts of Congress now in force, and of a permanent and general nature, might be revised and re-written, so as to be embraced in one volume (or at most, two volumes) of ordinary and convenient size. And I respectfully recommend to

Congress to consider of the subject, and, if my suggestion be approved, to devise such plan as to their wisdom shall seem most proper for the attainment of the end proposed.

One of the unavoidable consequences of the present insurrection is the entire suppression, in many places, of all the ordinary means of administering civil justice by the officers and in the forms of existing law. This is the case, in whole or in part, in all the insurgent States; and as our armies advance upon and take possession of parts of those States, the practical evil becomes more apparent. There are no courts nor officers to whom the citizens of other States may apply for the enforcement of their lawful claims against citizens of the insurgent States; and there is a vast amount of debt constituting such claims. Some have estimated it as high as two hundred million dollars, due, in large part, from insurgents, in open rebellion, to loyal citizens who are, even now, making great sacrifices in the discharge of their patriotic duty to support the government.

Under these circumstances, I have been urgently solicited to establish, by military power, courts to administer summary justice in such cases. I have thus far declined to do it, not because I had any doubt that the end proposed— the collection of the debts—was just and right in itself, but because I have been unwilling to go beyond the pressure of necessity in the unusual exercise of power. But the powers of Congress I suppose are equal to the anomalous occasion, and therefore I refer the whole matter to Congress, with the hope that a plan may be devised for the administration of justice in all such parts of the insurgent States and Territories as may be under the control of this government, whether by a voluntary return to allegiance and order or by the power of our arms. This, however, not to be a permanent institution, but a temporary substitute, and to cease as soon as the ordinary courts can be re-established in peace.

It is important that some more convenient means should be provided, if possible, for the adjustment of claims against the government, especially in view of their increased number by reason of the war. It is as much the duty of government to render prompt justice against itself, in favor of citizens, as it is to administer the same, between private individuals. The investigation and adjudication of claims, in their nature belong to the judicial department; besides it is apparent that the attention of Congress, will be more than usually engaged, for some time to come, with great national questions. It was intended, by the organization of the court of claims, mainly to remove this branch of business from the halls of Congress; but while the court has proved to be an effective, and valuable means of investigation, it in great degree fails to effect the object of its creation, for want of power to make its judgments final.

Fully aware of the delicacy, not to say the danger, of the subject, I commend to your careful consideration whether this power of making judgments final, may not properly be given to the court, reserving the right of appeal on questions of law to the Supreme Court, with such other provisions as experience may have shown to be necessary.

I ask attention to the report of the Postmaster General, the following being a summary statement of the condition of the department:

The revenue from all sources during the fiscal year ending June 30. 1861, including the annual permanent appropriation of seven hundred thousand dollars ($700,000) for the transportation of "free mail matter," was nine million, forty nine thousand, two hundred and ninety six dollars and forty cents ($9,049,296.40) being about two per cent. less than the revenue for 1860.

The expenditures were thirteen million, six hundred and six thousand, seven hundred and fifty nine dollars and eleven cents. ($13,606,759.11) showing a decrease of more than eight per cent. as compared with those of the previous year, and leaving an excess of expenditure over the revenue for the last fiscal year of four million, five hundred and fifty seven thousand, four hundred and sixty two dollars and seventy one cents ($4,557,462.71.)

The gross revenue for the year ending June 30, 1863, is estimated at an increase of four per cent. on that of 1861, making eight million, six hundred and eighty three thousand dollars ($8,683,000) to which should be added the earnings of the department in carrying free matter, viz: seven hundred thousand dollars ($700,000.) making nine million, three hundred and eighty three thousand dollars, ($9,383,000.)

The total expenditures for 1863 are estimated at $12,528,000, leaving an estimated deficiency of $3,145,000, to be supplied from the treasury, in addition to the permanent appropriation.

The present insurrection shows, I think, that the extension of this District across the Potomac river, at the time of establishing the capital here, was eminently wise, and consequently that the relinquishment of that portion of it which lies within the State of Virginia was unwise and dangerous. I submit for your consideration the expediency of regaining that part of the District, and the restoration of the original boundaries thereof, through negotiations with the State of Virginia.

The report of the Secretary of the Interior, with the accompanying documents, exhibits the condition of the several branches of the public business pertaining to that department. The depressing influences of the insurrection have been especially felt in the operations of the Patent and General Land Offices. The cash receipts from the sales of public lands during the past year have exceeded the expenses of our land system only about $200,000. The sales have been entirely suspended in the southern States, while the interruptions to the business of the country, and the diversion of large numbers of men from labor to military service, have obstructed settlements in the new States and Territories of the northwest.

The receipts of the Patent Office have declined in nine

months about $100,000, rendering a large reduction of the force employed necessary to make it self sustaining.

The demands upon the Pension Office will be largely increased by the insurrection. Numerous applications for pensions, based upon the casualties of the existing war, have already been made. There is reason to believe that many who are now upon the pension rolls and in receipt of the bounty of the government, are in the ranks of the insurgent army, or giving them aid and comfort. The Secretary of the Interior has directed a suspension of the payment of the pensions of such persons upon proof of their disloyalty. I recommend that Congress authorize that officer to cause the names of such persons to be stricken from the pension rolls.

The relations of the government with the Indian tribes have been greatly disturbed by the insurrection, especially in the southern superintendency and in that of New Mexico. The Indian country south of Kansas is in the possession of insurgents from Texas and Arkansas. The agents of the United States appointed since the 4th. of March for this superintendency have been unable to reach their posts, while the most of those who were in office before that time have espoused the insurrectionary cause, and assume to exercise the powers of agents by virtue of commissions from the insurrectionists. It has been stated in the public press that a portion of those Indians have been organized as a military force, and are attached to the army of the insurgents. Although the government has no official information upon this subject, letters have been written to the Commissioner of Indian Affairs by several prominent chiefs, giving assurance of their loyalty to the United States, and expressing a wish for the presence of federal troops to protect them. It is believed that upon the repossession of the country by the federal forces the Indians will readily cease all hostile demonstrations, and resume their former relations to the government.

Agriculture, confessedly the largest interest of the nation, has, not a department, nor a bureau, but a clerkship only, assigned to it in the government. While it is fortunate that this great interest is so independent in its nature as to not have demanded and extorted more from the government, I respectfully ask Congress to consider whether something more cannot be given voluntarily with general advantage.

Annual reports exhibiting the condition of our agriculture, commerce, and manufactures would present a fund of information of great practical value to the country. While I make no suggestion as to details, I venture the opinion that an agricultural and statistical bureau might profitably be organized.

The execution of the laws for the suppression of the African slave trade, has been confided to the Department of the Interior. It is a subject of gratulation that the efforts which have been made for the suppression of this inhuman traffic, have been recently attended with unusual success. Five vessels being fitted out for the slave trade have been seized and condemned. Two mates of vessels engaged in the trade, and one person in equipping a vessel as a slaver, have been convicted and subjected to the penalty of fine and imprisonment, and one captain, taken with a cargo of Africans on board his vessel, has been convicted of the highest grade of offence under our laws, the punishment of which is death.

The Territories of Colorado, Dakotah and Nevada, created by the last Congress, have been organized, and civil administration has been inaugurated therein under auspices especially gratifying, when it is considered that the leaven of treason was found existing in some of these new countries when the federal officers arrived there.

The abundant natural resources of these Territories, with the security and protection afforded by organized government, will doubtless invite to them a large immigration when peace shall restore the business of the country to its accustomed channels. I submit the resolutions of the legislature of Colorado, which evidence the patriotic spirit of the people of the Territory. So far the authority of the United States has been upheld in all the Territories, as it is hoped it will be in the future. I commend their interests and defence to the enlightened and generous care of Congress.

I recommend to the favorable consideration of Congress the interests of the District of Columbia. The insurrection has been the cause of much suffering and sacrifice to its inhabitants, and as they have no representative in Congress, that body should not overlook their just claims upon the government.

At your late session a joint resolution was adopted authorizing the President to take measures for facilitating a proper representation of the industrial interests of the United States at the exhibition of the industry of all nations to be holden at London in the year 1862. I regret to say I have been unable to give personal attention to this subject,—a subject at once so interesting in itself, and so extensively and intimately connected with the material prosperity of the world. Through the Secretaries of State and of the Interior a plan, or system, has been devised, and partly matured, and which will be laid before you.

Under and by virtue of the act of Congress entitled "An act to confiscate property used for insurrectionary purposes," approved August, 6, 1861, the legal claims of certain persons to the labor and service of certain other persons have become forfeited; and numbers of the latter, thus liberated, are already dependent on the United States, and must be provided for in some way. Besides this, it is not impossible that some of the States will pass similar enactments for their own benefit respectively, and by operation of which persons of the same class will be thrown upon them for disposal. In such case I recommend that Congress provide for accepting such persons from such States, according to some mode of valuation, in lieu, *pro tanto*, of direct taxes, or upon some other plan to be agreed on with such States respectively; that such persons, on such acceptance by the general government, be at once deemed free; and that, in any event, steps be taken for colonizing both classes, (or the one first mentioned, if the other shall not be brought into existence,) at some place, or places, in a climate congenial to them. It might be well to consider, too,—whether the free colored people already in the United States could not, so far as individuals may desire, be included in such colonization.

To carry out the plan of colonization may involve the acquiring of territory, and also the appropriation of money beyond that to be expended in the territorial acquisition. Having practiced the acquisition of territory for nearly sixty years, the question of constitutional power to do so is no longer an open one with us. The power was questioned at first by Mr. Jefferson, who, however, in the purchase of Louisiana, yielded his scruples on the plea of great expediency. If it be said that the only legitimate object of acquiring territory is to furnish homes for white men, this measure effects that object; for the emigration of colored men leaves additional room for white men remaining or coming here. Mr. Jefferson, however, placed the importance of procuring Louisiana more on political and commercial grounds than on providing room for population.

On this whole proposition,—including the appropriation of money with the acquisition of territory, does not the expediency amount to absolute necessity—that, without which the government itself cannot be perpetuated? The war continues. In considering the policy to be adopted for suppressing the insurrection, I have been anxious and careful that the inevitable conflict for this purpose shall not degenerate into a violent and remorseless revolutionary struggle. I have, therefore, in every case, thought it proper to keep the integrity of the Union prominent as the primary object of the contest on our part, leaving all questions which are not of vital military importance to the more deliberate action of the legislature.

In the exercise of my best discretion I have adhered to

the blockade of the ports held by the insurgents, instead of putting in force, by proclamation, the law of Congress enacted at the late session, for closing those ports.

So, also, obeying the dictates of prudence, as well as the obligations of law, instead of transcending, I have adhered to the act of Congress to confiscate property used for insurrectionary purposes. If a new law upon the same subject shall be proposed, its propriety will be duly considered.

The Union must be preserved, and hence, all indispensable means must be employed. We should not be in haste to determine that radical and extreme measures, which may reach the loyal as well as the disloyal, are indispensable.

The inaugural address at the beginning of the Administration, and the message to Congress at the late special session, were both mainly devoted to the domestic controversy out of which the insurrection and consequent war have sprung. Nothing now occurs to add or subtract, to or from, the principles or general purposes stated and expressed in those documents.

The last ray of hope for preserving the Union peaceably, expired at the assault upon Fort Sumter; and a general review of what has occurred since may not be unprofitable. What was painfully uncertain then, is much better defined and more distinct now; and the progress of events is plainly in the right direction. The insurgents confidently claimed a strong support from north of Mason and Dixon's line; and the friends of the Union were not free from apprehension on the point. This, however, was soon settled definitely and on the right side. South of the line, noble little Delaware led off right from the first. Maryland was made to *seem* against the Union. Our soldiers were assaulted, bridges were burned, and railroads torn up, within her limits; and we were many days, at one time, without the ability to bring a single regiment over her soil to the capital. Now, her bridges and railroads are repaired and open to the government; she already gives seven regiments to the cause of the Union and none to the enemy; and her people, at a regular election, have sustained the Union, by a larger majority, and a larger aggregate vote than they ever before gave to any candidate, or any question. Kentucky, too, for some time in doubt, is now decidedly, and, I think, unchangeably, ranged on the side of the Union. Missouri is comparatively quiet; and I believe cannot again be overrun by the insurrectionists. These three States of Maryland, Kentucky, and Missouri, neither of which would promise a single soldier at first, have now an aggregate of not less than forty thousand in the field, for the Union; while, of their citizens, certainly not more than a third of that number, and they of doubtful whereabouts, and doubtful existence, are in arms against it. After a somewhat bloody struggle of months, winter closes on the Union people of western Virginia, leaving them masters of their own country.

An insurgent force of about fifteen hundred, for months dominating the narrow peninsular region, constituting the counties of Accomac and Northampton, and known as eastern shore of Virginia, together with some contiguous parts of Maryland, have laid down their arms; and the people there have renewed their allegiance to, and accepted the protection of, the old flag. This leaves no armed insurrectionist north of the Potomac, or east of the Chesapeake.

Also we have obtained a footing at each of the isolated points, on the southern coast, of Hatteras, Port Royal, Tybee Island, near Savannah, and Ship Island; and we likewise have some general accounts of popular movements, in behalf of the Union, in North Carolina and Tennessee.

These things demonstrate that the cause of the Union is advancing steadily and certainly southward.

Since your last adjournment, Lieutenant General Scott has retired from the head of the army. During his long life, the nation has not been unmindful of his merit; yet, on calling to mind how faithfully, ably and brilliantly he has served the country, from a time far back in our history, when few of the now living had been born, and thenceforward continually, I cannot but think we are still his debtors. I submit, therefore, for your consideration, what further mark of recognition is due to him, and to ourselves, as a grateful people.

With the retirement of General Scott came the executive duty of appointing, in his stead, a general-in-chief of the army. It is a fortunate circumstance that neither in council nor country was there, so far as I know, any difference of opinion as to the proper person to be selected. The retiring chief repeatedly expressed his judgment in favor of General McClellan for the position; and in this the nation seemed to give a unanimous concurrence. The designation of General McClellan is therefore in considerable degree, the selection of the Country as well as of the Executive; and hence there is better reason to hope there will be given him, the confidence, and cordial support thus, by fair implication, promised, and without which, he cannot, with so full efficiency, serve the country.

It has been said that one bad general is better than two good ones; and the saying is true, if taken to mean no more than that an army is better directed by a single mind, though inferior, than by two superior ones, at variance, and crosspurposes with each other.

And the same is true, in all joint operations wherein those engaged, *can* have none but a common end in view, and *can* differ only as to the choice of means. In a storm at sea, no one on board *can* wish the ship to sink; and yet, not unfrequently, all go down together, because too many will direct, and no single mind can be allowed to control.

It continues to develop that the insurrection is largely, if not exclusively, a war upon the first principle of popular government—the rights of the people. Conclusive evidence of this is found in the most grave and maturely considered public documents, as well as in the general tone of the insurgents. In those documents we find the abridgement of the existing right of suffrage and the denial to the people of all right to participate in the selection of public officers, except the legislative boldly advocated, with labored arguments to prove that large control of the people in government, is the source of all political evil. Monarchy itself is sometimes hinted at as a possible refuge from the power of the people.

In my present position, I could scarcely be justified were I to omit raising a warning voice against this approach of returning despotism.

It is not needed, nor fitting here, that a general argument should be made in favor of popular institutions; but there is one point, with its connexions, not so hackneyed as most others, to which I ask a brief attention. It is the effort to place *capital* on an equal footing with, if not above *labor*, in the structure of government. It is assumed that labor is available only in connexion with capital; that nobody labors unless somebody else, owning capital, somehow by the use of it, induces him to labor. This assumed, it is next considered whether it is best that capital shall *hire* laborers, and thus induce them to work by their own consent, or *buy* them, and drive them to it without their consent. Having proceeded so far, it is naturally concluded that all laborers are either *hired* laborers, or what we call slaves. And further it is assumed that whoever is once a hired laborer, is fixed in that condition for life.

Now, there is no such relation between capital and labor as assumed; nor is there any such thing as a free man being fixed for life in the condition of a hired laborer. Both these assumptions are false, and all inferences from them are groundless.

Labor is prior to, and independent of, capital. Capital is only the fruit of labor, and could never have existed if labor had not first existed. Labor is the superior of capital, and deserves much the higher consideration. Capital has its rights, which are as worthy of protection as any other rights.

Nor is it denied that there is, and probably always will be, a relation between labor and capital, producing mutual benefits. The error is in assuming that the whole labor of community exists within that relation. A few men own capital, and that few avoid labor themselves, and, with their capital, hire or buy another few to labor for them. A large majority belong to neither class—neither work for others, nor have others working for them. In most of the southern States, a majority of the whole people of all colors are neither slaves nor masters; while in the northern a large majority are neither hirers nor hired. Men with their families—wives, sons, and daughters—work for themselves, on their farms, in their houses, and in their shops, taking the whole product to themselves, and asking no favors of capital on the one hand, nor of hired laborers or slaves on the other. It is not forgotten that a considerable number of persons mingle their own labor with capital—that is, they labor with their own hands, and also buy or hire others to labor for them; but this is only a mixed, and not a distinct class. No principle stated is disturbed by the existence of this mixed class.

Again: as has already been said, there is not, of necessity, any such thing as the free hired laborer being fixed to that condition for life. Many independent men everywhere in these States, a few years back in their lives, were hired laborers. The prudent, penniless beginner in the world, labors for wages awhile, saves a surplus with which to buy tools or land for himself; then labors on his own account another while, and at length hires another new beginner to help him. This is the just, and generous, and prosperous system, which opens the way to all—gives hope to all, and consequent energy, and progress, and improvement of condition to all. No men living are more worthy to be trusted than those who toil up from poverty—none less inclined to take, or touch, aught which they have not honestly earned. Let them beware of surrendering a political power which they already possess, and which, if surrendered, will surely be used to close the door of advancement against such as they, and to fix new disabilities and burdens upon them, till all of liberty shall be lost.

From the first taking of our national census to the last are seventy years; and we find our population at the end of the period eight times as great as it was at the beginning. The increase of those other things which men deem desirable has been even greater. We thus have at one view, what the popular principle applied to government, through the machinery of the States and the Union, has produced in a given time; and also what, if firmly maintained, it promises for the future. There are already among us those, who, if the Union be preserved, will live to see it contain two hundred and fifty millions. The struggle of today, is not altogether for today—it is for a vast future also. With a reliance on Providence, all the more firm and earnest, let us proceed in the great task which events have devolved upon us.

December 3, 1861

To David Hunter

Executive Mansion, Washington,
Major General Hunter.   Dec. 31, 1861.

Dear Sir: Yours of the 23rd. is received; and I am constrained to say it is difficult to answer so ugly a letter in good temper. I am, as you intimate, losing much of the great confidence I placed in you, not from any act or omission of yours touching the public service, up to the time you were sent to Leavenworth, but from the flood of grumbling despatches and letters I have seen from you since. I knew you were being ordered to Leavenworth at the time it was done; and I aver that with as tender a regard for your honor and your sensibilities as I had for my own, it never occurred to me that you were being "humiliated, insulted and disgraced"; nor have I, up to this day, heard an intimation that you have been wronged, coming from any one but yourself. No one has blamed you for the retrograde movement from Springfield, nor for the information you gave Gen. Cameron; and this you could readily understand, if it were not for your unwarranted assumption that the ordering you to Leavenworth must necessarily have been done as a *punishment* for some *fault*. I thought then, and think yet, the position assigned to you is as responsible, and as honorable, as that assigned to Buell. I know that Gen. McClellan expected more important results from it. My impression is that at the time you were assigned to the new Western Department, it had not been determined to re-place Gen. Sherman in Kentucky; but of this I am not certain, because the idea that a command in Kentucky was very desireable, and one in the farther West, very undesireable, had never occurred to me. You constantly speak of being placed in command of only 3000. Now tell me, is not this mere impatience? Have you not known all the while that you are to command four or five times that many?

I have been, and am sincerely your friend; and if, as such, I dare to make a suggestion, I would say you are adopting the best possible way to ruin yourself. "Act well your part, there all the honor lies." He who does *something* at the head of one Regiment, will eclipse him who does *nothing* at the head of a hundred. Your friend as ever,

To George B. McClellan

Executive Mansion,
Major General McClellan   Washington, Feb. 3, 1862.

My dear Sir: You and I have distinct, and different plans for a movement of the Army of the Potomac—yours to be down the Chesapeake, up the Rappahannock to Urbana, and across land to the terminus of the Railroad on the York River—, mine to move directly to a point on the Railroad South West of Manassas.

If you will give me satisfactory answers to the following questions, I shall gladly yield my plan to yours.

1st. Does not your plan involve a greatly larger expenditure of *time*, and *money* than mine?

2nd. Wherein is a victory *more certain* by your plan than mine?

3rd. Wherein is a victory *more valuable* by your plan than mine?

4th. In fact, would it not be *less* valuable, in this, that it would break no great line of the enemie's communications, while mine would?

5th. In case of disaster, would not a safe retreat be more difficult by your plan than by mine? Yours truly

————

1. Suppose the enemy should attack us in force *before* we reach the Ocoquan, what? In view of the possibility of this, might it not be safest to have our entire force to move together from above the Ocoquan.

2. Suppose the enemy, in force, shall dispute the crossing of the Ocoquan, what? In view of this, might it not be safest for us to cross the Ocoquan at Colchester rather than at the village of Ocoquan? This would cost the enemy two miles more of travel to meet us, but would, on the contrary, leave us two miles further from our ultimate destination.

3. Suppose we reach Maple valley without an attack, will we not be attacked there, in force, by the enemy marching by the several roads from Manassas? and if so, what?

Stay of Execution for Nathaniel Gordon

Abraham Lincoln,
President of the United States of America,

To all to whom these Presents shall come Greeting:

Whereas, it appears that at a Term of the Circuit Court of the United States of America for the Southern District of New York held in the month of November A.D. 1861, Nathaniel Gordon was indicted and convicted for being engaged in the Slave Trade, and was by the said Court sentenced to be put to death by hanging by the neck, on Friday the 7th. day of February, A.D. 1862;

And whereas, a large number of respectable citizens have earnestly besought me to commute the said sentence of the said Nathaniel Gordon to a term of imprisonment for life, which application I have felt it to be my duty to refuse;

And whereas, it has seemed to me probable that the unsuccessful application made for the commutation of his sentence may have prevented the said Nathaniel Gordon from making the necessary preparation for the awful change which awaits him:

Now, therefore, be it known, that I, Abraham Lincoln, President of the United States of America, have granted and do hereby grant unto him, the said Nathaniel Gordon, a respite of the above recited sentence, until Friday the twenty-first day of February, A.D. 1862, between the hours of twelve o'clock at noon and three o'clock in the afternoon of the said day, when the said sentence shall be executed.

In granting this respite, it becomes my painful duty to admonish the prisoner that, relinquishing all expectation of pardon by Human Authority, he refer himself alone to the mercy of the common God and Father of all men.

In testimony whereof, I have hereunto signed my name and caused the Seal of the United States to be affixed.

Done at the City of Washington, this Fourth day of February A.D. 1862, and of the Independence of the United States the Eighty-sixth.   ABRAHAM LINCOLN.

By the President:

WILLIAM H. SEWARD Secretary of State.

Message to Congress

Fellow-citizens of the Senate, and House of Representatives,

I recommend the adoption of a Joint Resolution by your honorable bodies which shall be substantially as follows:

"Resolved that the United States ought to co-operate with any state which may adopt gradual abolishment of slavery, giving to such state pecuniary aid, to be used by such state in it's discretion, to compensate for the inconveniences public and private, produced by such change of system"

If the proposition contained in the resolution does not meet the approval of Congress and the country, there is the end; but if it does command such approval, I deem it of importance that the states and people immediately interested, should be at once distinctly notified of the fact, so that they may begin to consider whether to accept or reject it. The federal government would find it's highest interest in such a measure, as one of the most efficient means of self-preservation. The leaders of the existing insurrection entertain the hope that this government will ultimately be forced to acknowledge the independence of some part of the disaffected region, and that all the slave states North of such part will then say "the Union, for which we have struggled, being already gone, we now choose to go with the Southern section." To deprive them of this hope, substantially ends the rebellion; and the initiation of emancipation completely deprives them of it, as to all the states initiating it. The point is not that *all* the states tolerating slavery would very soon, if at all, initiate emancipation; but that, while the offer is equally made to all, the more Northern shall, by such initiation, make it certain to the more Southern, that in no event, will the former ever join the latter, in their proposed confederacy. I say "initiation" because, in my judgment, gradual, and not sudden emancipation, is better for all. In the mere financial, or pecuniary view, any member of Congress, with the census-tables and Treasury-reports before him, can readily see for himself how very soon the current expenditures of this war would purchase, at fair valuation, all the slaves in any named State. Such a proposition, on the part of the general government, sets up no claim of a right, by federal authority, to interfere with slavery within state limits, referring, as it does, the absolute control of the subject, in each case, to the state and it's people, immediately interested. It is proposed as a matter of perfectly free choice with them.

In the annual message last December, I thought fit to say "The Union must be preserved; and hence all indispensable means must be employed." I said this, not hastily, but deliberately. War has been made, and continues to be, an indispensable means to this end. A practical re-acknowledgement of the national authority would render the war unnecessary, and it would at once cease. If, however, resistance continues, the war must also continue; and it is impossible to foresee all the incidents, which may attend and all the ruin which may follow it. Such as may seem indispensable, or may obviously promise great efficiency towards ending the struggle, must and will come.

The proposition now made, though an offer only, I hope it may be esteemed no offence to ask whether the pecuniary consideration tendered would not be of more value to the States and private persons concerned, than are the institution, and property in it, in the present aspect of affairs.

While it is true that the adoption of the proposed resolution would be merely initiatory, and not within itself a practical measure, it is recommended in the hope that it would soon lead to important practical results. In full view of my great responsibility to my God, and to my country, I earnestly beg the attention of Congress and the people to the subject.

March 6. 1862.

President's General War Order No. 3

President's General War Order No. 3   Executive Mansion Washington, March 8, 1862.

Ordered, that no change of the base of operations of the Army of the Potomac shall be made without leaving in, and about Washington, such a force as, in the opinion of the General-in-chief, and the commanders of all the Army corps, shall leave said City entirely secure.

That not more than two Army corps, (about fifty thousand troops) of said Army of the Potomac, shall be moved *en route* for a new base of operations until the navigation of the Potomac, from Washington to the Chesapeake bay shall be freed from enemies batteries and other obstructions, or, until the President shall hereafter give express permission.

That any movement, as aforesaid, *en route* for a new

base of operations, which may be ordered by the General-in-chief, & which may be intended to move upon the Chesapeake-bay, shall begin to move upon the bay as early as the 18th. day of March Inst.; and the General-in-chief shall be responsible that it so move as early as that day.

Ordered that the Army and Navy co-operate in an immediate effort to capture the enemies batteries upon the Potomac between Washington and the Chesapeake-bay.

To George B. McClellan

Private

Major General McClellan   Executive Mansion,
My dear Sir   Washington, March 31, 1862.

This morning I felt constrained to order Blenker's Division to Fremont; and I write this to assure you that I did so with great pain, understanding that you would wish it otherwise. If you could know the full pressure of the case, I am confident you would justify it—even beyond a mere acknowledgment that the Commander-in-chief, may order what he pleases. Yours very truly

To George B. McClellan

      Washington, D.C.,
Major Gen. McClellan   July 2 1862.

Your despatch of Tuesday morning induces me to hope your Army is having some rest. In this hope, allow me to reason with you a moment. When you ask for fifty thousand men to be promptly sent you, you surely labor under some gross mistake of fact. Recently you sent papers showing your disposal of forces, made last spring, for the defence of Washington, and advising a return to that plan. I find it included in, and about Washington seventyfive thousand men. Now please be assured, I have not men enough to fill that very plan by fifteen thousand. All of Fremont in the valley, all of Banks, all of McDowell, not with you, and all in Washington, taken together do not exceed, if they reach sixty thousand. With Wool and Dix added to those mentioned, I have not, outside of your Army, seventyfive thousand men East of the mountains. Thus, the idea of sending you fifty thousand, or any other considerable force promptly, is simply absurd. If in your frequent mention of responsibility, you have the impression that I blame you for not doing more than you can, please be relieved of such impression. I only beg that in like manner, you will not ask impossibilities of me. If you think you are not strong enough to take Richmond just now, I do not ask you to try just now. Save the Army, material and personal; and I will strengthen it for the offensive again, as fast as I can. The Governors of eighteen states offer me a new levy of three hundred thousand, which I accept.

To Edwin M. Stanton

Hon Sec of War   Executive Mansion
Sir   Washington Aug 9 1862
     I have examined and seen tried the "Rafael Repeater" and consider it a decided improvement upon what was called the "Coffee Mill Gun" in these particulars that it dispenses with the great cost and liability to loss of the Steel cartridges and that it is better arranged to prevent the escape of gas. Other advantages are claimed for it upon which I cannot so well speak. While I do not order it into the service I

think it well worthy of the attention of the Ordnance Bureau and should be rather pleased if it should be decided to put it into the service Yours Truly

Address on Colonization to a Committee of Colored Men, Washington, D.C.

This afternoon the President of the United States gave audience to a Committee of colored men at the White House. They were introduced by the Rev. J. Mitchell, Commissioner of Emigration. E. M. Thomas, the Chairman, remarked that they were there by invitation to hear what the Executive had to say to them. Having all been seated, the President, after a few preliminary observations, informed them that a sum of money had been appropriated by Congress, and placed at his disposition for the purpose of aiding the colonization in some country of the people, or a portion of them, of African descent, thereby making it his duty, as it had for a long time been his inclination, to favor that cause; and why, he asked, should the people of your race be colonized, and where? Why should they leave this country? This is, perhaps, the first question for proper consideration. You and we are different races. We have between us a broader difference than exists between almost any other two races. Whether it is right or wrong I need not discuss, but this physical difference is a great disadvantage to us both, as I think your race suffer very greatly, many of them by living among us, while ours suffer from your presence. In a word we suffer on each side. If this is admitted, it affords a reason at least why we should be separated. You here are freemen I suppose.

A VOICE: Yes, sir.

The President—Perhaps you have long been free, or all

your lives. Your race are suffering, in my judgment, the greatest wrong inflicted on any people. But even when you cease to be slaves, you are yet far removed from being placed on an equality with the white race. You are cut off from many of the advantages which the other race enjoy. The aspiration of men is to enjoy equality with the best when free, but on this broad continent, not a single man of your race is made the equal of a single man of ours. Go where you are treated the best, and the ban is still upon you.

I do not propose to discuss this, but to present it as a fact with which we have to deal. I cannot alter it if I would. It is a fact, about which we all think and feel alike, I and you. We look to our condition, owing to the existence of the two races on this continent. I need not recount to you the effects upon white men, growing out of the institution of Slavery. I believe in its general evil effects on the white race. See our present condition—the country engaged in war!—our white men cutting one another's throats, none knowing how far it will extend; and then consider what we know to be the truth. But for your race among us there could not be war, although many men engaged on either side do not care for you one way or the other. Nevertheless, I repeat, without the institution of Slavery and the colored race as a basis, the war could not have an existence.

It is better for us both, therefore, to be separated. I know that there are free men among you, who even if they could better their condition are not as much inclined to go out of the country as those, who being slaves could obtain their freedom on this condition. I suppose one of the principal difficulties in the way of colonization is that the free colored man cannot see that his comfort would be advanced by it. You may believe you can live in Washington or elsewhere in the United States the remainder of your life, perhaps more so than you can in any foreign country, and hence you may come to the conclusion that you have nothing to do with the idea of going to a foreign country. This is (I speak in no unkind sense) an extremely selfish view of the case.

But you ought to do something to help those who are not so fortunate as yourselves. There is an unwillingness on the part of our people, harsh as it may be, for you free colored people to remain with us. Now, if you could give a start to white people, you would open a wide door for many to be made free. If we deal with those who are not free at the beginning, and whose intellects are clouded by Slavery, we have very poor materials to start with. If intelligent colored men, such as are before me, would move in this matter, much might be accomplished. It is exceedingly important that we have men at the beginning capable of thinking as white men, and not those who have been systematically oppressed.

There is much to encourage you. For the sake of your race you should sacrifice something of your present comfort for the purpose of being as grand in that respect as the white people. It is a cheering thought throughout life that something can be done to ameliorate the condition of those who have been subject to the hard usage of the world. It is difficult to make a man miserable while he feels he is worthy of himself, and claims kindred to the great God who made him. In the American Revolutionary war sacrifices were made by men engaged in it; but they were cheered by the future. Gen. Washington himself endured greater physical hardships than if he had remained a British subject. Yet he was a happy man, because he was engaged in benefiting his race—something for the children of his neighbors, having none of his own.

The colony of Liberia has been in existence a long time. In a certain sense it is a success. The old President of Liberia, Roberts, has just been with me—the first time I ever saw him. He says they have within the bounds of that colony between 300,000 and 400,000 people, or more than in some of our old States, such as Rhode Island or Delaware, or in some of our newer States, and less than in some of our larger ones. They are not all American colonists, or their descendants. Something less than 12,000 have been sent thither from this country. Many of the original settlers have died, yet, like people elsewhere, their offspring outnumber those deceased.

The question is if the colored people are persuaded to go anywhere, why not there? One reason for an unwillingness to do so is that some of you would rather remain within reach of the country of your nativity. I do not know how much attachment you may have toward our race. It does not strike me that you have the greatest reason to love them. But still you are attached to them at all events.

The place I am thinking about having for a colony is in Central America. It is nearer to us than Liberia—not much more than one-fourth as far as Liberia, and within seven days' run by steamers. Unlike Liberia it is on a great line of travel—it is a highway. The country is a very excellent one for any people, and with great natural resources and advantages, and especially because of the similarity of climate with your native land—thus being suited to your physical condition.

The particular place I have in view is to be a great highway from the Atlantic or Caribbean Sea to the Pacific Ocean, and this particular place has all the advantages for a colony. On both sides there are harbors among the finest in the world. Again, there is evidence of very rich coal mines. A certain amount of coal is valuable in any country, and there may be more than enough for the wants of the country. Why I attach so much importance to coal is, it will afford an opportunity to the inhabitants for immediate employment till they get ready to settle permanently in their homes.

If you take colonists where there is no good landing, there is a bad show; and so where there is nothing to cultivate, and of which to make a farm. But if something is started so that you can get your daily bread as soon as you reach there, it is a great advantage. Coal land is the best thing I know of with which to commence an enterprise.

To return, you have been talked to upon this subject, and told that a speculation is intended by gentlemen, who have an interest in the country, including the coal mines. We have been mistaken all our lives if we do not know whites as well as blacks look to their self-interest. Unless among those deficient of intellect everybody you trade with makes something. You meet with these things here as elsewhere.

If such persons have what will be an advantage to them, the question is whether it cannot be made of advantage to you. You are intelligent, and know that success does not as much depend on external help as on self-reliance. Much, therefore, depends upon yourselves. As to the coal mines, I think I see the means available for your self-reliance.

I shall, if I get a sufficient number of you engaged, have provisions made that you shall not be wronged. If you will engage in the enterprise I will spend some of the money intrusted to me. I am not sure you will succeed. The Government may lose the money, but we cannot succeed unless we try; but we think, with care, we can succeed.

The political affairs in Central America are not in quite as satisfactory condition as I wish. There are contending factions in that quarter; but it is true all the factions are agreed alike on the subject of colonization, and want it, and are more generous than we are here. To your colored race they have no objection. Besides, I would endeavor to have you made equals, and have the best assurance that you should be the equals of the best.

The practical thing I want to ascertain is whether I can get a number of able-bodied men, with their wives and children, who are willing to go, when I present evidence of encouragement and protection. Could I get a hundred tolerably intelligent men, with their wives and children, to "cut their own fodder," so to speak? Can I have fifty? If I could find twenty-five able-bodied men, with a mixture of women and children, good things in the family relation, I think I could make a successful commencement.

I want you to let me know whether this can be done or not. This is the practical part of my wish to see you. These are subjects of very great importance, worthy of a month's study, instead of a speech delivered in an hour. I ask you then to consider seriously not pertaining to yourselves merely, nor for your race, and ours, for the present time, but as one of the things, if successfully managed, for the good of mankind—not confined to the present generation, but as

> "From age to age descends the lay,
>   To millions yet to be,
> Till far its echoes roll away,
>   Into eternity."

The above is merely given as the substance of the President's remarks.

The Chairman of the delegation briefly replied that "they would hold a consultation and in a short time give an answer." The President said: "Take your full time—no hurry at all."

The delegation then withdrew.

August 14, 1862

To Horace Greeley

Hon. Horace Greely: Executive Mansion,
Dear Sir   Washington, August 22, 1862.

I have just read yours of the 19th. addressed to myself through the New-York Tribune. If there be in it any statements, or assumptions of fact, which I may know to be erroneous, I do not, now and here, controvert them. If there be in it any inferences which I may believe to be falsely drawn, I do not now and here, argue against them. If there be perceptable in it an impatient and dictatorial tone, I waive it in deference to an old friend, whose heart I have always supposed to be right.

As to the policy I "seem to be pursuing" as you say, I have not meant to leave any one in doubt.

I would save the Union. I would save it the shortest way under the Constitution. The sooner the national authority can be restored; the nearer the Union will be "the Union as it was." If there be those who would not save the Union, unless they could at the same time *save* slavery, I do not agree with them. If there be those who would not save the Union unless they could at the same time *destroy* slavery, I do not agree with them. My paramount object in this struggle *is* to save the Union, and is *not* either to save or to destroy slavery. If I could save the Union without freeing *any* slave I would do it, and if I could save it by freeing *all* the slaves I would do it; and if I could save it by freeing some and leaving others alone I would also do that. What I do about slavery, and the colored race, I do because I believe it helps to save the Union; and what I forbear, I forbear because I do *not* believe it would help to save the Union. I shall do *less* whenever I shall believe what I am doing hurts the cause, and I shall do *more* whenever I shall believe doing more will help the cause. I shall try to correct errors when shown to be errors; and I shall adopt new views so fast as they shall appear to be true views.

I have here stated my purpose according to my view of *official* duty; and I intend no modification of my oft-expressed *personal* wish that all men every where could be free. Yours,

3.

THE GREAT EMANCIPATOR

Preliminary Emancipation Proclamation

By the President
of the United States of America
a proclamation.

I, Abraham Lincoln, President of the United States of America, and Commander-in-chief of the Army and Navy thereof, do hereby proclaim and declare that hereafter, as heretofore, the war will be prossecuted for the object of practically restoring the constitutional relation between the United States, and each of the states, and the people thereof, in which states that relation is, or may be suspended, or disturbed.

That it is my purpose, upon the next meeting of Congress to again recommend the adoption of a practical measure tendering pecuniary aid to the free acceptance or rejection of all slave-states, so called, the people whereof may not then be in rebellion against the United States, and which states, may then have voluntarily adopted, or thereafter may voluntarily adopt, immediate, or gradual abolishment of slavery within their respective limits; and that the effort to colonize persons of African descent, with their consent, upon this continent, or elsewhere, with the previously obtained consent of the Governments existing there, will be continued.

That on the first day of January in the year of our Lord, one thousand eight hundred and sixty-three, all persons held as slaves within any state, or designated part of a state, the people whereof shall then be in rebellion against the United States shall be then, thenceforward, and forever free; and the executive government of the United States, including the military and naval authority thereof, will recognize and maintain the freedom of such persons, and will do no act or acts to repress such persons, or any of them, in any efforts they may make for their actual freedom.

That the executive will, on the first day of January aforesaid, by proclamation, designate the States, and parts of states, if any, in which the people thereof respectively, shall then be in rebellion against the United States; and the fact that any state, or the people thereof shall, on that day be, in good faith represented in the Congress of the United States, by members chosen thereto, at elections wherein a majority of the qualified voters of such state shall have participated, shall, in the absence of strong countervailing testimony, be deemed conclusive evidence that such state and the people thereof, are not then in rebellion against the United States.

That attention is hereby called to an act of Congress entitled "An act to make an additional Article of War" approved March 13, 1862, and which act is in the words and figure following:

Be it enacted by the Senate and House of Representatives of the United States of America in Congress assembled, That hereafter the following shall be promulgated as an additional article of war for the government of the army of the United States, and shall be obeyed and observed as such:

Article—. All officers or persons in the military or naval service of the United States are prohibited from employing any of the forces under their respective commands for the purpose of returning fugitives from service or labor, who may have escaped from any persons to whom such service or labor is claimed to be due, and any officer who shall be found guilty by a court-martial of violating this article shall be dismissed from the service.

SEC. 2. *And be it further enacted,* That this act shall take effect from and after its passage.

Also to the ninth and tenth sections of an act entitled "An Act to suppress Insurrection, to punish Treason and Rebellion, to seize and confiscate property of rebels, and for other purposes," approved July 17, 1862, and which sections are in the words and figures following:

SEC. 9. *And be it further enacted,* That all slaves of persons who shall hereafter be engaged in rebellion against the government of the United States, or who shall in any way give aid or comfort thereto, escaping from such persons and taking refuge within the lines of the army; and all slaves captured from such persons or deserted by them and coming under the control of the government of the United States; and all slaves of such persons found *on* (or) being within any place occupied by rebel forces and afterwards occupied by the forces of the United States, shall be deemed captives of war, and shall be forever free of their servitude and not again held as slaves.

SEC. 10. *And be it further enacted,* That no slave escaping into any State, Territory, or the District of Columbia, from any other State, shall be delivered up, or in any way impeded or hindered of his liberty, except for crime, or some offence against the laws, unless the person claiming said fugitive shall first make oath that the person to whom the labor or service of such fugitive is alleged to be due is his lawful owner, and has not borne arms against the United States in the present rebellion, nor in any way given aid and comfort thereto; and no person engaged in the military or naval service of the United States shall, under any pretence whatever, assume to decide on the validity of the claim of any person to the service or labor of any other person, or surrender up any such person to the claimant, on pain of being dismissed from the service.

And I do hereby enjoin upon and order all persons engaged in the military and naval service of the United States to observe, obey, and enforce, within their respective spheres of service, the act, and sections above recited.

And the executive will in due time recommend that all citizens of the United States who shall have remained loyal thereto throughout the rebellion, shall (upon the restoration of the constitutional relation between the United States, and their respective states, and people, if that relation shall have been suspended or disturbed) be compensated for all losses by acts of the United States, including the loss of slaves.

In witness whereof, I have hereunto set my hand, and caused the seal of the United States to be affixed.

Done at the City of Washington, this twenty second day of September, in the year of our Lord, one thousand eight hundred and sixty two, and of the Independence of the United States, the eighty seventh.

ABRAHAM LINCOLN

By the President:

WILLIAM H. SEWARD, Secretary of State.

Proclamation Suspending the Writ of Habeas Corpus

BY THE PRESIDENT
OF THE UNITED STATES OF AMERICA:
A PROCLAMATION.

Whereas, it has become necessary to call into service not only volunteers but also portions of the militia of the States by draft in order to suppress the insurrection existing in the United States, and disloyal persons are not adequately restrained by the ordinary processes of law from hindering this measure and from giving aid and comfort in various ways to the insurrection;

Now, therefore, be it ordered, first, that during the existing insurrection and as a necessary measure for suppressing the same, all Rebels and Insurgents, their aiders and abettors within the United States, and all persons discouraging volunteer enlistments, resisting militia drafts, or guilty of any disloyal practice, affording aid and comfort to Rebels against the authority of the United States, shall be

subject to martial law and liable to trial and punishment by
Courts Martial or Military Commission:

Second. That the Writ of Habeas Corpus is suspended
in respect to all persons arrested, or who are now, or hereafter during the rebellion shall be, imprisoned in any fort,
camp, arsenal, military prison, or other place of confinement
by any military authority or by the sentence of any Court
Martial or Military Commission.

In witness whereof, I have hereunto set my hand, and
caused the seal of the United States to be affixed.

Done at the City of Washington this twenty fourth day
of September, in the year of our Lord one thousand eight
hundred and sixty-two, and of the Independence of the
United States the 87th.   ABRAHAM LINCOLN.

By the President:

WILLIAM H. SEWARD, Secretary of State.

To George B. McClellan

Major General McClellan   Executive Mansion,
My dear Sir   Washington, Oct. 13, 1862.

You remember my speaking to you of what I called your
over-cautiousness. Are you not over-cautious when you assume that you can not do what the enemy is constantly
doing? Should you not claim to be at least his equal in
prowess, and act upon the claim?

As I understand, you telegraph Gen. Halleck that you
can not subsist your army at Winchester unless the Railroad
from Harper's Ferry to that point be put in working order.
But the enemy does now subsist his army at Winchester at
a distance nearly twice as great from railroad transportation
as you would have to do without the railroad last named.
He now wagons from Culpepper C.H. which is just about

twice as far as you would have to do from Harper's Ferry. He is certainly not more than half as well provided with wagons as you are. I certainly should be pleased for you to have the advantage of the Railroad from Harper's Ferry to Winchester, but it wastes all the remainder of autumn to give it to you; and, in fact ignores the question of *time*, which can not, and must not be ignored.

Again, one of the standard maxims of war, as you know, is "to operate upon the enemy's communciations as much as possible without exposing your own." You seem to act as if this applies *against* you, but can not apply in your *favor*. Change positions with the enemy, and think you not he would break your communication with Richmond within the next twentyfour hours? You dread his going into Pennsylvania. But if he does so in full force, he gives up his communications to you absolutely, and you have nothing to do but to follow, and ruin him; if he does so with less than full force, fall upon, and beat what is left behind all the easier.

Exclusive of the water line, you are now nearer Richmond than the enemy is by the route that you *can*, and he *must* take. Why can you not reach there before him, unless you admit that he is more than your equal on a march. His route is the arc of a circle, while yours is the chord. The roads are as good on yours as on his.

You know I desired, but did not order, you to cross the Potomac below, instead of above the Shenandoah and Blue Ridge. My idea was that this would at once menace the enemies' communications, which I would seize if he would permit. If he should move Northward I would follow him closely, holding his communications. If he should prevent our seizing his communications, and move towards Richmond, I would press closely to him, fight him if a favorable opportunity should present, and, at least, try to beat him to Richmond on the inside track. I say "try"; if we never try, we

shall never succeed. If he make a stand at Winchester,
moving neither North or South, I would fight him there, on
the idea that if we can not beat him when he bears the
wastage of coming to us, we never can when we bear the
wastage of going to him. This proposition is a simple
truth, and is too important to be lost sight of for a moment. In coming to us, he tenders us an advantage which
we should not waive. We should not so operate as to
merely drive him away. As we must beat him somewhere,
or fail finally, we can do it, if at all, easier near to us,
than far away. If we can not beat the enemy where he
now is, we never can, he again being within the entrench-
ments of Richmond.

Recurring to the idea of going to Richmond on the inside
track, the facility of supplying from the side away from the
enemy is remarkable—as it were, by the different spokes of
a wheel extending from the hub towards the rim—and this
whether you move directly by the chord, or on the inside
arc, hugging the Blue Ridge more closely. The chord-line,
as you see, carries you by Aldie, Hay-Market, and Fredericksburg; and you see how turn-pikes, railroads, and finally,
the Potomac by Acquia Creek, meet you at all points from
Washington. The same, only the lines lengthened a little, if
you press closer to the Blue Ridge part of the way. The
gaps through the Blue Ridge I understand to be about the
following distances from Harper's Ferry, towit: Vestal's five
miles; Gregorie's, thirteen, Snicker's eighteen, Ashby's,
twenty-eight, Mannassas, thirty-eight, Chester fortyfive,
and Thornton's fifty-three. I should think it preferable to
take the route nearest the enemy, disabling him to make an
important move without your knowledge, and compelling
him to keep his forces together, for dread of you. The gaps
would enable you to attack if you should wish. For a great
part of the way, you would be practically between the
enemy and both Washington and Richmond, enabling us

to spare you the greatest number of troops from here.
When at length, running for Richmond ahead of him enables him to move this way; if he does so, turn and attack
him in rear. But I think he should be engaged long before
such point is reached. It is all easy if our troops march
as well as the enemy; and it is unmanly to say they can
not do it.

This letter is in no sense an order. Yours truly

To George B. McClellan

Washington City, D.C.

Majr. Genl. McClellan   Oct. 24. 1862

I have just read your despatch about sore tongued and
fatiegued horses. Will you pardon me for asking what the
horses of your army have done since the battle of Antietam
that fatigue anything?

October 25, 1862

To George B. McClellan

Executive Mansion, Washington,

Majr. Gen. McClellan.   Oct. 27. 1862

Yours of yesterday received. Most certainly I intend no
injustice to any; and if I have done any, I deeply regret it.
To be told after more than five weeks total inaction of the
Army, and during which period we had sent to that Army
every fresh horse we possibly could, amounting in the whole
to 7918 that the cavalry horses were too much fatiegued to
move, presented a very cheerless, almost hopeless, prospect

for the future; and it may have forced something of impatience into my despatches. If not recruited, and rested then, when could they ever be? I suppose the river is rising, and I am glad to believe you are crossing.

To John Pope

Major General Pope   Executive Mansion,
St. Paul, Minnesota   Washington, Nov. 10. 1862.
   Your despatch giving the names of three hundred Indians condemned to death, is received. Please forward, as soon as possible, the full and complete record of these convictions. And if the record does not fully indicate the more guilty and influential, of the culprits, please have a careful statement made on these points and forwarded to me. Send all by mail.

To Carl Schurz

Gen. Carl Schurz   Executive Mansion,
My dear Sir   Washington, Nov. 24. 1862.
   I have just received, and read, your letter of the 20th. The purport of it is that we lost the late elections, and the administration is failing, because the war is unsuccessful; and that I must not flatter myself that I am not justly to blame for it. I certainly know that if the war fails, the administration fails, and that I *will* be blamed for it, whether I deserve it or not. And I ought to be blamed, if I could do better. You think I could do better; therefore you blame me already. I think I could not do better; therefore I blame

you for blaming me. I understand you *now* to be willing to accept the help of men, who are not republicans, provided they have "heart in it." Agreed. I want no others. But who is to be the judge of hearts, or of "heart in it"? If I must discard my own judgment, and take yours, I must also take that of others; and by the time I should reject all I should be advised to reject, I should have none left, republicans, or others—not even yourself. For, be assured, my dear sir, there are men who have "heart in it" that think you are performing your part as poorly as you think I am performing mine. I certainly have been dissatisfied with the slowness of Buell and McClellan; but before I relieved them I had great fears I should not find successors to them, who would do better; and I am sorry to add, that I have seen little since to relieve those fears. I do not clearly see the prospect of any more rapid movements. I fear we shall at last find out that the difficulty is in our case, rather than in particular generals. I wish to disparage no one—certainly not those who sympathize with me; but I must say I need success more than I need sympathy, and that I have not seen the so much greater evidence of getting success from my sympathizers, than from those who are denounced as the contrary. It does seem to me that in the field the two classes have been very much alike, in what they have done, and what they have failed to do. In sealing their faith with their blood, Baker, and Lyon, and Bohlen, and Richardson, republicans, did all that men could do; but did they any more than Kearney, and Stevens, and Reno, and Mansfield, none of whom were republicans, and some, at least of whom, have been bitterly, and repeatedly, denounced to me as secession sympathizers? I will not perform the ungrateful task of comparing cases of failure.

In answer to your question "Has it not been publicly stated in the newspapers, and apparently proved as a fact, that from the commencement of the war, the enemy was continually supplied with information by some of the confidential subordinates of as important as officer as Adjutant General Thomas?" I must say "no" so far as my knowledge extends. And I add that if you can give any tangible evidence upon that subject, I will thank you to come to the City and do so. Very truly Your friend

Annual Message to Congress

Fellow-citizens of the Senate and House of Representatives:

Since your last annual assembling another year of health and bountiful harvests has passed. And while it has not pleased the Almighty to bless us with a return of peace, we can but press on, guided by the best light He gives us, trusting that in His own good time, and wise way, all will yet be well.

The correspondence touching foreign affairs which has taken place during the last year is herewith submitted, in virtual compliance with a request to that effect, made by the House of Representatives near the close of the last session of Congress.

If the condition of our relations with other nations is less gratifying than it has usually been at former periods, it is certainly more satisfactory than a nation so unhappily distracted as we are, might reasonably have apprehended. In the month of June last there were some grounds to expect that the maritime powers which, at the beginning of our domestic difficulties, so unwisely and unnecessarily, as we think, recognized the insurgents as a belligerent, would soon recede from that position, which has proved only less injurious to themselves, than to our own country. But the temporary reverses which afterwards befell the national arms, and which were exaggerated by our own disloyal citizens abroad have hitherto delayed that act of simple justice.

The civil war, which has so radically changed for the moment, the occupations and habits of the American people, has necessarily disturbed the social condition, and affected very deeply the prosperity of the nations with which we have carried on a commerce that has been steadily increasing throughout a period of half a century. It has, at the same time, excited political ambitions and apprehensions which have produced a profound agitation throughout the civilized world. In this unusual agitation we have forborne from taking part in any controversy between foreign states, and between parties or factions in such states. We have attempted no propagandism, and acknowledged no revolution. But we have left to every nation the exclusive conduct and management of its own affairs. Our struggle has been, of course, contemplated by foreign nations with reference less to its own merits, than to its supposed, and often exaggerated effects and consequences resulting to those nations themselves. Nevertheless, complaint on the part of this government, even if it were just, would certainly be unwise.

The treaty with Great Britain for the suppression of the slave trade has been put into operation with a good prospect of complete success. It is an occasion of special pleasure to acknowledge that the execution of it, on the part of Her Majesty's government, has been marked with a jealous respect for the authority of the United States, and the rights of their moral and loyal citizens.

The convention with Hanover for the abolition of the stade dues has been carried into full effect, under the act of Congress for that purpose.

A blockade of three thousand miles of sea-coast could not be established, and vigorously enforced, in a season of great commercial activity like the present, without committing occasional mistakes, and inflicting unintentional injuries upon foreign nations and their subjects.

A civil war occurring in a country where foreigners reside and carry on trade under treaty stipulations, is necessarily fruitful of complaints of the violation of neutral rights. All such collisions tend to excite misapprehensions, and possibly to produce mutual reclamations between nations which have a common interest in preserving peace and friendship. In clear cases of these kinds I have, so far as possible, heard and redressed complaints which have been presented by friendly powers. There is still, however, a large and an augmenting number of doubtful cases upon which the government is unable to agree with the governments whose protection is demanded by the claimants. There are, moreover, many cases in which the United States, or their citizens, suffer wrongs from the naval or military authorities of foreign nations, which the governments of those states are not at once prepared to redress. I have proposed to some of the foreign states, thus interested, mutual conventions to examine and adjust such complaints. This proposition has been made especially to Great Britain, to France, to Spain, and to Prussia. In each case it has been kindly received, but has not yet been formally adopted.

I deem it my duty to recommend an appropriation in behalf of the owners of the Norwegian bark Admiral P. Tordenskiold, which vessel was, in May, 1861, prevented by the commander of the blockading force off Charleston from leaving that port with cargo, notwithstanding a similar privilege had, shortly before, been granted to an English vessel. I have directed the Secretary of State to cause the papers in the case to be communicated to the proper committees.

Applications have been made to me by many free Americans of African descent to favor their emigration, with a view to such colonization as was contemplated in recent acts of Congress. Other parties, at home and abroad—some from interested motives, others upon patriotic considerations, and still others influenced by philanthropic sentiments—have suggested similar measures; while, on the other hand, several of the Spanish-American republics have protested against the sending of such colonies to their respective territories. Under these circumstances, I have declined to move any such colony to any state, without first obtaining the consent of its government, with an agreement on its part to receive and protect such emigrants in all the rights of freemen; and I have, at the same time, offered to the several states situated within the tropics, or having colonies there, to negotiate with them, subject to the advice and consent of the Senate, to favor the voluntary emigration of persons of that class to their respective territories, upon conditions which shall be equal, just, and humane. Liberia and Hayti are, as yet, the only countries to which colonists of African descent from here, could go with certainty of being received and adopted as citizens; and I regret to say such persons, contemplating colonization, do not seem so willing to migrate to those countries, as to some others, nor so willing as I think their interest demands. I believe, however, opinion among them, in this respect, is improving; and that, ere long, there will be an augmented, and considerable migration to both these countries, from the United States.

The new commercial treaty between the United States and the Sultan of Turkey has been carried into execution.

A commercial and consular treaty has been negotiated, subject to the Senate's consent, with Liberia; and a similar negotiation is now pending with the republic of Hayti. A considerable improvement of the national commerce is expected to result from these measures.

Our relations with Great Britain, France, Spain, Portugal, Russia, Prussia, Denmark, Sweden, Austria, the Netherlands, Italy, Rome, and the other European states, remain undisturbed. Very favorable relations also continue to be maintained with Turkey, Morocco, China and Japan.

During the last year there has not only been no change of our previous relations with the independent states of our own continent, but, more friendly sentiments than have heretofore existed, are believed to be entertained by these neighbors, whose safety and progress, are so intimately connected with our own. This statement especially applies to Mexico, Nicaragua, Costa Rica, Honduras, Peru, and Chile.

The commission under the convention with the republic of New Granada closed its session, without having audited and passed upon, all the claims which were submitted to it. A proposition is pending to revive the convention, that it may be able to do more complete justice. The joint commission between the United States and the republic of Costa Rica has completed its labors and submitted its report.

I have favored the project for connecting the United States with Europe by an Atlantic telegraph, and a similar project to extend the telegraph from San Francisco, to connect by a Pacific telegraph with the line which is being extended across the Russian empire.

The Territories of the United States, with unimportant exceptions, have remained undisturbed by the civil war, and they are exhibiting such evidence of prosperity as justifies an expectation that some of them will soon be in a condition to be organized as States, and be constitutionally admitted into the federal Union.

The immense mineral resources of some of those Territories ought to be developed as rapidly as possible. Every step in that direction would have a tendency to improve the revenues of the government, and diminish the burdens of the people. It is worthy of your serious consideration whether some extraordinary measures to promote that end cannot be adopted. The means which suggests itself as mostly likely to be effective, is a scientific exploration of the mineral regions in those Territories, with a view to the publication of its results at home and in foreign countries—results which cannot fail to be auspicious.

The condition of the finances will claim your most diligent consideration. The vast expenditures incident to the military and naval operations required for the suppression of the rebellion, have hitherto been met with a promptitude, and certainty, unusual in similar circumstances, and the public credit has been fully maintained. The continuance of the war, however, and the increased disbursements made necessary by the augmented forces now in the field, demand your best reflections as to the best modes of providing the necessary revenue, without injury to business and with the least possible burdens upon labor.

The suspension of specie payments by the banks, soon after the commencement of your last session, made large issues of United States notes unavoidable. In no other way could the payment of the troops, and the satisfaction of other just demands, be so economically, or so well provided for. The judicious legislation of Congress, securing the receivability of these notes for loans and internal duties, and making them a legal tender for other debts, has made them an universal currency; and has satisfied, partially, at least, and for the time, the long felt want of an uniform circulating medium, saving thereby to the people, immense sums in discounts and exchanges.

A return to specie payments, however, at the earliest period compatible with due regard to all interests concerned, should ever be kept in view. Fluctuations in the value of currency are always injurious, and to reduce these fluctuations to the lowest possible point will always be a leading purpose in wise legislation. Convertibility, prompt and certain convertibility into coin, is generally acknowledged to be the best and surest safeguard against them; and it is extremely doubtful whether a circulation of United States notes, payable in coin, and sufficiently large for the wants of the people, can be permanently, usefully and safely maintained.

Is there, then, any other mode in which the necessary provision for the public wants can be made, and the great advantages of a safe and uniform currency secured?

I know of none which promises so certain results, and is, at the same time, so unobjectionable, as the organization of banking associations, under a general act of Congress, well guarded in its provisions. To such associations the government might furnish circulating notes, on the security of United States bonds deposited in the treasury. These notes, prepared under the supervision of proper officers, being uniform in appearance and security, and convertible always into coin, would at once protect labor against the evils of a vicious currency, and facilitate commerce by cheap and safe exchanges.

A moderate reservation from the interest on the bonds would compensate the United States for the preparation and distribution of the notes and a general supervision of the system, and would lighten the burden of that part of the public debt employed as securities. The public credit, moreover, would be greatly improved, and the negotiation of new loans greatly facilitated by the steady market demand for government bonds which the adoption of the proposed system would create.

It is an additional recommendation of the measure, of considerable weight, in my judgment, that it would reconcile, as far as possible, all existing interests, by the opportunity offered to existing institutions to reorganize under the act, substituting only the secured uniform national circulation for the local and various circulation, secured and unsecured, now issued by them.

The receipts into the treasury from all sources, including loans and balance from the preceding year, for the fiscal year ending on the 30th June, 1862, were $583,885,247 06, of which sum $49,056,397 62 were derived from customs; $1,795,331,73 from the direct tax; from public lands $152,203,77; from miscellaneous sources, $931,787 64; from loans in all forms, $529,692,460 50. The remainder, $2,257,065 80, was the balance from last year.

The disbursements during the same period were for congressional, executive, and judicial purposes, $5,939,009 29; for foreign intercourse, $1,339,710,35;

for miscellaneous expenses, including the mints, loans, post office deficiencies, collection of revenue, and other like charges, $14,129,771 50; for expenses under the Interior Department, $3,102,985 52; under the War Department, $394,368,407,36; under the Navy Department, $42,674,569 69; for interest on public debt, $13,190,324 45; and for payment of public debt, including reimbursement of temporary loan, and redemptions, $96,096,922 09; making an aggregate of $570,841,700 25; and leaving a balance in the treasury on the first day of July, 1862, of $13,043,546,81.

It should be observed that the sum of $96,096,922 09, expended for reimbursements and redemption of public debt, being included also in the loans made, may be properly deducted, both from receipts and expenditures, leaving the actual receipts for the year $487,788,324,97; and the expenditures, $474,744,778 16.

Other information on the subject of the finances will be found in the report of the Secretary of the Treasury, to whose statements and views I invite your most candid and considerate attention.

The reports of the Secretaries of War, and of the Navy, are herewith transmitted. These reports, though lengthy, are scarcely more than brief abstracts of the very numerous and extensive transactions and operations conducted through those departments. Nor could I give a summary of them here, upon any principle, which would admit of its being much shorter than the reports themselves. I therefore content myself with laying the reports before you, and asking your attention to them.

It gives me pleasure to report a decided improvement in the financial condition of the Post Office Department, as compared with several preceding years. The receipts for the fiscal year 1861 amounted to $8,349,296 40, which embraced the revenue from all the States of the Union for three quarters of that year. Notwithstanding the cessation

of revenue from the so-called seceded States during the last
fiscal year, the increase of the correspondence of the loyal
States has been sufficient to produce a revenue during the
same year of $8,299,820 90, being only $50,000 less than
was derived from all the States of the Union during the
previous year. The expenditures show a still more favorable
result. The amount expended in 1861 was $13,606,759 11.
For the last year the amount has been reduced to
$11,125,364 13, showing a decrease of about $2,481,000
in the expenditures as compared with the preceding year
and about $3,750,000 as compared with the fiscal year
1860. The deficiency in the department for the previous
year was $4,551,966.98. For the last fiscal year it was
reduced to $2,112,814.57. These favorable results are in
part owing to the cessation of mail service in the insurrectionary States, and in part to a careful review of all expenditures in that department in the interest of economy. The
efficiency of the postal service, it is believed, has also been
much improved. The Postmaster General has also opened
a correspondence, through the Department of State, with
foreign governments, proposing a convention of postal representatives for the purpose of simplifying the rates of foreign
postage, and to expedite the foreign mails. This proposition,
equally important to our adopted citizens, and to the commercial interests of this country, has been favorably entertained, and agreed to, by all the governments from whom
replies have been received.

I ask the attention of Congress to the suggestions of the
Postmaster General in his report respecting the further legislation required, in his opinion, for the benefit of the postal
service.

The Secretary of the Interior reports as follows in regard
to the public lands:

"The public lands have ceased to be a source of revenue. From the 1st July, 1861, to the 30th September,
1862, the entire cash receipts from the sale of lands were

$137,476 26—a sum much less than the expenses of our land system during the same period. The homestead law, which will take effect on the 1st of January next, offers such inducements to settlers, that sales for cash cannot be expected, to an extent sufficient to meet the expenses of the General Land Office, and the cost of surveying and bringing the land into market"

The discrepancy between the sum here stated as arising from the sales of the public lands, and the sum derived from the same source as reported from the Treasury Department arises, as I understand, from the fact that the periods of time, though apparently, were not really, coincident at the beginning point—the Treasury report including a considerable sum now, which had previously been reported from the Interior—sufficiently large to greatly overreach the sum derived from the three months now reported upon by the Interior, and not by the Treasury.

The Indian tribes upon our frontiers have, during the past year, manifested a spirit of insubordination, and, at several points, have engaged in open hostilities against the white settlements in their vicinity. The tribes occupying the Indian country south of Kansas, renounced their allegiance to the United States, and entered into treaties with the insurgents. Those who remained loyal to the United States were driven from the country. The chief of the Cherokees has visited this city for the purpose of restoring the former relations of the tribe with the United States. He alleges that they were constrained, by superior force, to enter into treaties with the insurgents, and that the United States neglected to furnish the protection which their treaty stipulations required.

In the month of August last the Sioux Indians, in Minnesota, attacked the settlements in their vicinity with extreme ferocity, killing, indiscriminately, men, women, and children. This attack was wholly unexpected, and, therefore, no means of defence had been provided. It is estimated that not less than eight hundred persons were killed by the Indians, and a large amount of property was destroyed. How this outbreak was induced is not definitely known, and suspicions, which may be unjust, need not to be stated. Information was received by the Indian bureau, from different sources, about the time hostilities were commenced, that a simultaneous attack was to be made upon the white settlements by all the tribes between the Mississippi river and the Rocky mountains. The State of Minnesota has suffered great injury from this Indian war. A large portion of her territory has been depopulated, and a severe loss has been sustained by the destruction of property. The people of that State manifest much anxiety for the removal of the tribes beyond the limits of the State as a guarantee against future hostilities. The Commissioner of Indian Affairs will furnish full details. I submit for your especial consideration whether our Indian system shall not be remodelled. Many wise and good men have impressed me with the belief that this can be profitably done.

I submit a statement of the proceedings of commissioners, which shows the progress that has been made in the enterprise of constructing the Pacific railroad. And this suggests the earliest completion of this road, and also the favorable action of Congress upon the projects now pending before them for enlarging the capacities of the great canals in New York and Illinois, as being of vital, and rapidly increasing importance to the whole nation, and especially to the vast interior region hereinafter to be noticed at some greater length. I purpose having prepared and laid before you at an early day some interesting and valuable statistical information upon this subject. The military and commercial importance of enlarging the Illinois and Michigan canal, and improving the Illinois river, is presented in the report of Colonel Webster to the Secretary of War, and now transmitted to Congress. I respectfully ask attention to it.

To carry out the provisions of the act of Congress of the

15th of May last, I have caused the Department of Agriculture of the United States to be organized.

The Commissioner informs me that within the period of a few months this department has established an extensive system of correspondence and exchanges, both at home and aboard, which promises to effect highly beneficial results in the development of a correct knowledge of recent improvements in agriculture, in the introduction of new products, and in the collection of the agricultural statistics of the different States.

Also that it will soon be prepared to distribute largely seeds, cereals, plants and cuttings, and has already published, and liberally diffused, much valuable information in anticipation of a more elaborate report, which will in due time be furnished, embracing some valuable tests in chemical science now in progress in the laboratory.

The creation of this department was for the more immediate benefit of a large class of our most valuable citizens; and I trust that the liberal basis upon which it has been organized will not only meet your approbation, but that it will realize, at no distant day, all the fondest anticipations of its most sanguine friends, and become the fruitful source of advantage to all our people.

On the twenty-second day of September last a proclamation was issued by the Executive, a copy of which is herewith submitted.

In accordance with the purpose expressed in the second paragraph of that paper, I now respectfully recall your attention to what may be called "compensated emancipation."

A nation may be said to consist of its territory, its people, and its laws. The territory is the only part which is of certain durability. "One generation passeth away, and another generation cometh, but the earth abideth forever." It is of the first importance to duly consider, and estimate, this ever-enduring part. That portion of the earth's surface which is owned and inhabited by the people of the United States, is well adapted to be the home of one national family; and it is not well adapted for two, or more. Its vast extent, and its variety of climate and productions, are of advantage, in this age, for one people, whatever they might have been in former ages. Steam, telegraphs, and intelligence, have brought these, to be an advantageous combination, for one united people.

In the inaugural address I briefly pointed out the total inadequacy of disunion, as a remedy for the differences between the people of the two sections. I did so in language which I cannot improve, and which, therefore, I beg to repeat:

"One section of our country believes slavery is *right*, and ought to be extended, while the other believes it is *wrong*, and ought not to be extended. This is the only substantial dispute. The fugitive slave clause of the Constitution, and the law for the suppression of the foreign slave trade, are each as well enforced, perhaps, as any law can ever be in a community where the moral sense of the people imperfectly supports the law itself. The great body of the people abide by the dry legal obligation in both cases, and a few break over in each. This, I think, cannot be perfectly cured; and it would be worse in both cases *after* the separation of the sections, than before. The foreign slave trade, now imperfectly suppressed, would be ultimately revived without restriction in one section; while fugitive slaves, now only partially surrendered, would not be surrendered at all by the other.

"Physically speaking, we cannot separate. We cannot remove our respective sections from each other, nor build an impassable wall between them. A husband and wife may be divorced, and go out of the presence, and beyond the reach of each other; but the different parts of our country cannot do this. They cannot but remain face to face; and intercourse, either amicable or hostile, must continue between them. Is it possible, then, to make that intercourse more advantageous, or more satisfactory, *after* separation than *before?* Can aliens make treaties, easier than friends can make laws? Can treaties be more faithfully enforced between aliens, than laws can among friends? Suppose you go to war, you cannot fight always; and when, after much loss on both sides, and no gain on either, you cease fighting, the identical old questions, as to terms of intercourse, are again upon you."

There is no line, straight or crooked, suitable for a national boundary, upon which to divide. Trace through, from east to west, upon the line between the free and slave country, and we shall find a little more than one-third of its length are rivers, easy to be crossed, and populated, or soon to be populated, thickly upon both sides; while nearly all its remaining length, are merely surveyor's lines, over which people may walk back and forth without any consciousness of their presence. No part of this line can be made any more difficult to pass, by writing it down on paper, or parchment, as a national boundary. The fact of separation, if it comes, gives up, on the part of the seceding section, the fugitive slave clause, along with all other constitutional obligations upon the section seceded from, while I should expect no treaty stipulation would ever be made to take its place.

But there is another difficulty. The great interior region, bounded east by the Alleghenies, north by the British dominions, west by the Rocky mountains, and south by the line along which the culture of corn and cotton meets, and which includes part of Virginia, part of Tennessee, all of Kentucky, Ohio, Indiana, Michigan, Wisconsin, Illinois, Missouri, Kansas, Iowa, Minnesota and the Territories of Dakota, Nebraska, and part of Colorado, already has above ten millions of people, and will have fifty millions within fifty years, if not prevented by any political folly or mistake. It contains more than one-third of the country owned by the United States—certainly more than one million of square miles. Once half as populous as Massachusetts already is, it would have more than seventy-five millions of people. A glance at the map shows that, territorially speaking, it is the great body of the republic. The other parts are but marginal borders to it, the magnificent region sloping west from the rocky mountains to the Pacific, being the deepest, and also the richest, in undeveloped resources. In the production of provisions, grains, grasses, and all which proceed from them, this great interior region is naturally one of the most important in the world. Ascertain from the statistics the small proportion of the region which has, as yet, been brought into cultivation, and also the large and rapidly increasing amount of its products, and we shall be overwhelmed with the magnitude of the prospect presented. And yet this region has no sea-coast, touches no ocean anywhere. As part of one nation, its people now find, and may forever find, their way to Europe by New York, to South America and Africa by New Orleans, and to Asia by San Francisco. But separate our common country into two nations, as designed by the present rebellion, and every man of this great interior region is thereby cut off from some one or more of these outlets, not, perhaps, by a physical barrier, but by embarrassing and onerous trade regulations.

And this is true, *wherever* a dividing, or boundary line, may be fixed. Place it between the now free and slave country, or place it south of Kentucky, or north of Ohio, and still the truth remains, that none south of it, can trade to any port or place north of it, and none north of it, can trade to any port or place south of it, except upon terms dictated by a government foreign to them. These outlets, east, west, and south, are indispensable to the well-being of the people inhabiting, and to inhabit, this vast interior region. *Which* of the three may be the best, is no proper question. All, are better than either, and all, of right, belong to that people, and to their successors forever. True to themselves, they will not ask *where* a line of separation shall be, but will vow, rather, that there shall be no such line. Nor are the marginal regions less interested in these communications to, and through them, to the great outside world. They too, and each of them, must have access to this Egypt of the West, without paying toll at the crossing of any national boundary.

Our national strife springs not from our permanent part; not from the land we inhabit; not from our national homestead. There is no possible severing of this, but would multiply, and not mitigate, evils among us. In all its adaptations and aptitudes, it demands union, and abhors separation. In fact, it would, ere long, force reunion, however much of blood and treasure the separation might have cost.

Our strife pertains to ourselves—to the passing generations of men; and it can, without convulsion, be hushed forever with the passing of one generation.

In this view, I recommend the adoption of the following resolution and articles amendatory to the Constitution of the United States:

"*Resolved by the Senate and House of Representatives of the United States of America in Congress assembled,* (two thirds of both houses concurring,) That the following articles be proposed to the legislatures (or conventions) of the several States as amendments to the Constitution of the United States, all or any of which articles when ratified by three-fourths of the said legislatures (or conventions) to be valid as part or parts of the said Constitution, viz:

"Article——.

"Every State, wherein slavery now exists, which shall abolish the same therein, at any time, or times, before the first day of January, in the year of our Lord one thousand and nine hundred, shall receive compensation from the United States as follows, to wit:

"The President of the United States shall deliver to every such State, bonds of the United States, bearing interest at the rate of — per cent, per annum, to an amount equal to the aggregate sum of   for each slave shown to have been therein, by the eighth census of the United States, said bonds to be delivered to such State by instalments, or in one parcel, at the completion of the abolishment, accordingly as the same shall have been gradual, or at one time, within such State; and interest shall begin to run upon any such bond, only from the proper time of its delivery as aforesaid. Any State having received bonds as aforesaid, and afterwards reintroducing or tolerating slavery therein, shall refund to the United States the bonds so received, or the value thereof, and all interest paid thereon.

"Article——.

"All slaves who shall have enjoyed actual freedom by the chances of the war, at any time before the end of the rebellion, shall be forever free; but all owners of such, who shall not have been disloyal, shall be compensated for them, at the same rates as is provided for States adopting abolishment of slavery, but in such way, that no slave shall be twice accounted for.

"Article——.

"Congress may appropriate money, and otherwise provide, for colonizing free colored persons, with their own consent, at any place or places without the United States."

I beg indulgence to discuss these proposed articles at some length. Without slavery the rebellion could never have existed; without slavery it could not continue.

Among the friends of the Union there is great diversity, of sentiment, and of policy, in regard to slavery, and the African race amongst us. Some would perpetuate slavery; some would abolish it suddenly, and without compensation;

some would abolish it gradually, and with compensation; some would remove the freed people from us, and some would retain them with us; and there are yet other minor diversities. Because of these diversities, we waste much strength in struggles among ourselves. By mutual concession we should harmonize, and act together. This would be compromise; but it would be compromise among the friends, and not with the enemies of the Union. These articles are intended to embody a plan of such mutual concessions. If the plan shall be adopted, it is assumed that emancipation will follow, at least, in several of the States.

As to the first article, the main points are: first, the emancipation; secondly, the length of time for consummating it—thirty-seven years; and thirdly, the compensation.

The emancipation will be unsatisfactory to the advocates of perpetual slavery; but the length of time should greatly mitigate their dissatisfaction. The time spares both races from the evils of sudden derangement—in fact, from the necessity of any derangement—while most of those whose habitual course of thought will be disturbed by the measure will have passed away before its consummation. They will never see it. Another class will hail the prospect of emancipation, but will deprecate the length of time. They will feel that it gives too little to the now living slaves. But it really gives them much. It saves them from the vagrant destitution which must largely attend immediate emancipation in localities where their numbers are very great; and it gives the inspiring assurance that their posterity shall be free forever. The plan leaves to each State, choosing to act under it, to abolish slavery now, or at the end of the century, or at any intermediate time, or by degrees, extending over the whole or any part of the period; and it obliges no two states to proceed alike. It also provides for compensation, and generally the mode of making it. This, it would seem, must further mitigate the dissatisfaction of those who favor perpetual slavery, and especially of those who are to receive the compensation. Doubtless some of those who are to pay, and not to receive will object. Yet the measure is both just and economical. In a certain sense the liberation of slaves is the destruction of property—property acquired by descent, or by purchase, the same as any other property. It is no less true for having been often said, that the people of the south are not more responsible for the original introduction of this property, than are the people of the north; and when it is remembered how unhesitatingly we all use cotton and sugar, and share the profits of dealing in them, it may not be quite safe to say, that the south has been more responsible than the north for its continuance. If then, for a common object, this property is to be sacrificed is it not just that it be done at a common charge?

And if, with less money, or money more easily paid, we can preserve the benefits of the Union by this means, than we can by the war alone, is it not also economical to do it? Let us consider it then. Let us ascertain the sum we have expended in the war since compensated emancipation was proposed last March, and consider whether, if that measure had been promptly accepted, by even some of the slave States, the same sum would not have been done more to close the war, than has been otherwise done. If so the measure would save money, and, in that view, would be a prudent and economical measure. Certainly it is not so easy to pay *something* as it is to pay *nothing;* but it is easier to pay a *large* sum than it is to pay a larger one. And it is easier to pay any sum *when* we are able, than it is to pay it *before* we are able. The war requires large sums, and requires them at once. The aggregate sum necessary for compensated emancipation, of course, would be large. But it would require no ready cash; nor the bonds even, any faster than the emancipation progresses. This might not, and probably would not, close before the end of the thirty-seven years. At that time we shall probably have a hundred millions of people to share the burden, instead of thirty one millions, as now. And not only so, but the increase of our population may be expected to continue for a long time after that period, as rapidly as before; because our territory will not have become full. I do not state this inconsiderately. At the same ratio of increase which we have maintained, on an average, from our first national census, in 1790, until that of 1860, we should, in 1900, have a population of 103,208,415. And why may we not continue that ratio far beyond that period? Our abundant room—our broad national homestead—is our ample resource. Were our territory as limited as are the British Isles, very certainly our population could not expand as stated. Instead of receiving the foreign born, as now, we should be compelled to send part of the native born away. But such is not our condition. We have two millions nine hundred and sixty-three thousand square miles. Europe has three millions and eight hundred thousand, with a population averaging seventy-three and one-third persons to the square mile. Why may not our country, at some time, average as many? Is it less fertile? Has it more waste surface, by mountains, rivers, lakes, deserts, or other causes? Is it inferior to Europe in any natural advantage? If, then, we are, at some time, to be as populous as Europe, how soon? As to when this *may* be, we can judge by the past and the present; as to when it *will* be, if ever, depends much on whether we maintain the Union. Several of our States are already above the average of Europe—seventy three and a third to the square mile. Massachusetts has 157; Rhode Island, 133; Connecticut, 99; New York and New Jersey, each, 80; also two other great States, Pennsylvania and Ohio, are not far below, the former having 63, and the latter 59. The States already above the European average, except New York, have increased in as rapid a ratio, since passing that point, as ever before; while no one of them is equal to some other parts of our country, in natural capacity for sustaining a dense population.

Taking the nation in the aggregate, and we find its population and ratio of increase, for the several decennial periods, to be as follows:—

1790	3,929,827		
1800	5,305,937	35.02 per cent.	ratio of increase
1810	7,239,814	36.45	"
1820	9,638,131	33.13	"
1830	12,866,020	33.49	"
1840	17,069,453	32.67	"
1850	23,191,876	35.87	"
1860	31,443,790	35.58	"

This shows an average decennial increase of 34.60 per cent. in population through the seventy years from our first, to our last census yet taken. It is seen that the ratio of increase, at no one of these seven periods, is either two per cent. below, or two per cent. above, the average; thus showing how inflexible, and, consequently, how reliable, the law of increase, in our case, is. Assuming that it will continue, gives the following results:—

1870	42,323,341	1910	138,918,526
1880	56,967,216	1920	186,984,335
1890	76,677,872	1930	251,680,914
1900	103,208,415		

These figures show that our country *may* be as populous as Europe now is, at some point between 1920 and 1930—say about 1925—our territory, at seventy-three and a third persons to the square mile, being of capacity to contain 217,186,000.

And we *will* reach this, too, if we do not ourselves relinquish the chance, by the folly and evils of disunion, or by long and exhausting war springing from the only great element of national discord among us. While it cannot be fore-seen exactly how much one huge example of secession, breeding lesser ones indefinitely, would retard population, civilization, and prosperity, no one can doubt that the extent of it would be very great and injurious.

The proposed emancipation would shorten the war, per-petuate peace, insure this increase of population, and pro-portionately the wealth of the country. With these, we should pay all the emancipation would cost, together with our other debt, easier than we should pay our other debt, without it. If we had allowed our old national debt to run at six per cent. per annum, simple interest, from the end of our revolutionary struggle until to day, without paying anything on either principal or interest, each man of us would owe less upon that debt now, than each man owed upon it then; and this because our increase of men, through the whole period, has been greater than six per cent.; has run faster than the interest upon the debt. Thus, time alone relieves a debtor nation, so long as its population increases faster than unpaid interest accumu-lates on its debt.

This fact would be no excuse for delaying payment of what is justly due; but it shows the great importance of time in this connexion—the great advantage of a policy by which we shall not have to pay until we number a hundred millions, what, by a different policy, we would have to pay now, when we number but thirty one millions. In a word, it shows that a dollar will be much harder to pay for the war, than will be a dollar for emancipation on the proposed plan. And then the latter will cost no blood, no precious life. It will be a saving of both.

As to the second article, I think it would be impracticable to return to bondage the class of persons therein contem-plated. Some of them, doubtless, in the property sense, belong to loyal owners; and hence, provision is made in this article for compensating such.

The third article relates to the future of the freed people. It does not oblige, but merely authorizes, Congress to aid in colonizing such as may consent. This ought not to be regarded as objectionable, on the one hand, or on the other, in so much as it comes to nothing, unless by the mutual consent of the people to be deported, and the American voters, through their representatives in Congress.

I cannot make it better known than it already is, that I strongly favor colonization. And yet I wish to say there is an objection urged against free colored persons remaining in the country, which is largely imaginary, if not sometimes malicious.

It is insisted that their presence would injure, and displace white labor and white laborers. If there ever could be a proper time for mere catch arguments, that time surely is not now. In times like the present, men should utter nothing for which they would not willingly be responsible through time and in eternity. Is it true, then, that colored people can displace any more white labor, by being free, than by remaining slaves? If they stay in their old places, they jostle no white laborers; if they leave their old places, they leave them open to white laborers. Logically, there is neither more nor less of it. Emancipation, even without deportation, would probably enhance the wages of white labor, and, very surely, would not reduce them. Thus, the customary amount of labor would still have to be performed; the freed people would surely not do more than their old proportion of it, and very probably, for a time, would do less, leaving an increased part to white laborers, bringing their labor into greater demand, and, consequently, enhancing the wages of it. With deportation, even to a limited extent, enhanced wages to white labor is mathematically certain. Labor is like any other commodity in the market—increase the demand for it, and you increase the price of it. Reduce the supply of black labor, by colonizing the black laborer out of the country, and, by precisely so much, you increase the demand for, and wages of, white labor.

But it is dreaded that the freed people will swarm forth, and cover the whole land? Are they not already in the land? Will liberation make them any more numerous? Equally distributed among the whites of the whole country, and there would be but one colored to seven whites. Could the one, in any way, greatly disturb the seven? There are many communities now, having more than one free colored person, to seven whites; and this, without any apparent consciousness of evil from it. The District of Columbia, and the States of Maryland and Delaware, are all in this condition. The District has more than one free colored to six whites; and yet, in its frequent petitions to Congress, I believe it has never presented the presence of free colored persons as one of its grievances. But why should emancipation south, send the free people north? People, of any color, seldom run, unless there be something to run from. *Heretofore* colored people, to some extent, have fled north from bondage; and *now*, perhaps, from both bondage and destitution. But if gradual emancipation and deportation be adopted, they will have neither to flee from. Their old masters will give them wages at least until new laborers can be procured; and the freed men, in turn, will gladly give their labor for the wages, till new homes can be found for them, in congenial climes, and with people of their own blood and race. This proposition can be trusted on the mutual interests involved. And, in any event, cannot the north decide for itself, whether to receive them?

Again, as practice proves more than theory, in any case, has there been any irruption of colored people northward, because of the abolishment of slavery in this District last spring?

What I have said of the proportion of free colored persons to the whites, in the District, is from the census of 1860, having no reference to persons called contrabands, not to those made free by the act of Congress abolishing slavery here.

The plan consisting of these articles is recommended, not but that a restoration of the national authority would be accepted without its adoption.

Nor will the war, nor proceedings under the proclamation of September 22, 1862, be stayed because of the *recommendation* of this plan. Its timely *adoption*, I doubt not, would bring restoration and thereby stay both.

And, notwithstanding this plan, the recommendation that Congress provide by law for compensating any State which may adopt emancipation, before this plan shall have been acted upon, is hereby earnestly renewed. Such would be only an advance part of the plan, and the same arguments apply to both.

This plan is recommended as a means, not in exclusion of, but additional to, all others for restoring and preserving the national authority throughout the Union. The subject is presented exclusively in its economical aspect. The plan would, I am confident, secure peace more speedily, and maintain it more permanently, than can be done by force alone; while all it would cost, considering amounts, and manner of payment, and times of payment, would be easier paid than will be the additional cost of the war, if we rely solely upon force. It is much—very much—that it would cost no blood at all.

The plan is proposed as permanent constitutional law. It cannot become such without the concurrence of, first, two-thirds of Congress, and, afterwards, three-fourths of the States. The requisite three-fourths of the States will necessarily include seven of the Slave states. Their concurrence, if obtained, will give assurance of their severally adopting emancipation, at no very distant day, upon the new constitutional terms. This assurance would end the struggle now, and save the Union forever.

I do not forget the gravity which should characterize a

paper addressed to the Congress of the nation by the Chief Magistrate of the nation. Nor do I forget that some of you are my seniors, nor that many of you have more experience than I, in the conduct of public affairs. Yet I trust that in view of the great responsibility resting upon me, you will perceive no want of respect to yourselves, in any undue earnestness I may seem to display.

Is it doubted, then, that the plan I propose, if adopted, would shorten the war, and thus lessen its expenditure of money and of blood? Is it doubted that it would restore the national authority and national prosperity, and perpetuate both indefinitely? Is it doubted that we here—Congress and Executive—can secure its adoption? Will not the good people respond to a united, and earnest appeal from us? Can we, can they, by any other means, so certainly, or so speedily, assure these vital objects? We can succeed only by concert. It is not "can *any* of us *imagine* better?" but "can we *all* do better?" Object whatsoever is possible, still the question recurs "can we do better?" The dogmas of the quiet past, are inadequate to the stormy present. The occasion is piled high with difficulty, and we must rise with the occasion. As our case is new, so we must think anew, and act anew. We must disenthrall ourselves, and then we shall save our country.

Fellow-citizens, *we* cannot escape history. We of this Congress and this administration, will be remembered in spite of ourselves. No personal significance, or insignificance, can spare one or another of us. The fiery trial through which we pass, will light us down, in honor or dishonor, to the latest generation. We *say* we are for the Union. The world will not forget that we say this. We know how to save the Union. The world knows we do know how to save it. We—even *we here*—hold the power, and bear the responsibility. In *giving* freedom to the *slave*, we *assure* freedom to the *free*—honorable alike in what we give, and what we preserve. We shall nobly save, or meanly lose, the last best, hope of earth. Other means may succeed; this could not fail. The way is plain, peaceful, generous, just—a way which, if followed, the world will forever applaud, and God must forever bless.

December 1, 1862.

Message to Senate on Minnesota Indians

To the Senate of the United States:

In compliance with your resolution of December 5th, 1862, requesting the President "to furnish the Senate with all information in his possession touching the late Indian barbarities in the State of Minnesota, and also the evidence in his possession upon which some of the principal actors and head men were tried and condemned to death," I have the honor to state, that on receipt of said resolution I transmitted the same to the Secretary of the Interior, accompanied by a note, a copy of which is herewith inclosed, marked "A.," and in response to which I received, through that Department, a letter of the Commissioner of Indian Affairs, a copy of which is herewith inclosed, marked "B."

I further state, that on the 8th. day of November last I received a long telegraphic dispatch from Major General Pope, at St. Paul, Minnesota, simply announcing the names of the persons sentenced to be hanged. I immediately telegraphed to have transcripts of the records in all the cases forwarded to me, which transcripts, however, did not reach me until two or three days before the present meeting of Congress. Meantime I received, through telegraphic dispatches and otherwise, appeals in behalf of the condemned, appeals for their execution, and expressions of opinion as to proper policy in regard to them, and to the Indians generally in that vicinity, none of which, as I understand, falls within the scope of your inquiry. After the arrival of the transcripts of records, but before I had sufficient opportunity to examine them, I received a joint letter from one of the Senators and two of the Representatives from Minnesota, which contains some statements of fact not found in the records of the trials, and for which reason I herewith transmit a copy, marked "C." I also, for the same reason, inclose a printed memorial of the citizens of St. Paul, addressed to me, and forwarded with the letter aforesaid.

Anxious to not act with so much clemency as to encourage another outbreak on the one hand, nor with so much severity as to be real cruelty on the other, I caused a careful examination of the records of trials to be made, in view of first ordering the execution of such as had been proved guilty of violating females. Contrary to my expectations, only two of this class were found. I then directed a further examination, and a classification of all who were proven to have participated in *massacres*, as distinguished from participation in *battles*. This class numbered forty, and included the two convicted of female violation. One of the number is strongly recommended by the Commission which tried them, for commutation to ten years' imprisonment. I have ordered the other thirty-nine to be executed on Friday, the 19th. instant. The order was dispatched from here on Monday, the 8th. instant, by a messenger to General Sibley; and a copy of which order is herewith transmitted, marked "D."

An abstract of the evidence as to the forty is herewith enclosed, marked "E."

To avoid the immense amount of copying, I lay before the Senate the original transcripts of the records of trials, as received by me.

This is as full and complete a response to the resolution as it is in my power to make.

December 11, 1862

To William H. Seward and Salmon P. Chase

(COPY)

Hon. William H. Seward, &   Executive Mansion,
Hon. Salmon P. Chase.   Washington, December 20. 1862.

Gentlemen: You have respectively tendered me your resignations, as Secretary of State, and Secretary of the Treasury of the United States. I am apprised of the circumstances which may render this course personally desireable to each of you; but, after most anxious consideration, my deliberate judgment is, that the public interest does not admit of it. I therefore have to request that you will resume the duties of your Departments respectively. Your Obt. Servt.

P.S. Same as above sent to Gov. Chase
P.S. Same as above sent to Gov. Seward.
Note—Postscripts, like the above are to respective letters.

Message to the Army of the Potomac

Executive Mansion, Washington, December 22, 1862.

To the Army of the Potomac: I have just read your Commanding General's preliminary report of the battle of Fredericksburg. Although you were not successful, the attempt was not an error, nor the failure other than an accident. The courage with which you, in an open field, maintained the contest against an entrenched foe, and the consummate skill and success with which you crossed and re-crossed the river, in face of the enemy, show that you possess all the qualities of a great army, which will yet give victory to the cause of the country and of popular government. Condoling with the mourners for the dead, and sympathizing with the severely wounded, I congratulate you that the number of both is comparatively so small.

I tender to you, officers and soldiers, the thanks of the nation.

To Fanny McCullough

Executive Mansion,
Dear Fanny   Washington, December 23, 1862.

It is with deep grief that I learn of the death of your kind and brave Father; and, especially, that it is affecting your young heart beyond what is common in such cases. In this sad world of ours, sorrow comes to all; and, to the young, it comes with bitterest agony, because it takes them unawares. The older have learned to ever expect it. I am anxious to afford some alleviation of your present distress. Perfect relief is not possible, except with time. You can not now realize that you will ever feel better. Is not this so? And yet it is a mistake. You are sure to be happy again. To know this, which is certainly true, will make you some less miserable now. I have had experience enough to know what I say; and you need only to believe it, to feel better at once. The memory of your dear Father, instead of an agony, will yet be a sad sweet feeling in your heart, of a purer, and holier sort than you have known before.

Please present my kind regards to your afflicted mother.

Your sincere friend

Final Emancipation Proclamation

By the President
of the United States of America:
a Proclamation.

Whereas, on the twentysecond day of September, in the year of our Lord one thousand eight hundred and sixty two, a proclamation was issued by the President of the United States, containing, among other things, the following, towit:

"That on the first day of January, in the year of our Lord one thousand eight hundred and sixty-three, all persons held as slaves within any State or designated part of a State, the people whereof shall then be in rebellion against the United States, shall be then, thenceforward, and forever free; and the Executive Government of the United States, including the military and naval authority thereof, will recognize and maintain the freedom of such persons, and will do no act or acts to repress such persons, or any of them, in any efforts they may make for their actual freedom.

"That the Executive will, on the first day of January aforesaid, by proclamation, designate the States and parts of States, if any, in which the people thereof, respectively, shall then be in rebellion against the United States; and the fact that any State, or the people thereof, shall on that day be, in good faith, represented in the Congress of the United States by members chosen thereto at elections wherein a majority of the qualified voters of such State shall have participated, shall, in the absence of strong countervailing testimony, be deemed conclusive evidence that such State, and the people thereof, are not then in rebellion against the United States."

Now, therefore, I, Abraham Lincoln, President of the United States, by virtue of the power in me vested as Commander-in-Chief, of the Army and Navy of the United States in time of actual armed rebellion against authority and government of the United States, and as a fit and necessary war measure for suppressing said rebellion, do, on this first day of January, in the year of our Lord one thousand eight hundred and sixty three, and in accordance with my purpose so to do publicly proclaimed for the full period of one hundred days, from the day first above mentioned, order and designate as the States and parts of States wherein the people thereof respectively, are this day in rebellion against the United States, the following, towit:

Arkansas, Texas, Louisiana, (except the Parishes of St. Bernard, Plaquemines, Jefferson, St. Johns, St. Charles, St. James, Ascension, Assumption, Terrebonne, Lafourche, St. Mary, St. Martin, and Orleans, including the City of New-Orleans) Mississippi, Alabama, Florida, Georgia, South-Carolina, North-Carolina, and Virginia, (except the fortyeight counties designated as West Virginia, and also the counties of Berkley, Accomac, Northampton, Elizabeth-City, York, Princess Ann, and Norfolk, including the cities of Norfolk & Portsmouth); and which excepted parts are, for the present, left precisely as if this proclamation were not issued.

And by virtue of the power, and for the purpose aforesaid, I do order and declare that all persons held as slaves within said designated States, and parts of States, are, and henceforward shall be free; and that the Executive government of the United States, including the military and naval authorities thereof, will recognize and maintain the freedom of said persons.

And I hereby enjoin upon the people so declared to be free to abstain from all violence, unless in necessary self-defence; and I recommend to them that, in all cases when allowed, they labor faithfully for reasonable wages.

And I further declare and make known, that such persons of suitable condition, will be received into the armed service of the United States to garrison forts, positions, stations, and other places, and to man vessels of all sorts in said service.

And upon this act, sincerely believed to be an act of justice, warranted by the Constitution, upon military necessity, I invoke the considerate judgment of mankind, and the gracious favor of Almighty God.

In witness whereof, I have hereunto set my hand and caused the seal of the United States to be affixed.

Done at the City of Washington, this first day of January, in the year of our Lord one thousand eight hundred and sixty three, and of the Independence of the United States of America the eighty-seventh.

By the President: ABRAHAM LINCOLN
WILLIAM H. SEWARD, Secretary of State.

To the Workingmen of Manchester, England

Executive Mansion, Washington,
To the workingmen of Manchester: January 19, 1863.

I have the honor to acknowledge the receipt of the address and resolutions which you sent me on the eve of the new year.

When I came, on the fourth day of March, 1861, through a free and constitutional election, to preside in the government of the United States, the country was found at the verge of civil war. Whatever might have been the cause, or whosoever the fault, one duty paramount to all others was before me, namely, to maintain and preserve at once the Constitution and the integrity of the federal republic. A conscientious purpose to perform this duty is a key to all the measures of administration which have been, and to all which will hereafter be pursued. Under our form of government, and my official oath, I could not depart from this purpose if I would. It is not always in the power of governments to enlarge or restrict the scope of moral results which follow the policies that they may deem it necessary for the public safety, from time to time, to adopt.

I have understood well that the duty of self-preservation rests solely with the American people. But I have at the same time been aware that favor or disfavor of foreign nations might have a material influence in enlarging and prolonging the struggle with disloyal men in which the country is engaged. A fair examination of history has seemed to authorize a belief that the past action and influences of the United States were generally regarded as having been beneficent towards mankind. I have therefore reckoned upon the forbearance of nations. Circumstances, to some of which you kindly allude, induced me especially to expect that if justice and good faith should be practiced by the United States, they would encounter no hostile influence on the part of Great Britain. It is now a pleasant duty to acknowledge the demonstration you have given of your desire that a spirit of peace and amity towards this country may prevail in the councils of your Queen, who is respected and esteemed in your own country only more than she is by the kindred nation which has its home on this side of the Atlantic.

I know and deeply deplore the sufferings which the workingmen at Manchester and in all Europe are called to endure in this crisis. It has been often and studiously represented that the attempt to overthrow this government, which was built upon the foundation of human rights, and to substitute for it one which should rest exclusively on the basis of human slavery, was likely to obtain the favor of Europe. Through the actions of our disloyal citizens the workingmen of Europe have been subjected to a severe trial, for the purpose of forcing their sanction to that attempt. Under these circumstances, I cannot but regard your decisive utterance upon the question as an instance of sublime Christian heroism which has not been surpassed in any age or in any country. It is, indeed, an energetic and reinspiring assurance of the inherent power of truth and of the ultimate and universal

triumph of justice, humanity, and freedom. I do not doubt
that the sentiments you have expressed will be sustained by
your great nation, and, on the other hand, I have no hesitation
in assuring you that they will excite admiration, esteem, and
the most reciprocal feelings of friendship among the American
people. I hail this interchange of sentiment, therefore, as an
augury that, whatever else may happen, whatever misfortune
may befall your country or my own, the peace and friendship
which now exist between the two nations will be, as it shall
be my desire to make them, perpetual.

To Joseph Hooker

Major General Hooker: Executive Mansion,
General.   Washington, January 26, 1863.

I have placed you at the head of the Army of the Potomac. Of course I have done this upon what appear to me
to be sufficient reasons. And yet I think it best for you to
know that there are some things in regard to which, I am
not quite satisfied with you. I believe you to be a brave
and a skilful soldier, which, of course, I like. I also believe
you do not mix politics with your profession, in which you
are right. You have confidence in yourself, which is a valuable, if not an indispensable quality. You are ambitious,
which, within reasonable bounds, does good rather than
harm. But I think that during Gen. Burnside's command of
the Army, you have taken counsel of your ambition, and
thwarted him as much as you could, in which you did a
great wrong to the country, and to a most meritorious and
honorable brother officer. I have heard, in such way as to
believe it, of your recently saying that both the Army and
the Government needed a Dictator. Of course it was not
for this, but in spite of it, that I have given you the com-

mand. Only those generals who gain successes, can set up dictators. What I now ask of you is military success, and I will risk the dictatorship. The government will support you to the utmost of it's ability, which is neither more nor less than it has done and will do for all commanders. I much fear that the spirit which you have aided to infuse into the Army, of criticising their Commander, and withholding confidence from him, will now turn upon you. I shall assist you as far as I can, to put it down. Neither you, nor Napoleon, if he were alive again, could get any good out of an army, while such a spirit prevails in it.

And now, beware of rashness. Beware of rashness, but with energy, and sleepless vigilance, go forward, and give us victories. Yours very truly

To Andrew Johnson

Private

Hon. Andrew Johnson   Executive Mansion,
My dear Sir: Washington, March 26. 1863.

I am told you have at least *thought* of raising a negro military force. In my opinion the country now needs no specific thing so much as some man of your ability, and position, to go to this work. When I speak of your position, I mean that of an eminent citizen of a slave-state, and himself a slave-holder. The colored population is the great *available* and yet *unavailed* of, force for restoring the Union. The bare sight of fifty thousand armed, and drilled black soldiers on the banks of the Mississippi, would end the rebellion at once. And who doubts that we can present that sight, if we but take hold in earnest? If you *have* been thinking of it please do not dismiss the thought. Yours truly

Speech to Indian Chiefs, Washington, D.C.

"You have all spoken of the strange sights you see here, among your pale-faced brethren; the very great number of people that you see; the big wigwams; the difference between our people and your own. But you have seen but a very small part of the pale-faced people. You may wonder when I tell you that there are people here in this wigwam, now looking at you, who have come from other countries a great deal farther off than you have come.

"We pale-faced people think that this world is a great, round ball, and we have people here of the pale-faced family who have come almost from the other side of it to represent their nations here and conduct their friendly intercourse with us, as you now come from your part of the round ball."

Here a globe was introduced, and the President, laying his hand upon it, said:

"One of our learned men will now explain to you our notions about this great ball, and show you where you live."

Professor Henry then gave the delegation a detailed and interesting explanation of the formation of the earth, showing how much of it was water and how much was land; and pointing out the countries with which we had intercourse. He also showed them the position of Washington and that of their own country, from which they had come.

The President then said:

"We have people now present from all parts of the globe—here, and here, and here. There is a great difference between this pale-faced people and their red brethren, both as to numbers and the way in which they live. We know not whether your own situation is best for your race, but this is what has made the difference in our way of living.

"The pale-faced people are numerous and prosperous because they cultivate the earth, produce bread, and depend upon the products of the earth rather than wild game for a subsistence.

"This is the chief reason of the difference; but there is another. Although we are now engaged in a great war between one another, we are not, as a race, so much disposed to fight and kill one another as our red brethren.

"You have asked for my advice. I really am not capable of advising you whether, in the providence of the Great Spirit, who is the great Father of us all, it is best for you to maintain the habits and customs of your race, or adopt a new mode of life.

"I can only say that I can see no way in which your race is to become as numerous and prosperous as the white race except by living as they do, by the cultivation of the earth.

"It is the object of this Government to be on terms of peace with you, and with all our red brethren. We constantly endeavor to be so. We make treaties with you, and will try to observe them; and if our children should sometimes behave badly, and violate these treaties, it is against our wish.

"You know it is not always possible for any father to have his children do precisely as he wishes them to do.

"In regard to being sent back to your own country, we have an officer, the Commissioner of Indian Affairs, who will take charge of that matter, and make the necessary arrangements."

The President's remarks were received with frequent marks of applause and approbation. "Ugh," "Aha" sounded along the line as the interpreter proceeded, and their countenances gave evident tokens of satisfaction.

March 27, 1863

To Mary Todd Lincoln

Mrs. Lincoln   Executive Mansion,
Philadelphia, Pa.   Washington, June 9. 1863.
  Think you better put "Tad's" pistol away. I had an ugly
dream about him.

To Lorenzo Thomas

Gen. Thomas   Washington, D.C.,
Harrisburg, Penn.   July 8 1863
  Your despatch of this morning to the Sec. of War is
before me. The forces you speak of, will be of no immagi-
neable service, if they can not go forward with a little more
expedition. Lee is now passing the Potomac faster than the
forces you mention are passing Carlyle. Forces now beyond
Carlyle, to be joined by regiments still at Harrisburg, and
the united force again to join Pierce somewhere, and the
whole to move down the Cumberland Valley, will, in my
unprofessional opinion, be quite as likely to capture the
Man-in-the-Moon, as any part of Lee's Army

To Ulysses S. Grant

Major General Grant   Executive Mansion,
My dear General   Washington, July 13, 1863.
  I do not remember that you and I ever met personally.
I write this now as a grateful acknowledgment for the almost
inestimable service you have done the country. I wish to

say a word further. When you first reached the vicinity of Vicksburg, I thought you should do, what you finally did—march the troops across the neck, run the batteries with the transports, and thus go below; and I never had any faith, except a general hope that you knew better than I, that the Yazoo Pass expedition, and the like, could succeed. When you got below, and took Port-Gibson, Grand Gulf, and vicinity, I thought you should go down the river and join Gen. Banks; and when you turned Northward East of the Big Black, I feared it was a mistake. I now wish to make the personal acknowledgment that you were right, and I was wrong. Yours very truly

To George G. Meade

Executive Mansion,
Major General Meade   Washington, July 14, 1863.

I have just seen your despatch to Gen. Halleck, asking to be relieved of your command, because of a supposed censure of mine. I am very—*very*—grateful to you for the magnificent success you gave the cause of the country at Gettysburg; and I am sorry now to be the author of the slightest pain to you. But I was in such deep distress myself that I could not restrain some expression of it. I had been oppressed nearly ever since the battles at Gettysburg, by what appeared to be evidences that yourself, and Gen. Couch, and Gen. Smith, were not seeking a collision with the enemy, but were trying to get him across the river without another battle. What these evidences were, if you please, I hope to tell you at some time, when we shall both feel better. The case, summarily stated is this. You fought and beat the enemy at Gettysburg; and, of course, to say the least, his loss was as great as yours. He retreated; and you did not, as it seemed to me, pressingly pursue him; but a flood in the river detained him, till, by slow degrees, you were again upon him. You had at least twenty thousand veteran troops directly with you, and as many more raw ones within supporting distance, all in addition to those who fought with you at Gettysburg; while it was not possible that he had received a single recruit; and yet you stood and let the flood run down, bridges be built, and the enemy move away at his leisure, without attacking him. And Couch and Smith! The latter left Carlisle in time, upon all ordinary calculation, to have aided you in the last battle at Gettysburg; but he did not arrive. At the end of more than ten days, I believe twelve, under constant urging, he reached Hagerstown from Carlisle, which is not an inch over fiftyfive miles, if so much. And Couch's movement was very little different.

Again, my dear general, I do not believe you appreciate the magnitude of the misfortune involved in Lee's escape. He was within your easy grasp, and to have closed upon him would, in connection with our other late successes, have ended the war. As it is, the war will be prolonged indefinitely. If you could not safely attack Lee last monday, how can you possibly do so South of the river, when you can take with you very few more than two thirds of the force you then had in hand? It would be unreasonable to expect, and I do not expect you can now effect much. Your golden opportunity is gone, and I am distressed immeasureably because of it.

I beg you will not consider this a prossecution, or persecution of yourself. As you had learned that I was dissatisfied, I have thought it best to kindly tell you why.

Verse on Lee's Invasion of the North

Gen. Lees invasion of the North written by himself—

> In eighteen sixty three, with pomp,
>   and mighty swell,
> Me and Jeff's Confederacy, went
>   forth to sack Phil-del,
> The Yankees they got arter us, and
>   giv us particular hell,
> And we skedaddled back again,
>   and didn't sack Phil-del.

July 19, 1863

To Edwin M. Stanton

Hon Secretary of War   Executive Mansion
My dear Sir: Washington July 28 1863
   A young son of the Senator Brown of Mississippi, not yet twenty, as I understand, was wounded, and made a prisoner at Gettysburg. His mother is sister of Mrs P. R. Fendall, of this city. Mr Fendall, on behalf of himself and family, asks that he and they may have charge of the boy, to cure him up, being responsible for his person and good behavior. Would it not be rather a grateful and graceful thing to let them have him? Yours truly

Order of Retaliation

Executive Mansion, Washington D.C July 30. 1863

It is the duty of every government to give protection to its citizens, of whatever class, color, or condition, and especially to those who are duly organized as soldiers in the public service. The law of nations and the usages and customs of war as carried on by civilized powers, permit no distinction as to color in the treatment of prisoners of war as public enemies. To sell or enslave any captured person, on account of his color, and for no offense against the laws of war, is a relapse into barbarism and a crime against the civilization of the age.

The government of the United States will give the same protection to all its soldiers, and if the enemy shall sell or enslave anyone because of his color, the offense shall be punished by retaliation upon the enemy's prisoners in our possession.

It is therefore ordered that for every soldier of the United States killed in violation of the laws of war, a rebel soldier shall be executed; and for every one enslaved by the enemy or sold into slavery, a rebel soldier shall be placed at hard labor on the public works and continued at such labor until the other shall be released and receive the treatment due to a prisoner of war

Proclamation of Thanksgiving

By the President
of the United States of America
a proclamation.

The year that is drawing towards its close, has been filled with the blessings of fruitful fields and healthful skies. To these bounties, which are so constantly enjoyed that we are prone to forget the source from which they come, others have been added, which are of so extraordinary a nature, that they cannot fail to penetrate and soften even the heart which is habitually insensible to the ever watchful providence of Almighty God. In the midst of a civil war of unequalled magnitude and severity, which has sometimes seemed to foreign States to invite and to provoke their aggression, peace has been preserved with all nations, order has been maintained, the laws have been respected and obeyed, and harmony has prevailed everywhere except in the theatre of military conflict; while that theatre has been greatly contracted by the advancing armies and navies of the Union. Needful diversions of wealth and of strength from the fields of peaceful industry to the national defence, have not arrested the plough, the shuttle or the ship; the axe has enlarged the borders of our settlements, and the mines, as well of iron and coal as of the precious metals, have yielded even more abundantly than heretofore. Population has steadily increased, notwithstanding the waste that has been made in the camp, the siege and the battle-field; and the country, rejoicing in the consciousness of augmented strength and vigor, is permitted to expect continuance of years with large increase of freedom. No human counsel hath devised nor hath any mortal hand worked out these great things. They are the gracious gifts of the Most High God, who, while dealing with us in anger for our sins, hath nevertheless remembered mercy. It has seemed to me fit and proper that they should be solemnly, reverently and gratefully acknowledged as with one heart and one voice by the whole American People. I do therefore invite my fellow citizens in every part of the United States, and also those who are at sea and those who are sojourning in foreign lands, to set apart and observe the last Thursday of November next, as a day of Thanksgiving and Praise to our beneficent Father who dwelleth in the Heavens. And I recommend to them that while offering up the ascriptions justly due to Him for such singular deliverances and blessings, they do also, with humble penitence of our national perverseness and disobedience, commend to His tender care all those who have become widows, orphans, mourners or sufferers in the lamentable civil strife in which we are unavoidably engaged, and fervently implore the interposition of the Almighty Hand to heal the wounds of the nation and to restore it as soon as may be consistent with the Divine purposes to the full enjoyment of peace, harmony, tranquillity and Union.

In testimony whereof, I have hereunto set my hand and caused the Seal of the United States to be affixed.

Done at the city of Washington, this Third day of October, in the year of our Lord one thousand eight hundred and sixty-three, and of the Independence of the United States the Eighty-eighth.

By the President: ABRAHAM LINCOLN
WILLIAM H. SEWARD, Secretary of State.

4.

THE SYMBOL OF AMERICA

Address at Gettysburg, Pennsylvania

Address delivered at the dedication of the Cemetery at Gettysburg.

Four score and seven years ago our fathers brought forth on this continent, a new nation, conceived in Liberty, and dedicated to the proposition that all men are created equal.

Now we are engaged in a great civil war, testing whether that nation, or any nation so conceived and so dedicated, can long endure. We are met on a great battle-field of that war. We have come to dedicate a portion of that field, as a final resting place for those who here gave their lives that that nation might live. It is altogether fitting and proper that we should do this.

But, in a larger sense, we can not dedicate—we can not consecrate—we can not hallow—this ground. The brave men, living and dead, who struggled here, have consecrated it, far above our poor power to add or detract. The world will little note, nor long remember what we say here, but it can never forget what they did here. It is for us the living, rather, to be dedicated here to the unfinished work which they who fought here have thus far so nobly advanced. It is rather for us to be here dedicated to the great task remaining before us—that from these honored dead we take increased devotion to that cause for which they gave the last full measure of devotion— that we here highly resolve that these dead shall not have died in vain—that this nation, under God, shall have a new birth of freedom—and that government of the people, by the people, for the people, shall not perish from the earth.

November 19. 1863.

Annual Message to Congress

Fellow citizens of the Senate and House of Representatives:

Another year of health, and of sufficiently abundant harvests has passed. For these, and especially for the improved condition of our national affairs, our renewed, and profoundest gratitude to God is due.

We remain in peace and friendship with foreign powers.

The efforts of disloyal citizens of the United States to involve us in foreign wars, to aid an inexcusable insurrection, have been unavailing. Her Britannic Majesty's government, as was justly expected, have exercised their authority to prevent the departure of new hostile expeditions from British ports. The Emperor of France has, by a like proceeding, promptly vindicated the neutrality which he proclaimed at the beginning of the contest. Questions of great intricacy and importance have arisen out of the blockade, and other belligerent operations, between the government and several of the maritime powers, but they have been discussed, and, as far as was possible, accommodated in a spirit of frankness, justice, and mutual good will. It is especially gratifying that our prize courts, by the impartiality of their adjudications, have commanded the respect and confidence of maritime powers.

The supplemental treaty between the United States and Great Britain for the suppression of the African slave trade, made on the 17th. day of February last, has been duly ratified, and carried into execution. It is believed that, so far as American ports and American citizens are concerned, that inhuman and odious traffic has been brought to an end.

I shall submit, for the consideration of the Senate, a convention for the adjustment of possessory claims in Washington Territory, arising out of the treaty of the 15th. June, 1846, between the United States and Great Britain, and which have been the source of some disquiet among the citizens of that now rapidly improving part of the country.

A novel and important question, involving the extent of the maritime jurisdiction of Spain in the waters which surround the island of Cuba, has been debated without reaching an agreement, and it is proposed in an amicable spirit to refer it to the arbitrament of a friendly power. A convention for that purpose will be submitted to the Senate.

I have thought it proper, subject to the approval of the Senate, to concur with the interested commercial powers in an arrangement for the liquidation of the Scheldt dues upon the principles which have been heretofore adopted in regard to the imposts upon navigation in the waters of Denmark.

The long pending controversy between this government and that of Chili touching the seizure at Sitana, in Peru, by Chilian officers, of a large amount in treasure belonging to citizens of the United States, has been brought to a close by the award of His Majesty, the King of the Belgians, to whose arbitration the question was referred by the parties. The subject was thoroughly and patiently examined by that justly respected magistrate, and although the sum awarded to the claimants may not have been as large as they expected, there is no reason to distrust the wisdom of his Majesty's decision. That decision was promptly complied with by Chili, when intelligence in regard to it reached that country.

The joint commission, under the act of the last session, for carrying into effect the convention with Peru on the subject of claims, has been organized at Lima, and is engaged in the business intrusted to it.

Difficulties concerning inter-oceanic transit through Nicaragua are in course of amicable adjustment.

In conformity with principles set forth in my last annual message, I have received a representative from the United States of Colombia, and have accredited a minister to that republic.

Incidents occurring in the progress of our civil war have forced upon my attention the uncertain state of international questions, touching the rights of foreigners in this country and of United States citizens abroad. In regard to some governments these rights are at least partially defined by treaties. In no instance, however, is it expressly stipulated that, in the event of civil war, a foreigner residing in this country, within the lines of the insurgents, is to be exempted from the rule which classes him as a belligerent, in whose behalf the government of his country cannot expect any privileges or immunities distinct from that character. I regret to say, however, that such claims have been put forward, and, in some instances, in behalf of foreigners who have lived in the United States the greater part of their lives.

There is reason to believe that many persons born in foreign countries, who have declared their intention to become citizens, or who have been fully naturalized, have evaded the military duty required of them by denying the fact, and thereby throwing upon the government the burden of proof. It has been found difficult or impracticable to obtain this proof from the want of guides to the proper sources of information. These might be supplied by requiring clerks of courts, where declarations of intention may be made or naturalizations effected, to send, periodically, lists of the names of the persons naturalized, or declaring their intention to become citizens, to the Secretary of the Interior, in whose department those names might be arranged and printed for general information.

There is also reason to believe that foreigners frequently

become citizens of the United States for the sole purpose of evading duties imposed by the laws of their native countries, to which, on becoming naturalized here, they at once repair, and though never returning to the United States, they still claim the interposition of this government as citizens. Many altercations and great prejudices have heretofore arisen out of this abuse. It is therefore, submitted to your serious consideration. It might be advisable to fix a limit, beyond which no Citizen of the United States residing abroad may claim the interposition of his government.

The right of suffrage has often been assumed and exercised by aliens, under pretences of naturalization, which they have disavowed when drafted into the military service. I submit the expediency of such an amendment of the law as will make the fact of voting an estoppel against any plea of exemption from military service, or other civil obligation, on the ground of alienage.

In common with other western powers, our relations with Japan have been brought into serious jeopardy, through the perverse opposition of the hereditary aristocracy of the empire, to the enlightened and liberal policy of the Tycoon designed to bring the country into the society of nations. It is hoped, although not with entire confidence, that these difficulties may be peacefully overcome. I ask your attention to the claim of the Minister residing there for the damages he sustained in the destruction by fire of the residence of the legation at Yedo.

Satisfactory arrangements have been made with the Emperor of Russia, which, it is believed, will result in effecting a continuous line of telegraph through that empire from our Pacific coast.

I recommend to your favorable consideration the subject of an international telegraph across the Atlantic ocean; and also of a telegraph between this capital and the national forts along the Atlantic seaboard and the Gulf of Mexico.

Such communications, established with any reasonable out-lay, would be economical as well as effective aids to the diplomatic, military, and naval service.

The consular system of the United States, under the en-actments of the last Congress, begins to be self-sustaining; and there is reason to hope that it may become entirely so, with the increase of trade which will ensue whenever peace is restored. Our ministers abroad have been faithful in de-fending American rights. In protecting commercial interests, our Consuls have necessarily had to encounter increased la-bors and responsibilities, growing out of the war. These they have, for the most part, met and discharged with zeal and efficiency. This acknowledgment justly includes those Consuls who, residing in Morocco, Egypt, Turkey, Japan, China, and other oriental countries, are charged with com-plex functions and extraordinary powers.

The condition of the several organized Territories is gen-erally satisfactory, although Indian disturbances in New Mexico have not been entirely suppressed. The mineral re-sources of Colorado, Nevada, Idaho, New Mexico, and Arizona are proving far richer than has been heretofore understood. I lay before you a communication on this subject from the governor of New Mexico. I again submit to your consideration the expediency of establishing a system for the encouragement of immigration. Although this source of national wealth and strength is again flowing with greater freedom than for several years before the insurrection oc-curred, there is still a great deficiency of laborers in every field of industry, especially in agriculture and in our mines, as well of iron and coal as of the precious metals. While the demand for labor is thus increased here, tens of thousands of persons, destitute of remunerative occupation, are thronging our foreign consulates, and offering to emigrate to the United States if essential, but very cheap, assistance can be afforded them. It is easy to see that, under the sharp discipline of civil war, the nation is beginning a new life.

This noble effort demands the aid, and ought to receive the attention and support of the government.

Injuries, unforseen by the government and unintended, may, in some cases, have been inflicted on the subjects or citizens of foreign countries, both at sea and on land, by persons in the service of the United States. As this government expects redress from other powers when similar injuries are inflicted by persons in their service upon citizens of the United States, we must be prepared to do justice to foreigners. If the existing judicial tribunals are inadequate to this purpose, a special court may be authorized, with power to hear and decide such claims of the character referred to as may have arisen under treaties and the public law. Conventions for adjusting the claims by joint commission have been proposed to some governments, but no definitive answer to the proposition has yet been received from any.

In the course of the session I shall probably have occasion to request you to provide indemnification to claimants where decrees of restitution have been rendered, and damages awarded by admiralty courts; and in other cases where this government may be acknowledged to be liable in principle, and where the amount of that liability has been ascertained by an informal arbitration.

The proper officers of the treasury have deemed themselves required, by the law of the United States upon the subject, to demand a tax upon the incomes of foreign consuls in this country. While such a demand may not, in strictness, be in derogation of public law, or perhaps of any existing treaty between the United States and a foreign country, the expediency of so far modifying the act as to exempt from tax the income of such consuls as are not citizens of the United States, derived from the emoluments of their office, or from property not situated in the United States, is submitted to your serious consideration. I make this suggestion upon the ground that a comity which ought to be reciprocated exempts our Consuls, in all other countries, from taxation to the extent thus indicated. The United States, I think, ought not to be exceptionally illiberal to international trade and commerce.

The operations of the treasury during the last year have been successfully conducted. The enactment by Congress of a national banking law has proved a valuable support of the public credit; and the general legislation in relation to loans has fully answered the expectations of its favorers. Some amendments may be required to perfect existing laws; but no change in their principles or general scope is believed to be needed.

Since these measures have been in operation, all demands on the treasury, including the pay of the army and navy, have been promptly met and fully satisfied. No considerable body of troops, it is believed, were ever more amply provided, and more liberally and punctually paid; and it may be added that by no people were the burdens incident to a great war ever more cheerfully borne.

The receipts during the year from all sources, including loans and the balance in the treasury at its commencement, were $901,125,674.86, and the aggregate disbursements $895,796,630.65, leaving a balance on the 1st. July, 1863, of $5,329,044.21. Of the receipts there were derived from customs, $69,059,642.40; from internal revenue, $37,640,787.95; from direct tax, $1,485,103.61; from lands, $167,617.17; from miscellaneous sources, $3,046,615.35; and from loans, $776,682,361.57; making the aggregate, $901,125,674.86. Of the disbursements there were for the civil service, $23,253,922.08; for pensions and Indians, $4,216,520.79; for interest on public debt, $24,729,846.51; for the War Department, $599,298,600.83; for the Navy Department, $63,211,105.27; for payment of funded and temporary debt, $181,086,635.07; making the aggregate, $895,796,630.65, and leaving the balance of $5,329,044.21. But the payment of funded and temporary debt, having been made from moneys borrowed during the year, must be regarded as merely nominal payments, and the moneys borrowed to make them as merely nominal receipts; and their amount, $181,086,635.07, should therefore be deducted both from receipts and disbursements. This being done, there remains as actual receipts $720,039,039.79; and the actual disbursements, $714,709,995.58, leaving the balance as already stated.

The actual receipts and disbursements for the first quarter, and the estimated receipts and disbursements for the remaining three quarters, of the current fiscal year, 1864, will be shown in detail by the report of the Secretary of the Treasury, to which I invite your attention. It is sufficient to say here that it is not believed that actual results will exhibit a state of the finances less favorable to the country than the estimates of that officer heretofore submitted; while it is confidently expected that at the close of the year both disbursements and debt will be found very considerably less than has been anticipated.

The report of the Secretary of War is a document of great interest. It consists of—

1. The military operations of the year, detailed in the report of the general-in-chief.

2. The organization of colored persons into the war service.

3. The exchange of prisoners, fully set forth in the letter of General Hitchcock.

4. The operations under the act for enrolling and calling out the national forces, detailed in the report of the provost marshal general.

5. The organization of the invalid corps; and

6. The operation of the several departments of the quartermaster general, commissary general, paymaster general, chief of engineers, chief of ordnance, and surgeon general.

It has appeared impossible to make a valuable summary of this report except such as would be too extended for this place, and hence I content myself by asking your careful attention to the report itself.

The duties devolving on the naval branch of the service during the year, and throughout the whole of this unhappy contest, have been discharged with fidelity and eminent success. The extensive blockade has been constantly increasing in efficiency, as the navy has expanded; yet on so long a line it has so far been impossible to entirely suppress illicit trade. From returns received at the Navy Department, it appears that more than one thousand vessels have been captured since the blockade was instituted, and that the value of prizes already sent in for adjudication amounts to over thirteen millions of dollars.

The naval force of the United States consists at this time of five hundred and eighty-eight vessels, completed and in the course of completion, and of these seventy-five are iron-clad or armored steamers. The events of the war give an increased interest and importance to the navy which will probably extend beyond the war itself.

The armored vessels in our navy completed and in service, or which are under contract and approaching completion, are believed to exceed in number those of any other power. But while these may be relied upon for harbor defence and coast service, others of greater strength and capacity will be necessary for cruising purposes, and to maintain our rightful position on the ocean.

The change that has taken place in naval vessels and naval warfare, since the introduction of steam as a motive-power for ships-of-war, demands either a corresponding change in some of our existing navy yards, or the establishment of new ones, for the construction and necessary repair of modern naval vessels. No inconsiderable embarrassment, delay, and public injury have been experienced from the want of such governmental establishments. The necessity of such a navy yard, so furnished, at some suitable place upon

the Atlantic seaboard, has on repeated occasions been
brought to the attention of Congress by the Navy Department, and is again presented in the report of the Secretary
which accompanies this communication. I think it my duty
to invite your special attention to this subject, and also to
that of establishing a yard and depot for naval purposes
upon one of the western rivers. A naval force has been
created on those interior waters, and under many disadvan-
tages, within little more than two years, exceeding in numbers the whole naval force of the country at the commencement
of the present administration. Satisfactory and important as
have been the performances of the heroic men of the navy
at this interesting period, they are scarcely more wonderful
than the success of our mechanics and artisans in the production of war vessels which has created a new form of naval
power.

Our country has advantages superior to any other nation
in our resources of iron and timber, with inexhaustible quan-
tities of fuel in the immediate vicinity of both, and all available and in close proximity to navigable waters. Without
the advantage of public works the resources of the nation
have been developed and its power displayed in the construction of a navy of such magnitude which has, at the very
period of its creation, rendered signal service to the Union.

The increase of the number of seamen in the public service, from seven thousand five hundred men, in the spring
of 1861, to about thirty four thousand at the present time
has been accomplished without special legislation, or extraordinary bounties to promote that increase. It has been
found, however, that the operation of the draft, with the
high bounties paid for army recruits, is beginning to affect
injuriously the naval service, and will, if not corrected, be
likely to impair its efficiency, by detaching seamen from their
proper vocation and inducing them to enter the Army. I
therefore respectfully suggest that Congress might aid both

the army and naval services by a definite provision on this subject, which would at the same time be equitable to the communities more especially interested.

I commend to your consideration the suggestions of the Secretary of the Navy in regard to the policy of fostering and training seamen, and also the education of officers and engineers for the naval service. The Naval Academy is rendering signal service in preparing midshipmen for the highly responsible duties which in after life they will be required to perform. In order that the country should not be deprived of the proper quota of educated officers, for which legal provision has been made at the naval school, the vacancies caused by the neglect or omission to make nominations from the States in insurrection have been filled by the Secretary of the Navy.

The school is now more full and complete than at any former period, and in every respect entitled to the favorable consideration of Congress.

During the past fiscal year the financial condition of the Post office Department has been one of increasing prosperity, and I am gratified in being able to state that the actual postal revenue has nearly equalled the entire expenditures; the latter amounting to $11,314,206.84, and the former to $11,163,789 59, leaving a deficiency of but $150,417 25. In 1860, the year immediately preceding the rebellion the deficiency amounted to $5,656,705 49, the postal receipts of that year being $2,645,722 19 less than those of 1863. The decrease since 1860 in the annual amount of transportation has been only about 25 per cent, but the annual expenditure on account of the same has been reduced 35 per cent. It is manifest, therefore, that the Post Office Department may become self-sustaining in a few years, even with the restoration of the whole service.

The international conference of postal delegates from the principal countries of Europe and America, which was called at the suggestion of the Postmaster General, met at

Paris on the 11th of May last, and concluded its deliberations on the 8th of June. The principles established by the conference as best adapted to facilitate postal intercourse between nations, and as the basis of future postal conventions, inaugurate a general system of uniform international charges, at reduced rates of postage, and cannot fail to produce beneficial results.

I refer you to the report of the Secretary of the Interior, which is herewith laid before you, for useful and varied information in relation to the public lands, Indian affairs, patents, pensions, and other matters of public concern pertaining to his department.

The quantity of land disposed of during the last and first quarter of the present fiscal year was three million eight hundred and forty one thousand five hundred and forty nine acres, of which one hundred and sixty one thousand nine hundred and eleven acres were sold for cash, one million four hundred and fifty six thousand five hundred and fourteen acres were taken up under the homestead law, and the residue disposed of under laws granting lands for military bounties, for railroad and other purposes. It also appears that the sale of the public lands is largely on the increase.

It has long been a cherished opinion of some of our wisest statesmen that the people of the United States had a higher and more enduring interest in the early settlement and substantial cultivation of the public lands than in the amount of direct revenue to be derived from the sale of them. This opinion has had a controlling influence in shaping legislation upon the subject of our national domain. I may cite, as evidence of this, the liberal measures adopted in reference to actual settlers; the grant to the States of the overflowed lands within their limits in order to their being reclaimed and rendered fit for cultivation; the grants to railway companies of alternate sections of land upon the contemplated lines of their roads which, when completed, will so largely multiply the facilities for reaching our distant possessions. This policy has received its most signal and beneficent illustration in the recent enactment granting homesteads to actual settlers.

Since the first day of January last the before-mentioned quantity of one million four hundred and fifty-six thousand five hundred and fourteen acres of land have been taken up under its provisions. This fact and the amount of sales furnish gratifying evidence of increasing settlement upon the public lands, notwithstanding the great struggle in which the energies of the nation have been engaged, and which has required so large a withdrawal of our citizens from their accustomed pursuits. I cordially concur in the recommendation of the Secretary of the Interior suggesting a modification of the act in favor of those engaged in the military and naval service of the United States. I doubt not that Congress will cheerfully adopt such measures as will, without essentially changing the general features of the system, secure to the greatest practicable extent, its benefits to those who have left their homes in the defence of the country in this arduous crisis.

I invite your attention to the views of the Secretary as to the propriety of raising by appropriate legislation a revenue from the mineral lands of the United States.

The measures provided at your last session for the removal of certain Indian tribes have been carried into effect. Sundry treaties have been negotiated which will, in due time, be submitted for the constitutional action of the Senate. They contain stipulations for extinguishing the possessory rights of the Indians to large and valuable tracts of land. It is hoped that the effect of these treaties will result in the establishment of permanent friendly relations with such of these tribes as have been brought into frequent and bloody collision with our outlying settlements and emigrants.

Sound policy and our imperative duty to these wards of the government demand our anxious and constant attention to their material well-being, to their progress in the arts of civilization, and, above all, to that moral training which, under the blessing of Divine Providence, will confer upon them the elevated and sanctifying influences, the hopes and consolation of the Christian faith.

I suggested in my last annual message the propriety of remodelling our Indian system. Subsequent events have satisfied me of its necessity. The details set forth in the report of the Secretary evince the urgent need for immediate legislative action.

I commend the benevolent institutions, established or patronized by the government in this District, to your generous and fostering care.

The attention of Congress, during the last session, was engaged to some extent with a proposition for enlarging the water communication between the Mississippi river and the northeastern seaboard, which proposition, however, failed for the time. Since then, upon a call of the greatest respectability a convention has been held at Chicago upon the same subject, a summary of whose views is contained in a memorial addressed to the President and Congress, and which I now have the honor to lay before you. That this interest is one which, ere long, will force its own way, I do not entertain a doubt, while it is submitted entirely to your wisdom as to what can be done now. Augmented interest is given to this subject by the actual commencement of work upon the Pacific railroad, under auspices so favorable to rapid progress and completion. The enlarged navigation becomes a palpable need to the great road.

I transmit the second annual report of the Commissioner of the Department of Agriculture, asking your attention to the developments in that vital interest of the nation.

When Congress assembled a year ago the war had already lasted nearly twenty months, and there had been many conflicts on both land and sea, with varying results.

The rebellion had been pressed back into reduced limits; yet the tone of public feeling and opinion, at home and abroad, was not satisfactory. With other signs, the popular elections, then just past, indicated uneasiness among ourselves, while amid much that was cold and menacing the kindest words coming from Europe were uttered in accents of pity, that we were too blind to surrender a hopeless cause. Our commerce was suffering greatly by a few armed vessels built upon and furnished from foreign shores, and we were threatened with such additions from the same quarter as would sweep our trade from the sea and raise our blockade. We had failed to elicit from European governments anything hopeful upon this subject. The preliminary emancipation proclamation, issued in September, was running its assigned period to the beginning of the new year. A month later the final proclamation came, including the announcement that colored men of suitable condition would be received into the war service. The policy of emancipation, and of employing black soldiers, gave to the future a new aspect, about which hope, and fear, and doubt contended in uncertain conflict. According to our political system, as a matter of civil administration, the general government had no lawful power to effect emancipation in any State, and for a long time it had been hoped that the rebellion could be suppressed without resorting to it as a military measure. It was all the while deemed possible that the necessity for it might come, and that if it should, the crisis of the contest would then be presented. It came, and as was anticipated, it was followed by dark and doubtful days. Eleven months having now passed, we are permitted to take another review. The rebel borders are pressed still further back, and by the complete opening of the Mississippi the country dominated by the rebellion is divided into distinct parts, with no practical communication between them. Tennessee and Arkansas have been substantially cleared of insurgent control, and influential citizens in each, owners of slaves and advocates of slavery at the beginning of the rebellion, now declare openly for emancipation in their respective States. Of those States not included in the emancipation proclamation, Maryland, and Missouri, neither of which three years ago would tolerate any restraint upon the extention of slavery into new territories, only dispute now as to the best mode of removing it within their own limits.

Of those who were slaves at the beginning of the rebellion, full one hundred thousand are now in the United States military service, about one-half of which number actually bear arms in the ranks; thus giving the double advantage of taking so much labor from the insurgent cause, and supplying the places which otherwise must be filled with so many white men. So far as tested, it is difficult to say they are not as good soldiers as any. No servile insurrection, or tendency to violence or cruelty, has marked the measures of emancipation and arming the blacks. These measures have been much discussed in foreign countries, and contemporary with such discussion the tone of public sentiment there is much improved. At home the same measures have been fully discussed, supported, criticised, and denounced, and the annual elections following are highly encouraging to those whose official duty it is to bear the country through this great trial. Thus we have the new reckoning. The crisis which threatened to divide the friends of the Union is past.

Looking now to the present and future, and with reference to a resumption of the national authority within the States wherein that authority has been suspended, I have thought fit to issue a proclamation, a copy of which is herewith transmitted. On examination of this proclamation it will appear, as is believed, that nothing is attempted beyond what is amply justified by the Constitution. True, the form of an oath is given, but no man is coerced to take it. The man is only promised a pardon in case he voluntarily takes the oath. The Constitution authorizes the Executive to grant or withhold the pardon at his own absolute discretion; and this includes the power to grant on terms, as is fully established by judicial and other authorities.

It is also proffered that if, in any of the States named, a State government shall be, in the mode prescribed, set up, such government shall be recognized and guarantied by the United States, and that under it the State shall, on the constitutional conditions, be protected against invasion and domestic violence. The constitutional obligation of the United States to guaranty to every State in the Union a republican form of government, and to protect the State, in the cases stated, is explicit and full. But why tender the benefits of this provision only to a State government set up in this particular way? This section of the Constitution contemplates a case wherein the element within a State, favorable to republican government, in the Union, may be too feeble for an opposite and hostile element external to, or even within the State; and such are precisely the cases with which we are now dealing.

An attempt to guaranty and protect a revived State government, constructed in whole, or in preponderating part, from the very element against whose hostility and violence it is to be protected, is simply absurd. There must be a test by which to separate the opposing elements, so as to build only from the sound; and that test is a sufficiently liberal one, which accepts as sound whoever will make a sworn recantation of his former unsoundness.

But if it be proper to require, as a test of admission to the political body, an oath of allegiance to the Constitution of the United States, and to the Union under it, why also to the laws and proclamations in regard to slavery? Those laws and proclamations were enacted and put forth for the purpose of aiding in the suppression of the rebellion. To give them their fullest effect, there had to be a pledge for their maintenance. In my judgment they have aided, and will further aid, the cause for which they were intended. To now abandon them would be not only to relinquish a lever of power, but would also be a cruel and an astounding breach of faith. I may add at this point, that while I remain in my present position I shall not attempt to retract or modify the emancipation proclamation; nor shall I return to slavery any person who is free by the terms of that proclamation, or by any of the acts of Congress. For these and other reasons it is thought best that support of these measures shall be included in the oath; and it is believed the Executive may lawfully claim it in return for pardon and restoration of forfeited rights, which he has clear constitutional power to withhold altogether, or grant upon the terms which he shall deem wisest for the public interest. It should be observed, also, that this part of the oath is subject to the modifying and abrogating power of legislation and supreme judicial decision.

The proposed acquiescence of the national Executive in any reasonable temporary State arrangement for the freed people is made with the view of possibly modifying the confusion and destitution which must, at best, attend all classes by a total revolution of labor throughout whole States. It is hoped that the already deeply afflicted people in those States may be somewhat more ready to give up the cause of their affliction, if, to this extent, this vital matter be left to themselves; while no power of the national Executive to prevent an abuse is abridged by the proposition.

The suggestion in the proclamation as to maintaining the political framework of the States on what is called reconstruction, is made in the hope that it may do good without danger of harm. It will save labor and avoid great confusion.

But why any proclamation now upon this subject? This question is beset with the conflicting views that the step might be delayed too long or be taken too soon. In some States the elements for resumption seem ready for action, but remain inactive, apparently for want of a rallying point—a plan of action. Why shall A adopt the plan of B, rather than B that of A? And if A and B should agree, how can they know but that the general government here will reject their plan? By the proclamation a plan is presented which may be accepted by them as a rallying point, and which they are assured in advance will not be rejected here. This may bring them to act sooner than they otherwise would.

The objections to a premature presentation of a plan by the national Executive consists in the danger of committals on points which could be more safely left to further developments. Care has been taken to so shape the document as to avoid embarrassments from this source. Saying that, on certain terms, certain classes will be pardoned, with rights restored, it is not said that other classes, or other terms, will never be included. Saying that reconstruction will be accepted if presented in a specified way, it is not said it will never be accepted in any other way.

The movements, by State action, for emancipation in several of the States, not included in the emancipation proclamation, are matters of profound gratulation. And while I do not repeat in detail what I have heretofore so earnestly urged upon this subject, my general views and feelings remain unchanged; and I trust that Congress will omit no fair opportunity of aiding these important steps to a great consummation.

In the midst of other cares, however important, we must not lose sight of the fact that the war power is still our main reliance. To that power alone can we look, yet for a time, to give confidence to the people in the contested regions, that the insurgent power will not again overrun them. Until that confidence shall be established, little can be done anywhere for what is called reconstruction. Hence our chiefest care must still be directed to the army and navy, who have thus far borne their harder part so nobly and well. And it may be esteemed fortunate that in giving the greatest efficiency to these indispensable arms, we do also honorably recognize the gallant men, from commander to sentinel, who compose them, and to whom, more than to others, the world must stand indebted for the home of freedom disenthralled, regenerated, enlarged, and perpetuated.

Washington, December 8, 1863.

Proclamation of Amnesty and Reconstruction

BY THE PRESIDENT
OF THE UNITED STATES OF AMERICA:
A PROCLAMATION.

Whereas, in and by the Constitution of the United States, it is provided that the President "shall have power to grant reprieves and pardons for offences against the United States, except in cases of impeachment;" and

Whereas a rebellion now exists whereby the loyal State governments of several States have for a long time been subverted, and many persons have committed and are now guilty of treason against the United States; and

Whereas, with reference to said rebellion and treason, laws have been enacted by Congress declaring forfeitures and confiscation of property and liberation of slaves, all upon terms and conditions therein stated, and also declaring that the President was thereby authorized at any time thereafter, by proclamation, to extend to persons who may have participated in the existing rebellion, in any State or part thereof, pardon and amnesty, with such exceptions and at such times and on such conditions as he may deem expedient for the public welfare; and

Whereas the congressional declaration for limited and

conditional pardon accords with well-established judicial exposition of the pardoning power; and

Whereas, with reference to said rebellion, the President of the United States has issued several proclamations, with provisions in regard to the liberation of slaves; and

Whereas it is now desired by some persons heretofore engaged in said rebellion to resume their allegiance to the United States, and to reinaugurate loyal State governments within and for their respective States; therefore,

I, Abraham Lincoln, President of the United States, do proclaim, declare, and make known to all persons who have, directly or by implication, participated in the existing rebellion, except as hereinafter excepted, that a full pardon is hereby granted to them and each of them, with restoration of all rights and property, except as to slaves, and in property cases where rights of third parties shall have intervened, and upon the condition that every such person shall take and subscribe an oath, and thenceforward keep and maintain said oath inviolate; and which oath shall be registered for permanent preservation, and shall be of the tenor and effect following, to wit:

"I, ———, do solemnly swear, in presence of Almighty God, that I will henceforth faithfully support, protect and defend the Constitution of the United States, and the union of the States thereunder; and that I will, in like manner, abide by and faithfully support all acts of Congress passed during the existing rebellion with reference to slaves, so long and so far as not repealed, modified or held void by Congress, or by decision of the Supreme Court; and that I will, in like manner, abide by and faithfully support all proclamations of the President made during the existing rebellion having reference to slaves, so long and so far as not modified or declared void by decision of the Supreme Court. So help me God."

The persons excepted from the benefits of the foregoing provisions are all who are, or shall have been, civil or diplomatic officers or agents of the so-called confederate government; all who have left judicial stations under the United States to aid the rebellion; all who are, or shall have been, military or naval officers of said so-called confederate government above the rank of colonel in the army, or of lieutenant in the navy; all who left seats in the United States Congress to aid the rebellion; all who resigned commissions in the army or navy of the United States, and afterwards aided the rebellion; and all who have engaged in any way in treating colored persons or white persons, in charge of such, otherwise than lawfully as prisoners of war, and which persons may have been found in the United States service, as soldiers, seamen, or in any other capacity.

And I do further proclaim, declare, and make known, that whenever, in any of the States of Arkansas, Texas, Louisiana, Mississippi, Tennessee, Alabama, Georgia, Florida, South Carolina, and North Carolina, a number of persons, not less than one-tenth in number of the votes cast in such State at the Presidential election of the year of our Lord one thousand eight hundred and sixty, each having taken the oath aforesaid and not having since violated it, and being a qualified voter by the election law of the State existing immediately before the so-called act of secession, and excluding all others, shall re-establish a State government which shall be republican, and in no wise contravening said oath, such shall be recognized as the true government of the State, and the State shall receive thereunder the benefits of the constitutional provision which declares that "The United States shall guaranty to every State in this union a republican form of government, and shall protect each of them against invasion; and, on application of the legislature, or the executive, (when the legislature cannot be convened,) against domestic violence."

And I do further proclaim, declare, and make known that any provision which may be adopted by such State government in relation to the freed people of such State, which shall recognize and declare their permanent freedom, provide for their education, and which may yet be consistent, as a temporary arrangement, with their present condition as a laboring, landless, and homeless class, will not be objected to by the national Executive. And it is suggested as not improper, that, in constructing a loyal State government in any State, the name of the State, the boundary, the subdivisions, the constitution, and the general code of laws, as before the rebellion, be maintained, subject only to the modifications made necessary by the conditions hereinbefore stated, and such others, if any, not contravening said conditions, and which may be deemed expedient by those framing the new State government.

To avoid misunderstanding, it may be proper to say that this proclamation, so far as it relates to State governments, has no reference to States wherein loyal State governments have all the while been maintained. And for the same reason, it may be proper to further say that whether members sent to Congress from any State shall be admitted to seats, constitutionally rests exclusively with the respective Houses, and not to any extent with the Executive. And still further, that this proclamation is intended to present the people of the States wherein the national authority has been suspended, and loyal State governments have been subverted, a mode in and by which the national authority and loyal State governments may be re-established within said States, or in any of them; and, while the mode presented is the best the Executive can suggest, with his present impressions, it must not be understood that no other possible mode would be acceptable.

Given under my hand at the city, of Washington, the 8th. day of December, A.D. one thousand eight hundred and sixty-three, and of the independence of the United States of America the eighty-eighth.

By the President: ABRAHAM LINCOLN
WILLIAM H. SEWARD, Secretary of State.

To Mrs. Esther Stockton

Executive Mansion,
Mrs. Esther Stockton.   Washington Jany. 8, 1864.

Madam: Learning that you who have passed the eighty-fourth year of life, have given to the soldiers, some three hundred pairs of stockings, knitted by yourself, I wish to offer you my thanks. Will you also convey my thanks to those young ladies who have done so much in feeding our soldiers while passing through your city? Yours truly,

To Albert G. Hodges

A. G. Hodges, Esq   Executive Mansion,
Frankfort, Ky.   Washington, April 4, 1864.

My dear Sir: You ask me to put in writing the substance of what I verbally said the other day, in your presence, to Governor Bramlette and Senator Dixon. It was about as follows:

"I am naturally anti-slavery. If slavery is not wrong, nothing is wrong. I can not remember when I did not so think, and feel. And yet I have never understood that the Presidency conferred upon me an unrestricted right to act officially upon this judgment and feeling. It was in the oath I took that I would, to the best of my ability, preserve, protect, and defend the Constitution of the United States. I could not take the office without taking the oath. Nor was it my view that I might take an oath to get power, and break the oath in using the power. I understood, too, that in ordinary civil administration this oath even forbade me to practically indulge my primary abstract judgment on the moral question of slavery. I had publicly declared this many times, and in many ways. And I aver that, to this day, I have done no official act in mere deference to my abstract judgment and feeling on slavery. I did understand however, that my oath to preserve the constitution to the best of my ability, imposed upon me the duty of preserving, by every indispensable means, that government—that nation—of which that constitution was the organic law. Was it possible to lose the nation, and yet preserve the constitution? By general law life *and* limb must be protected; yet often a limb must be amputated to save a life; but a life is never wisely given to save a limb. I felt that measures, otherwise unconstitutional, might become lawful, by becoming indispensable to the preservation of the constitution, through the preservation of the nation. Right or wrong, I assumed this ground, and now avow it. I could not feel that, to the best of my ability, I had even tried to preserve the constitution, if, to save slavery, or any minor matter, I should permit the wreck of government, country, and Constitution all together. When, early in the war, Gen. Fremont attempted military emancipation, I forbade it, because I did not then think it an indispensable necessity. When a little later, Gen. Cameron, then Secretary of War, suggested the arming of the blacks, I objected, because I did not yet think it an indispensable necessity. When, still later, Gen. Hunter attempted military emancipation, I again forbade it, because I did not yet think the indispensable necessity had come. When, in March, and May, and July 1862 I made earnest, and successive appeals to the border states to favor compensated emancipation, I believed the indispensable necessity for military emancipation, and arming the blacks would come, unless averted by that measure. They declined the proposition; and I was, in my best judgment, driven to the alternative of either surrendering the Union, and with it, the Constitution, or of laying strong hand upon the colored element. I chose the latter. In choosing it, I hoped for greater gain than loss; but of this, I was not entirely confident. More than a year of trial now shows no loss by it in our foreign relations, none in our home popular sentiment, none in our white military force,—no loss by it any how or any where. On the contrary, it shows a gain of quite a hundred and thirty thousand soldiers, seamen, and laborers. These are palpable facts, about which, as facts, there can be no cavilling. We have the men; and we could not have had them without the measure.

"And now let any Union man who complains of the measure, test himself by writing down in one line that he is for subduing the rebellion by force of arms; and in the next, that he is for taking these hundred and thirty thousand men from the Union side, and placing them where they would be but for the measure he condemns. If he can not face his case so stated, it is only because he can not face the truth."

I add a word which was not in the verbal conversation. In telling this tale I attempt no compliment to my own sagacity. I claim not to have controlled events, but confess plainly that events have controlled me. Now, at the end of three years struggle the nation's condition is not what either party, or any man devised, or expected. God alone can claim it. Whither it is tending seems plain. If God now wills the removal of a great wrong, and wills also that we of the North as well as you of the South, shall pay fairly for our complicity in that wrong, impartial history will find therein new cause to attest and revere the justice and goodness of God. Yours truly

Address at Sanitary Fair, Baltimore, Maryland

Ladies and Gentlemen—Calling to mind that we are in Baltimore, we can not fail to note that the world moves. Looking upon these many people, assembled here, to serve, as they best may, the soldiers of the Union, it occurs at once that three years ago, the same soldiers could not so much as pass through Baltimore. The change from then till now, is both great, and gratifying. Blessings on the brave men who have wrought the change, and the fair women who strive to reward them for it.

But Baltimore suggests more than could happen within Baltimore. The change within Baltimore is part only of a far wider change. When the war began, three years ago, neither party, nor any man, expected it would last till now. Each looked for the end, in some way, long ere to-day. Neither did any anticipate that domestic slavery would be much affected by the war. But here we are; the war has not ended, and slavery has been much affected—how much needs not now to be recounted. So true is it that man proposes, and God disposes.

But we can see the past, though we may not claim to have directed it; and seeing it, in this case, we feel more hopeful and confident for the future.

The world has never had a good definition of the word liberty, and the American people, just now, are much in want of one. We all declare for liberty; but in using the same *word* we do not all mean the same *thing*. With some the word liberty may mean for each man to do as he pleases with himself, and the product of his labor; while with others the same word may mean for some men to do as they please with other men, and the product of other men's labor. Here are two, not only different, but incompatable things, called by the same name—liberty. And it follows that each of the things is, by the respective parties, called by two different and incompatable names—liberty and tyranny.

The shepherd drives the wolf from the sheep's throat, for which the sheep thanks the shepherd as a *liberator*, while the wolf denounces him for the same act as the destroyer of liberty, especially as the sheep was a black one. Plainly the sheep and the wolf are not agreed upon a definition of the word liberty; and precisely the same difference prevails to-day among us human creatures, even in the North, and all professing to love liberty. Hence we behold the processes by which thousands are daily passing from under the yoke of bondage, hailed by some as the advance of liberty, and bewailed by others as the destruction of all liberty. Recently, as it seems, the people of Maryland have been doing something to define liberty; and thanks to them that, in what they have done, the wolf's dictionary, has been repudiated.

It is not very becoming for one in my position to make speeches at great length; but there is another subject upon which I feel that I ought to say a word. A painful rumor, true I fear, has reached us of the massacre, by the rebel forces, at Fort Pillow, in the West end of Tennessee, on the Mississippi river, of some three hundred colored soldiers and white officers, who had just been overpowered by their assailants. There seems to be some anxiety in the public mind whether the government is doing it's duty to the colored soldier, and to the service, at this point. At the beginning of the war, and for some time, the use of colored troops was not contemplated; and how the change of purpose was wrought, I will not now take time to explain. Upon a clear conviction of duty I resolved to turn that element of strength to account; and I am responsible for it to the American people, to the christian world, to history, and on my final account to God. Having determined to use the negro as a soldier, there is no way but to give him all the protection given to any other soldier. The difficulty is not in stating the principle, but in practically applying it. It is a mistake to suppose the government is indifferent to this matter, or is not doing the best it can in regard to it. We do not to-day *know* that a colored soldier, or white officer command-ing colored soldiers, has been massacred by the rebels when made a prisoner. We fear it, believe it, I may say, but we do not *know* it. To take the life of one of their prisoners, on the assumption that they murder ours, when it is short of certainty that they do murder ours, might be too serious, too cruel a mistake. We are having the Fort-Pillow affair thoroughly investigated; and such investigation will probably show conclusively how the truth is. If, after all that has been said, it shall turn out that there has been no massacre at Fort-Pillow, it will be almost safe to say there has been none, and will be none elsewhere. If there has been the massacre of three hundred there, or even the tenth part of three hundred, it will be conclusively proved; and being so proved, the retribution shall as surely come. It will be matter of grave consideration in what exact course to apply the retribution; but in the supposed case, it must come.

April 18, 1864

To Edwin M. Stanton

Hon. Secretary of War: Executive Mansion
Sir.   Washington, D.C. May 17. 1864

Please notify the insurgents, through the proper military channels and forms, that the government of the United States has satisfactory proof of the massacre, by insurgent forces, at Fort-Pillow, on the 12th. and 13th. days of April last, of fully   white and colored officers and soldiers of the United States, after the latter had ceased resistance, and asked quarter of the former.

That with reference to said massacre, the government of the United States has assigned and set apart by name   insurgent officers, theretofore, and up to that time, held by said government as prisoners of war.

That, as blood can not restore blood, and government should not act for revenge, any assurance, as nearly perfect as the case admits, given on or before the first day of July next, that there shall be no similar massacre, nor any officer or soldier of the United States, whether white or colored, now held, or hereafter captured by the insurgents, shall be treated other than according to the laws of war, will insure the replacing of said   insurgent officers in the simple condition of prisoners of war.

That the insurgents having refused to exchange, or to give any account or explanation in regard to colored soldiers of the United States captured by them, a number of insurgent prisoners equal to the number of such colored soldiers supposed to have been captured by said insurgents will, from time to time, be assigned and set aside, with reference to such captured colored soldiers, and will, if the insurgents assent, be exchanged for such colored soldiers; but that if no satisfactory attention shall be given to this notice, by said insurgents, on or before the first day of July next, it will be assumed by the government of the United States, that said captured colored troops shall have been murdered, or subjected to Slavery, and that said government will, upon said assumption, take such action as may then appear expedient and just.

To Charles Sumner

Hon. Charles Sumner,   Executive Mansion,
My dear Sir: Washington, May 19, 1864.
The bearer of this is the widow of Major Booth, who fell at Fort-Pillow. She makes a point, which I think very worthy of consideration which is, widows and children *in fact*, of colored soldiers who fall in our service, be placed in law, the same as if their marriages were legal, so that they can have the benefit of the provisions made the widows & orphans of white soldiers. Please see & hear Mrs. Booth. Yours truly

To Horace Greeley

Hon. Horace Greely   Washington, D.C.
Dear Sir   July 9. 1864

Your letter of the 7th., with inclosures, received. If you can find, any person anywhere professing to have any proposition of Jefferson Davis in writing, for peace, embracing the restoration of the Union and abandonment of slavery, what ever else it embraces, say to him he may come to me with you, and that if he really brings such proposition, he shall, at the least, have safe conduct, with the paper (and without publicity, if he choose) to the point where you shall have met him. The same, if there be two or more persons. Yours truly

To Ulysses S. Grant

              United States Military Telegraph,
Lieut. Gen. Grant   War Department.
City Point, Va.   July 17. 11/25. AM. 1864

In your despatch of yesterday to Gen. Sherman, I find the following, towit: "I shall make a desparate effort to get a position here which will hold the enemy without the necessity of so many men."

Pressed as we are by lapse of time, I am glad to hear you say this; and yet I do hope you may find a way that the effort shall not be desparate in the sense of great loss of life.

To Edwin M. Stanton

I know not how much is within the legal power of the government in this case; but it is certainly true in equity, that the laboring women in our employment, should be paid at the least as much as they were at the beginning of the war. Will the Secretary of War please have the case fully examined, and so much relief given as can be consistently with the law and the public service.

July 27. 1864

To Ulysses S. Grant

"Cypher"   Office U.S. Military Telegraph,
Lieut. Genl. Grant   War Department,
City-Point, Va.   Washington, D.C., August 14 1864.

The Secretary of War and I concur that you better confer with Gen. Lee and stipulate for a mutual discontinuance of house-burning and other destruction of private property. The time and manner of conference, and particulars of stipulation we leave, on our part, to your convenience and judgment.

To Ulysses S. Grant

"Cypher"

Lieut. Gen. Grant   Executive Mansion,
City Point, Va.   Washington, August 17. 1864.

I have seen your despatch expressing your unwillingness to break your hold where you are. Neither am I willing. Hold on with a bull-dog gripe, and chew & choke, as much as possible.

Speech to the 166th Ohio Regiment, Washington, D.C.

I suppose you are going home to see your families and friends. For the service you have done in this great struggle in which we are engaged I present you sincere thanks for myself and the country. I almost always feel inclined, when I happen to say anything to soldiers, to impress upon them in a few brief remarks the importance of success in this contest. It is not merely for to-day, but for all time to come that we should perpetuate for our children's children this great and free government, which we have enjoyed all our lives. I beg you to remember this, not merely for my sake, but for yours. I happen temporarily to occupy this big White House. I am a living witness that any one of your children may look to come here as my father's child has. It is in order that each of you may have through this free government which we have enjoyed, an open field and a fair chance for your industry, enterprise and intelligence; that you may all have equal privileges in the race of life, with all its desirable human aspirations. It is for this the struggle should be maintained, that we may not lose our birthright—not only for one, but for two or three years. The nation is worth fighting for, to secure such an inestimable jewel.

August 22, 1864

Memorandum on Probable Failure of Re-election

Executive Mansion
Washington, Aug. 23, 1864.

This morning, as for some days past, it seems exceedingly probable that this Administration will not be re-elected. Then it will be my duty to so co-operate with the President elect, as to save the Union between the election and the inauguration; as he will have secured his election on such ground that he can not possibly save it afterwards.

To Henry J. Raymond

Executive Mansion,
Sir: Washington, August 24. 1864.

You will proceed forthwith and obtain, if possible, a conference for peace with Hon. Jefferson Davis, or any person by him authorized for that purpose.

You will address him in entirely respectful terms, at all events, and in any that may be indispensable to secure the conference.

At said conference you will propose, on behalf this government, that upon the restoration of the Union and the national authority, the war shall cease at once, all remaining questions to be left for adjustment by peaceful modes. If this be accepted hostilities to cease at once.

If it be not accepted, you will then request to be informed what terms, if any embracing the restoration of the Union, would be accepted. If any such be presented you in answer, you will forthwith report the same to this government, and await further instructions.

If the presentation of any terms embracing the restoration of the Union be declined, you will then request to be informed what terms of peace would, be accepted; and on receiving any answer, report the same to this government, and await further instructions.

Response to Serenade, Washington, D.C.

It has long been a grave question whether any government, not *too* strong for the liberties of its people, can be strong *enough* to maintain its own existence, in great emergencies.

On this point the present rebellion brought our republic to a severe test; and a presidential election occurring in regular course during the rebellion added not a little to the strain. If the loyal people, *united*, were put to the utmost of their strength by the rebellion, must they not fail when *divided*, and partially paralized, by a political war among themselves?

But the election was a necessity.

We can not have free government without elections; and if the rebellion could force us to forego, or postpone a national election, it might fairly claim to have already conquered and ruined us. The strife of the election is but human-nature practically applied to the facts of the case. What has occurred in this case, must ever recur in similar cases. Human-nature will not change. In any future great national trial, compared with the men of this, we shall have as weak, and as strong; as silly and as wise; as bad and good. Let us, therefore, study the incidents of this, as philosophy to learn wisdom from, and none of them as wrongs to be revenged.

But the election, along with its incidental, and undesirable strife, has done good too. It has demonstrated that a people's government can sustain a national election, in the midst of a great civil war. Until now it has not been known to the world that this was a possibility. It shows also how *sound*, and how *strong* we still are. It shows that, even among candidates of the same party, he who is most devoted to the Union, and most opposed to treason, can receive most of the people's votes. It shows also, to the extent yet known, that we have more men now, than we had when the war began. Gold is good in its place; but living, brave, patriotic men, are better than gold.

But the rebellion continues; and now that the election is over, may not all, having a common interest, re-unite in a common effort, to save our common country? For my own part I have striven, and shall strive to avoid placing any obstacle in the way. So long as I have been here I have not willingly planted a thorn in any man's bosom.

While I am deeply sensible to the high compliment of a re-election; and duly grateful, as I trust, to Almighty God for having directed my countrymen to a right conclusion, as I think, for their own good, it adds nothing to my satisfaction that any other man may be disappointed or pained by the result.

May I ask those who have not differed with me, to join with me, in this same spirit towards those who have?

And now, let me close by asking three hearty cheers for our brave soldiers and seamen and their gallant and skillful commanders.

November 10, 1864

To Mrs. Lydia Bixby

Executive Mansion,
Washington, Nov. 21, 1864.

Dear Madam,—I have been shown in the files of the War Department a statement of the Adjutant General of Massachusetts, that you are the mother of five sons who have died gloriously on the field of battle.

I feel how weak and fruitless must be any words of mine which should attempt to beguile you from the grief of a loss so overwhelming. But I cannot refrain from tendering to you the consolation that may be found in the thanks of the Republic they died to save.

I pray that our Heavenly Father may assuage the anguish of your bereavement, and leave you only the cherished memory of the loved and lost, and the solemn pride that must be yours, to have laid so costly a sacrifice upon the altar of Freedom. Yours, very sincerely and respectfully,

Reply to a Southern Woman

THE PRESIDENT'S LAST, SHORTEST,
AND BEST SPEECH.

On thursday of last week two ladies from Tennessee came before the President asking the release of their husbands held as prisoners of war at Johnson's Island. They were put off till friday, when they came again; and were again put off to saturday. At each of the interviews one of the ladies urged that her husband was a religious man. On saturday the President ordered the release of the prisoners, and then said to this lady "You say your husband is a religious man; tell him when you meet him, that I say I am not much of a judge of religion, but that, in my opinion, the religion that sets men to rebel and fight against their government, because, as they think, that government does not sufficiently help *some* men to eat their bread on the sweat of *other* men's faces, is not the sort of religion upon which people can get to heaven!"

December 6, 1864, or before

To William T. Sherman

Executive Mansion, Washington,
My dear General Sherman.   Dec. 26, 1864.

Many, many, thanks for your Christmas-gift—the capture of Savannah.

When you were about leaving Atlanta for the Atlantic coast, I was *anxious*, if not fearful; but feeling that you were the better judge, and remembering that "nothing risked, nothing gained" I did not interfere. Now, the undertaking being a success, the honor is all yours; for I believe none of us went farther than to acquiesce. And, taking the work of Gen. Thomas into the count, as it should be taken, it is indeed a great success. Not only does it afford the obvious and immediate military advantages; but, in showing to the world that your army could be divided, putting the stronger part to an important new service, and yet leaving enough to vanquish the old opposing force of the whole—Hood's army—it brings those who sat in darkness, to see a great light. But what next? I suppose it will be safer if I leave Gen. Grant and yourself to decide.

Please make my grateful acknowledgments to your whole army, officers and men. Yours very truly

To Ulysses S. Grant

Executive Mansion, Washington,
Lieut. General Grant: Jan. 19, 1865.

Please read and answer this letter as though I was not President, but only a friend. My son, now in his twenty second year, having graduated at Harvard, wishes to see something of the war before it ends. I do not wish to put him in the ranks, nor yet to give him a commission, to which those who have already served long, are better entitled, and better qualified to hold. Could he, without embarrassment to you, or detriment to the service, go into your Military family with some nominal rank, I, and not the public, furnishing his necessary means? If no, say so without the least hesitation, because I am as anxious, and as deeply interested, that you shall not be encumbered as you can be yourself. Yours truly

To John Glenn

"Cypher"
Lt. Col. Glenn.   Executive Mansion
Commanding Post at   Washington,
Henderson, Ky.   Feb. 7. 1865

Complaint is made to me that you are forcing negroes into the Military service, and even torturing them—riding them on rails and the like—to extort their consent. I hope this may be a mistake. The like must not be done by you, or any one under you. You must not force negroes any more than white men. Answer me on this.

To Ulysses S. Grant

Lieutenant General Grant   March 3. 1865

The President directs me to say to you that he wishes you to have no conference with General Lee unless it be for the capitulation of Gen. Lee's army, or on some minor, and purely, military matter. He instructs me to say that you are not to decide, discuss, or confer upon any political question. Such questions the President holds in his own hands; and will submit them to no military conferences or conventions. Meantime you are to press to the utmost, your military advantages.   EDWIN M STANTON
                                    Secretary of War

Second Inaugural Address

Fellow Countrymen:

At this second appearing to take the oath of the presidential office, there is less occasion for an extended address than there was at the first. Then a statement, somewhat in detail, of a course to be pursued, seemed fitting and proper. Now, at the expiration of four years, during which public declarations have been constantly called forth on every point and phase of the great contest which still absorbs the attention, and engrosses the energies of the nation, little that is new could be presented. The progress of our arms, upon which all else chiefly depends, is as well known to the public as to myself; and it is, I trust, reasonably satisfactory and encouraging to all. With high hope for the future, no prediction in regard to it is ventured.

On the occasion corresponding to this four years ago, all thoughts were anxiously directed to an impending civil-war. All dreaded it—all sought to avert it. While the inaugeral

address was being delivered from this place, devoted altogether to *saving* the Union without war, insurgent agents
were in the city seeking to *destroy* it without war—seeking
to dissolve the Union, and divide effects, by negotiation.
Both parties deprecated war; but one of them would
make war rather than let the nation survive; and the other
would *accept* war rather than let it perish. And the war
came.

One eighth of the whole population were colored slaves,
not distributed generally over the Union, but localized in
the Southern part of it. These slaves constituted a peculiar
and powerful interest. All knew that this interest was, somehow, the cause of the war. To strengthen, perpetuate, and
extend this interest was the object for which the insurgents
would rend the Union, even by war; while the government
claimed no right to do more than to restrict the territorial
enlargement of it. Neither party expected for the war, the
magnitude, or the duration, which it has already attained.
Neither anticipated that the *cause* of the conflict might cease
with, or even before, the conflict itself should cease. Each
looked for an easier triumph, and a result less fundamental
and astounding. Both read the same Bible, and pray to the
same God; and each invokes His aid against the other. It
may seem strange that any men should dare to ask a just
God's assistance in wringing their bread from the sweat of
other men's faces; but let us judge not that we be not judged.
The prayers of both could not be answered; that of neither
has been answered fully. The Almighty has His own purposes. "Woe unto the world because of offences! for it must
needs be that offences come; but woe to that man by whom
the offence cometh!" If we shall suppose that American
Slavery is one of those offences which, in the providence of
God, must needs come, but which, having continued through
His appointed time, He now wills to remove, and that He
gives to both North and South, this terrible war, as the
woe due to those by whom the offence came, shall we dis-

cern therein any departure from those divine attributes which
the believers in a Living God always ascribe to Him?
Fondly do we hope—fervently do we pray—that this mighty
scourge of war may speedily pass away. Yet, if God wills
that it continue, until all the wealth piled by the bond-man's
two hundred and fifty years of unrequited toil shall be sunk,
and until every drop of blood drawn with the lash, shall be
paid by another drawn with the sword, as was said three
thousand years ago, so still it must be said "the judgments
of the Lord, are true and righteous altogether"

With malice toward none; with charity for all; with firmness in the right, as God gives us to see the right, let us
strive on to finish the work we are in; to bind up the nation's
wounds; to care for him who shall have borne the battle,
and for his widow, and his orphan—to do all which may
achieve and cherish a just, and a lasting peace, among ourselves, and with all nations.

March 4, 1865

To Thurlow Weed

Thurlow Weed, Esq   Executive Mansion,
My dear Sir.   Washington, March 15, 1865.

Every one likes a compliment. Thank you for yours on
my little notification speech, and on the recent Inaugeral
Address. I expect the latter to wear as well as—perhaps
better than—any thing I have produced; but I believe it is
not immediately popular. Men are not flattered by being
shown that there has been a difference of purpose between
the Almighty and them. To deny it, however, in this case,
is to deny that there is a God governing the world. It is a
truth which I thought needed to be told; and as whatever
of humiliation there is in it, falls most directly on myself, I
thought others might afford for me to tell it. Yours truly

Speech to the 140th Indiana Regiment, Washington, D.C.

FELLOW CITIZENS—It will be but a very few words that I shall undertake to say. I was born in Kentucky, raised in Indiana and lived in Illinois. (Laughter.) And now I am here, where it is my business to care equally for the good people of all the States. I am glad to see an Indiana regiment on this day able to present the captured flag to the Governor of Indiana. (Applause.) I am not disposed, in saying this, to make a distinction between the States, for all have done equally well. (Applause.) There are but few views or aspects of this great war upon which I have not said or written something whereby my own opinions might be known. But there is one—the recent attempt of our erring brethren, as they are sometimes called—(laughter)—to employ the negro to fight for them. I have neither written nor made a speech on that subject, because that was their business, not mine; and if I had a wish upon the subject I had not the power to introduce it, or make it effective. The great question with them was, whether the negro, being put into the army, would fight for them. I do not know, and therefore cannot decide. (Laughter.) They ought to know better than we. I have in my lifetime heard many arguments why the negroes ought to be slaves; but if they fight for those who would keep them in slavery it will be a better argument than any I have yet heard. (Laughter and applause.) He who will fight for that ought to be a slave. (Applause.) They have concluded at last to take one out of four of the slaves, and put them in the army; and that one out of the four who will fight to keep the others in slavery ought to be a slave himself unless he is killed in a fight. (Applause.) While I have often said that all men ought to be free, yet I would allow those colored persons to be slaves who want to be; and next to them those white persons who argue in favor of making other people slaves. (Applause.) I am in favor of giving an opportunity to such white men to try it on for themselves. (Applause.) I will say one thing in regard to the negro being employed to fight for them. I do know he cannot fight and stay at home and make bread too—(laughter and applause)—and as one is about as important as the other to them, I don't care which they do. (Renewed applause.) I am rather in favor of having them try them as soldiers. (Applause.) They lack one vote of doing that, and I wish I could send my vote over the river so that I might cast it in favor of allowing the negro to fight. (Applause.) But they cannot fight and work both. We must now see the bottom of the enemy's resources. They will stand out as long as they can, and if the negro will fight for them, they must allow him to fight. They have drawn upon their last branch of resources. (Applause.) And we can now see the bottom. (Applause.) I am glad to see the end so near at hand. (Applause.) I have said now more than I intended, and will therefore bid you goodby.

March 17, 1865

To Ulysses S. Grant

Head Quarters Armies of the United States,

City-Point,

Lieut Gen. Grant.   April 7. 11 A.M. 1865

Gen. Sheridan says "If the thing is pressed I think that Lee will surrender." Let the *thing* be pressed.

Response to Serenade, Washington, D.C.

"FELLOW CITIZENS: I am very greatly rejoiced to find that an occasion has occurred so pleasurable that the people cannot restrain themselves. [Cheers.] I suppose that arrangements are being made for some sort of a formal demonstration, this, or perhaps, to-morrow night. [Cries of 'We can't wait,' 'We want it now,' &c.] If there should be such a demonstration, I, of course, will be called upon to respond, and I shall have nothing to say if you dribble it all out of me before. [Laughter and applause.] I see you have a band of music with you. [Voices, 'We have two or three.'] I propose closing up this interview by the band performing a particular tune which I will name. Before this is done, however, I wish to mention one or two little circumstances connected with it. I have always thought 'Dixie' one of the best tunes I have ever heard. Our adversaries over the way attempted to appropriate it, but I insisted yesterday that we fairly captured it. [Applause.] I presented the question to the Attorney General, and he gave it as his legal opinion that it is our lawful prize. [Laughter and applause.] I now request the band to favor me with its performance."

April 10, 1865